Trauma, Collective Trauma and Refugee Trajectories in the Digital Era

Development of the Trauma Recovery Understanding Self-Help Therapy (TRUST)

Selam Kidane

PhD Thesis, Tilburg University
2021

Langaa Research & Publishing CIG
Mankon, Bamenda

Publisher:
Langaa RPCIG
Langaa Research & Publishing Common Initiative Group
P.O. Box 902 Mankon
Bamenda
North West Region
Cameroon
Langaagrp@gmail.com
www.langaa-rpcig.net

Distributed in and outside N. America by African Books Collective
orders@africanbookscollective.com
www.africanbookscollective.com

ISBN-10: 9956-552-50-x

ISBN-13: 978-9956-552-50-4

Copy-editor: Susan Sellars-Shrestra
Picture cover: Mirjam van Reisen (May Ayni Refugee camp, Tigray, 22 July 2015)
Graphic design all figures: Selam Kidane (edited by: Klara Smits, Asa Splinter)

Cite as:
Kidane, S. (2021) *Trauma, Collective Trauma and Refugee Trajectories
in the Digital Era. Development of the Trauma Recovery Understanding Self-Help Therapy
(TRUST).* PhD Thesis. Tilburg University. Bamenda, Cameroon: Langaa RPCIG.

Disclaimer: Great care was taken to factually represent the research findings of
the author. The content of the book is the sole responsibility of the author. If
there are any factual errors or if you have other comments, please address them
to: selamkidane@hotmail.com

PROEFSCHRIFT

ter verkrijging van de graad van doctor
aan Tilburg University
op gezag van de Rector Magnificus,
prof. dr. W.B.H.J. van de Donk,
in het openbaar te verdedigen ten overstaan van een
door het college voor promoties aangewezen commissie
in de Aula van de Universiteit

op vrijdag 5 november 2021 om 13.30 uur

door

Selam Kidane

geboren te Addis Abeba, Ethiopië

Promotores

    Prof. dr. M.E.H. van Reisen

    Prof. dr. J.W.M. Kroon

Co-promotor

    Dr. M.J.W. Stokmans

Overige leden van de promotiecommissie

    Dr. S. Ashaba

    Prof. dr. M.H. Braakman

    Prof. dr. M. Dekker

    Prof. dr. G.T.M. Mooren

    Prof. dr. C.R.J.J. Rijken

Book Series

Connected and Mobile:
Migration and Human Trafficking in Africa

Book 1
Human Trafficking and Traula in the Digital Era. The Ongoing Tragedy of the Trade in Refugees from Eritrea. (2017). Mirjam van Reisen & Munyaradzi Mawere (eds)

Book 2
Roaming Africa: Migration, Resilience and Social Protection. (2019). Mirjam van Reisen Munyaradzi Mawere, Mia Stokmans & Kinfe Abraha Gebre-Egziabher (eds)

Book 3
Mobile Africa: Human Trafficking and the Digital Divide. (2019). Mirjam van Reisen Munyaradzi Mawere, Mia Stokmans & Kinfe Abraha Gebre-Egziabher (eds)

Book 4
Trauma, Collective Trauma and Refugee Trajectories in the Digital Era. Development of the Trauma Recovery Understanding Self-Help Therapy (TRUST). (2021). Selam Kidane (author).

Summary

Trauma, Collective Trauma and Refugee Trajectories in the Digital Era

Development of the Trauma Recovery Understanding Self-Help Therapy (TRUST)

This study investigates the effectiveness of the Trauma Recovery Understanding Self-Help Therapy (TRUST). The intervention was specifically developed to treat Traumatic Stress in highly traumatised populations, residing in settings where there are few resources and limited, if any, mental health support provisions. The study found that the intervention is highly effective and can be used in remote settings with little cost.

The background to the study was the observation that Eritrean refugees take very high risks, often life threatening, during their search for a safe heaven. This raised the question whether PTSD symptoms could impair decision-making in refugees causing them to make risky. Another question that was raised was whether the Eritrean refugees were engaging maladaptive behaviours as coping strategies. Underpinning these questions was the fact that hypervigilance, which is a symptom of PTSD, causes people to become oversensitive to the presence of risk and danger and can cause an exaggerated response. The question therefore was whether Eritrean refugees, did suffer from high levels of post-traumatic stress disorder (PTSD), and if so, whether resilience could be enhanced by an intervention, adapted to the context, to treat PTSD.

The research consists of three phases: (i) an exploration to understand the prevalence of PTSD among Eritrean refugees and an investigation of the occurrence of collective trauma and how traumatic stories are communicated; (ii) a design of a pilot of an intervention (TRUST) to treat PTSD and (iii) the test of the intervention among Eritrean refugees in a real-life setting.

The research was conducted among Eritrean refugees residing in different locations. A pilot of TRUST was carried out in North Uganda. The prevalence of PTSD was measured using the Impact of Events Scale-Revised (IES-R). It was found that almost without exception, the scores indicated high levels of PTSD. The extensive prevalence of PTSD also indicated collective trauma, which was researched by investigating the narration of traumatising memories on digital channels, such as Facebook. It was found that social media platforms were important communication channels, despite the fact that traumatic memories were also shared through these mediums causing high levels of collective trauma.

As a subsequent step, an intervention was designed. This therapy took into account the nature of the context and utilising the available communication channels – such as the mobile phones, that were in high use and trusted. The utilisation of these communication channels was intended to overcome the challenge of the unavailability of mental health workers to provide support. Based on techniques from Eye Movement Desensitisation and Reprocessing (EMDR), TRUST was designed with the objective of offering self-help techniques. Instructions were adapted taking the cultural and linguistic context into account. The program consists of three parts: understanding of the cause and symptoms of traumatic stress, the provision of techniques to cope with the symptoms of trauma and a social reintegration program.

Following its development, TRUST was first tested as a pilot in Northern Uganda among female returnees after the civil war. Self-perceived resilience was measured using the Social and Economic Resilience Scale (SER). SER is a self-reporting questionnaire with five constructs: social, income, empowerment, access to justice and capacity. In addition IES-R was used to measure levels of traumatic stress. The study was conducted in a real-life setting in a controlled pre-test post-test experimental design. TRUST was administered alongside an intervention of a social protection program, in the form of cash transfers and in-kind support packages. This allowed us to isolate and measure the various factors affecting resilience as well as compare their effect.

Prior to the implementation of TRUST the impact of other psycho-social support methods was tested. In this first phase, 471 women participated and were divided into four groups in a post-experimental design. The results compared the impact of the various interventions on socio-economic resilience. The groups that had psycho-social support for trauma scored significantly higher on socio-economic resilience than the groups that only participated in social protection interventions. The group that received a combination of income support interventions for social protection and psycho-social support scored the highest for improvements on socio-economic resilience.

We then compared the psycho-social support received in phase one with TRUST. In this phase, 356 participants were divided into eight groups and were given different combinations of interventions. TRUST was, contextualised to the culture and was offered in local languages through an audio program, recorded by trusted and familiar local radio presenters. Findings indicated a significant impact of TRUST on socio- economic resilience, with varying implications for the different constructs of resilience. Moreover, the results of the study pointed to the relevance of collective trauma in addition to individual traumatic stress.

Subsequently, the intervention was adapted and implemented in two refugee camps in Ethiopia (Hitsats and Shimelba camps in the Tigray region) with 103 young, Eritrean participants. TRUST was made available via videos on mobile phones. This had been proven to be a familiar and trusted communication channel for refugee youth in the camps.

The study in Ethiopia implemented TRUST within the framework of livelihood support programmes, which allowed the isolation of several variables that influence resilience. Participants were divided into four groups, with the trauma intervention being administered in two ways: group 1 received only the first stage of the intervention, group 2 completed the entire intervention. The research was a pre test-post test-experimental study with repeated measurements. Both IES-R and SER were shortened, taking into account the high mobility of participants. Additionally, in this research the collective nature of trauma was investigated as an independent variable and measured using the Internet Social Capital Scale (ISCS).

The results of this study are similar to the previous results from Uganda: the participants who completed the TRUST intervention scored significantly higher on the Socio-Economic Resilience Scale. Interestingly the availability of livelihood support packages had no influence on the socio-economic resilience of the respondents, indicating that the improvements are caused by psychological rather that material support. The intervention also dramatically decreased the score on the IES-R, indicating that it may decrease the symptoms of PTSD. It was also found that collective trauma decreased as a result of the TRUST treatment and that the decrease negatively correlated with enhanced socio-economic resilience.

The three experimental studies confirm the hypothesis that trauma affects perceived social and economic resilience and that psycho-social support alleviates the situation and contributes to enhanced socio-economic resilience (SER scores). The study further finds that the treatment TRUST, designed as a low-cost self-help intervention, has significant impact on socio-economic resilience and more so than social protection support in the form of cash transfers, in-kind support or livelihood support. Additionally, the study points to the relevance of collective trauma as a factor in improving socio-economic resilience.

The study concludes that high levels of traumatic stress can be a factor that influences refugee decision-making. High levels of PTSD are not conducive for refugees settling down; in fact, they may keep fleeing to avert the trauma-induced danger that haunts them, taking their trauma along with them. Current policies developed to discourage refugees to move away from the first point of safety that they flee to, can exacerbate the stress of traumatised refugees. To understand the risky behaviours of refugees and to develop approaches that generate more resilience, greater attention is needed for the treatment of Post-Traumatic Stress in refugee communities. Based on the findings in this study, it may be postulated that it would be more prudent to improve the mental health state of refugees with PTSD symptoms, by treating trauma and thus increasing their resilience, rather than instituting preventive measures restricting their movement and enhancing their feelings of insecurity. TRUST offers a viable option to help address trauma, decrease risky decision-making and increase the socio-economic resilience of refugees and their communities.

About the Author

Selam KIDANE

Selam Kidane is a systemic psychotherapist trained at the Institute of Family Therapy in London, UK. She is a researcher in various programmes related to refugees resilience and mental health with the Globalisation, Accessibility, Innovation and Care (GAIC)-Research Network at the Faculty of Humanities and Digital Sciences at the Tilburg University.

Selam Kidane has worked with various refugee communities and particularly with separated refugee children in the UK and has authored practice guides and training manuals in relation to that work. Currently she works as a systemic therapist for an integrated clinical service in London.

Acknowledgement

This research was undertaken in an area that spans Eritrea, Ethiopia, Uganda, Sudan and Israel. Therefore, the list of people and organisations that I owe gratitude to is long and reflects the many links and networks I had at my disposal. It is impossible to list all of the local, regional and international organisations working with refugees that have contributed to this work. My hope is that I have made a meaningful contribution to our understanding of how best to support refugees and that this will go some way towards thanking them.

I am very grateful to the Netherlands Organisation for Scientific Research, Science for Global Development (NWO-WOTRO) for the grant (Project number W 08.400.159) 'Causes and dynamics of mixed unskilled migrants trafficked within the Horn of Africa region', which enabled me to conduct parts of this research in the depth that I have been able to. I also thank NWO, European Commission and EEPA for additional research support (see p. 306).

Colleagues at Mekelle University, Ethiopia, particularly Professor Kinfe and Dr Aradom, played a pivotal role in connecting this research to their institution and the rich research activities there. I thank them for their interest and their support. The teams of research assistants and colleagues in Eritrea, Ethiopia, Sudan, Uganda and Israel were invaluable in coordinating the registration of participants and supporting participants as they waited for their interview. They truly went above and beyond the call of duty to make the collection of data possible, sometimes at great personal cost to themselves. Without their intimate local knowledge and understanding of the context none of this would have been possible and, for that, I am grateful.

I received a lot of language support throughout and I appreciate the efficiency of those involved, particularly Zekarias Gerrima, for understanding the concepts as well as the language. I would also like to thank Zekarias for his keen involvement in making the material accessible.

Yohaness Alula recorded, edited and uploaded the videos, painstakingly editing the various versions and supporting the seamless transition from the original idea to subsequent adaptations. I am grateful for his support and touched by his patience and eagerness to help.

Rick Schoenmaecker was in the region for the duration of the Ethiopia research and was instrumental in ensuring that the videos continued to be distributed in accordance with the agreements. His insight into connectivity and access were influential in the development of the adaptation to overcome the barriers posed by connectivity. I thank ZOA and MSF who provided practical support to the research in the camps in Ethiopia.

Dr Primrose Nakazibwe and the research team in Uganda allowed me to learn from their work and contribute to it, enabling me to gain both insight and inspiration. I am forever indebted to them for their generosity in beautifully grafting my work onto theirs.

I also owe thanks to 24COMS, in particular Norbert Wilmering, for making their App available free of charge. I learnt a great deal about the possibility of providing assistance via an App, as well as the pitfalls, from them. Wenqing Yin played a key role in the development of our content on 24COMS and she also collected and collated the data that came through it. This was central to my understanding of how we can use an App for the kind of work we are doing. I thank her for her patience in responding to the constant needs that emerged.

Dr Mia Stokmans' contribution to the development of the theoretical underpinning of this thesis and the research instruments, as well as the analysis of the data gathered, was invaluable. All this was crucial in helping me make sense of the data and interpret the findings. I am sincerely grateful to her for her patience and expertise.

Professor Sjaak Kroon's input in guiding me through the writing of my thesis and capturing the essence of my findings was crucial. I am grateful for his insight, which shaped the research, as well as his encouragement throughout the process.

It was an honour and a great learning experience to work with Professor Dr Mirjam van Reisen. Her relentless work in shaping the direction of the research, the professional and academic rigor she provided, and the passion with which she drove the work forward is evident in what has been achieved. I thank her for her professional input and friendship throughout the years. I am grateful to all colleagues of the Research Network Globalisation, Accessibility, Innovation and Care (GAIC) and especially to Klara Smits, Kristína Melicherová and Bertha Vallejo for their support and friendship. I am very grateful to Susan Sellars who is a wonderful editor and copy-editor, thank you for going over this manuscript in such detail.

I simply have no words to thank my family. My husband and best friend, Asheber Tesfay, supported me every step of the way and held the fort, ensuring our children were supported as they were going through their transitions into young adulthood. Amen, Wintana and Eddy, I am proud of the way you accommodated my many absences and showed immense maturity in supporting each other when there was a need. My parents laid the foundations for all this long before I got here myself; I am grateful and I hope I have lived up to the dreams you had for your children. I could not have wished for better parents, my only regret is the fact that Baba is not here to witness the realisation of our shared dream. Lydia, Aida, Didi and Baby, together with your respective families (the Hageresebs) – my fellow travellers, my sisters and my friends – without you I would be lost and would not even know where to begin. I thank you for your support and for filling in the many gaps I left.

Finally, and most importantly, I am grateful to the hundreds of Eritrean refugees and Ugandan internally displaced persons who shared some of their most painful experiences, allowing me to gain insight into their lives as refugees. I am truly grateful for this and I sincerely hope that this research will contribute to the improvement of the support available to people in vulnerable situations who need protection.

Thank you all, thank God for you.

Selam Kidane
London, September 2021

Acronyms

CBT	cognitive behavioural therapy
COI	Commission of Inquiry
COR	conservation of resources
EMDR	Eye Movement Desensitisation Reordering
HAP	Humanitarian Assistance Programmes
ICC	International Criminal Court
ICT	information and communication technology
IDP	internally displaced person
IES-R	Impact of Events Scale-Revised
IES-S	Impact of Events Scale-Short
ISCS	Internet Social Capital Scale
LRA	Lord's Resistance Army
MANOVA	multivariate analysis of variance
MH	mental health
MSF	Medecins Sans Frontières
NGO	non-governmental organisation
NWO	Netherlands Organisation for Scientific Research
PFC	prefrontal cortex
PSE	perceived self-efficacy
PTS	post-traumatic stress
PTSD	post-traumatic stress disorder
SER	Social and Economic Resilience Scale
SER-S	Social and Economic Resilience Scale-Short
SES	socio-economic standing
SUD	Subjective Unit of Distress
UN	United Nations
UNHCR	United Nations High Commissioner for Refugees
WHO	World Health Organization
WOTRO	Science for Global Development
ZOA	Zuid Oost Azië

Table of Contents

Chapter 1

Introduction

The simple truth is that refugees would not risk their lives on a journey so dangerous if they could thrive where they are.

Melissa Fleming, UNHCR

Refugee Go Home!

Like the river that passes through
I have no place to call my own
I stop where life wills
to let them take what they want...
And dump what they will
...then on I lumber
Changing names along the way
...Recruit
...Deserter
...Objector
...Asylum seeker
Illegal immigrant
...Homeless
...Stateless
...Trafficked
...Smuggled
...Hired
...Bought
...Sold
...Donated
...Lent
...Refugee
I don't remember my name anymore
I don't recall my dreams
Never had the luxury of a vision

1

Have lost count of the case files kept on me
I have no history…I have no legacy…
Is home really where the heart is?
Me… I have no use for a heart
Home?
I have no home

I wrote the above poem many years ago, the sentiments are my own, the various contexts of a refugee existence are borrowed from the many refugees I have known, either as personal acquaintances or through my professional career working with many refugees from all over the world. I find that we often fail to see the world from the perspective of a refugee. This research is my attempt to begin to address this imbalance.

1.1 The refugee-making process

Why do refugees take the risks they do, taking dangerous journeys to places they believe to be safer? The quote at the top of this chapter is from a speech by Melissa Fleming (Fleming, 2015), the chief spokesperson for the United Nations High Commissioner for Refugees (UNHCR). The 'simple truth' referred to by Fleming – that refugees will not move on if they can thrive where they are – does not always hold true. The reality on the ground, as told even in the UNHCR's own data, indicates that refugees *do* risk their lives, taking dangerous journeys, when it seems that perhaps they could stay where they are. There seems to be something missing in our understanding of why refugees continue to take such risks, despite the UNHCR and others' best efforts to enable them to "thrive where they are".

There is an African fable about a young monkey who fell out of a tree into a bush of thorns. As he tried to extricate himself, his entire body became covered in thorns. When he eventually got out, he could not sit or stand in one spot long enough to be able to start plucking the thorns out. A passer-by asked how he could help, but added that he only had enough time to pluck a single thorn out and so the young monkey had to think hard about which one to choose.

It did not take long, as he was very clear which one he wanted to be removed. Pointing to his bottom, he said: "I want you to take the one on my bottom out. With that one out I can settle and take all of the others out myself".

This is an apt analogy to describe the situation that many refugees find themselves in: thrown out of their home into a bush of thorns. There is a great deal of ambiguity over what to do to help them get out of the impossible situation they find themselves in. However, unlike the fable, there does not seem to be anyone asking the refugees what would be most useful to them. Instead, most attempt to impose their own array of solutions to resolve 'the refugee crisis'. Some of these solutions make the situation worse. Similar to the monkey who, when left entirely to his own devices, found himself in an impossible situation, refugees need help so that they can help themselves. But, unlike the monkey, refugees are usually not enabled to do so. Part of the problem is the way many refugee-hosting communities try to help refugees, which results from the way migration is seen as a simple cause and effect dynamic – a set of 'push' and 'pull' factors. This leads to a failure to understand the reasons why refugees move and, as a result, solutions that do not address the causes.

This research aims to provide an alternative approach to conceptualising the reasons for the ongoing mobility of refugees and, in particular, the often unimaginable risks that many take in attempt to reach a place where they feel safe and can build a future. It aims to build on what we know about the traumatic experiences of refugees and examines the potential benefits of advancements in technology to see if the combination of the two could enhance protection and support, even in the most difficult circumstances. Many questions will continue to be asked and will require multi-faceted answers. It is my hope that this book will provide some of these answers.

Political violence, state repression, and civil wars have devastating consequences for the individuals and communities embroiled in such situations. These periods of upheaval can result in the massive dislocation of people, forced to flee their homes in search of security and prospects elsewhere. A closer analysis of refugee migration rates indicates that in recent conflicts, such as the conflicts in Eritrea,

Rwanda, Afghanistan, Kosovo, Darfur, and Syria, displacement is often far greater than the number killed and injured. This makes forced migration and the displacement of people an important dimension of these conflicts, not only affecting the individuals displaced, but also impacting on the causes and dynamics of these conflicts and with long-term implications for the social, economic and political environment in their place of origin as well as their place of refuge. Moreover, when conflicts continue to rage, eluding lasting solutions, the refugee crises they cause can drag on for decades, leaving many people without a permanent home (Salehyan, 2007).

While the above link between conflict and the outflow of refugees is obvious, there is still a gap in our understanding of refugees and their motivations, perspectives, and decisions to flee. Even though the international flow of people has been on the international agenda for many years (Teitelbaum, 1984), it is still an under researched area (Neumayer, 2005). This gap in our understanding also extends to what motivates refugees to either stay where they end up after their initial flight or keep moving, even when this involves great risk.

Much of our understanding of conflict-induced migration is focused on the consequences of the instability, such as poverty, inequality, economic restructuring and development pressures, often considered to be the 'root causes' of such migration (Hamilton & Chinchilla, 1991). However, this is a rather narrow interpretation based on push and pull theory (Lee, 1966). As a result we often find that refugee migration is described from the perspective of an outsider commentator, rather than from the perspectives of the refugees themselves, failing to take into account the factors internal to the refugee. For instance, the impact of trauma and traumatic stress as a factor in the decision to migrate and settle is hardly ever considered, despite the fact that war and conflict are prime causes of trauma and traumatic stress. The refugee is not seen as having agency and, hence, analyses of their evaluation of the costs and benefits of ongoing mobility are incomplete. This results in a gap in our understanding of the impact of refugees' migration experiences on the mental processes that affect information processing and decision making. There also a gap in the research that incorporates the consideration of the agency of the refugee in the refugee-making

4

process (which includes the circumstances that make it unsafe for the refugee to stay in their place of origin, their decision to move, and the direction of that move).

The magnitude of the experiences involved in the refugee-making process, ranging from persecution and harassment to torture and mass killing, are known to result in persistent symptoms that damage the victim's self-esteem, as well as their trust in others, leading many to experience changes to their identity (Barudy, 1989). Studies indicate that the prevalence of depression and post-traumatic stress disorder (PTSD) in refugee communities is as high as 40 to 70% (Baingana, 2003). Unfortunately, displacement could compound these symptoms; nonetheless, such a high prevalence of PTSD is indicative of how conflict and political violence can cause psychiatric illness and trigger severe psychological reactions to trauma, with debilitating effects (Silove, Ekblad & Mollica, 2000).

Such a high prevalence of trauma has implications for the wider community, which often succumbs to maladaptations that can be detrimental to wellbeing in the long term. This phenomenon has been documented in various locations. A study in Cambodia, following the long history of violence and civil war in the 1960s that culminated in the Khmer Rouge rule, which devastated the social fabric of the society, found high levels of psychiatric symptoms in refugees, even 10 years after the events (Boehnlein et al., 2004). Similarly, a survey of 993 adults from the largest Cambodian internally displaced person (IDP) camp on the Thailand-Cambodia border identified that 80% felt depressed, as well as experiencing somatic complaints, despite good access to medical services (Mollica et al., 1999). Another example is a Mayan village in Guatemala where everyone was observed to be experiencing a tremendous sense of guilt, fear, depression, loss, abandonment, despair, humiliation, anger and solitude, as well as a shattered faith in God. This population had been the target of a genocidal campaign from 1981 to 1983, during which more than 600 massacres were carried out, mostly by Guatemalan troops. This resulted in people retreating to passivity, conformity, and mistrust, incubating a cycle of vulnerability that continued to threaten recovery long after the events had taken place (Manz, 2002).

5

Despite this stark reality of significant and multi-layered trauma and collective trauma, migration is seldom discussed in the light of the impact of traumatic stress on refugees and their communities. Failure to consider such a significant factor in the refugee-making process has resulted in a gap in policies and practices that seek to provide refugees with protection and support. It also feeds into negative portrayals of refugees in the media, thus negatively affecting their integration (Steimel, 2010).

As mentioned above, the aim of this research is to offer a different perspective than the traditional approach to viewing migration and the organisation and delivery of refugee support. The specific refugee population of concern here are the traumatised Eritrean refugees who have been making headlines, both because of the sheer number of refugees leaving the country as well as the enormous risks they have been taking to do so. The researcher also had the opportunity to work with traumatised women in Northern Uganda and this research has also been included.

1.2 Context of the research: Traumatised Eritrean refugees

In 2015, I led a march of tens of thousands of fellow Eritrean refugees who rallied in Geneva-Switzerland in support of a report by the UN Human Rights Commission that investigated the gross human rights violations occurring in Eritrea and declared that they potentially amount to 'crimes against humanity'. The report called for accountability on behalf of the millions of Eritreans who have suffered atrocities that were untold or ignored when told. For the first time we felt that the world dared to see what we had experienced in silence for so long. It is a bitter-sweet memory of a time when we felt visible and significant and our pain was finally quantifiable in a language that the world understood. We felt vindicated.

Having outlined the systematic use of extrajudicial killing, torture, rape, indefinite national service and forced labour, the report by the UN Commission of Inquiry on Human Rights in Eritrea (COI) concluded that "It is not law that rules Eritreans – it is fear" (UN Human Rights Council, 2015). The report also states that these violations could amount to crimes against humanity. In what makes

6

absolute grim reading, cataloguing the harrowing violations committed against groups and individuals in Eritrea, the report details experiences that have had a devastating traumatic impact on Eritreans.

The COI report states that the violations, including a programme of imprisonments and forced disappearances, perpetrated by the regime of President Isaias Afwerki, are "on a scope and scale seldom witnessed elsewhere". The government was found to be using extreme surveillance and censorship to create a culture of fear to crush all forms of dissent, including at the level of thought. Spying and surveillance are conducted to such a degree that Eritreans live in constant fear of arbitrary arrest, detention, torture, disappearance and death. This surveillance culture has given rise to a poisonous climate of self-censorship and mistrust that permeates communities and families.

In addition to draconian limits on freedom of speech, media, movement and assembly, the report states that, only four religious denominations – the Eritrean Orthodox Church, Catholic Church, Lutheran Church and Sunni Islam – are tolerated. All other religious communities are restricted or attacked by the government. Another source of fear for Eritreans, including minors, is the policy of forced conscription, which has trapped an entire generation of young Eritreans in indefinite national service, in which conditions during training and deployment are reported to including lack of sufficient food and water and inadequate hygiene facilities, accommodation and medical facilities. The hardships are further compounded by the abuse and ill-treatment of both men and women. Women, however, additionally suffer gender-based violence perpetrated against them, in some cases, the Commission found, amounting to torture. The findings indicate that: "Sexual violence against women and girls is widespread and indeed notorious in military training camps. [...] Furthermore, the enforced domestic service of women and girls who are also sexually abused in these camps amounts to sexual slavery" (UN Human Rights Council, 2015, p. 13). In addition, the report identified that Eritrean officials regularly use beating and rape as a way to inflict severe physical and psychological pain, extract confessions and information, as well as punish, intimidate and coerce detainees and conscripts.

Regarding the mass exodus of Eritreans fleeing their country, the COI report makes it clear that the root cause is inside the country. It states that: "Faced with a seemingly hopeless situation they [Eritreans] feel powerless to change, hundreds of thousands of Eritreans are fleeing their country", despite the fact that "Eritreans who attempt to leave the country are seen as traitors", and that "the government has implemented a shoot-to-kill policy in border areas to prevent people from fleeing" (*ibid.*, p. 6).

Indeed, tens of thousands of Eritrean citizens are leaving Eritrea, taking enormous risks to do so and facing further hazards along the routes to destinations they deem 'safe' (Van Reisen, Estefanos & Rijken, 2012, 2014; Van Reisen & Rijken, 2015; Connel, 2012; Hotline for Migrant Workers, 2011). Many are young and are deserting indefinite national service or fleeing to avoid forced conscription (Kibreab, 2009; Van Reisen, Saba & Smits, 2019). Sadly, there does not seem to be an end in sight; nearly three decades after winning its independence from Ethiopia, Eritrea has yet to implement the Constitution ratified in 1997, the government routinely jails critics, including top government and party officials, and has banned non-state media as well as independent organisations (Connel, 2012). While not everyone in Eritrea has first-hand experience of imprisonment, torture, sexual exploitation or rape (Human Rights Watch, 2009), everyone knows someone who is in prison, has been tortured, or has been raped or sexually assaulted (Hepner, 2009). The general sense of uncertainty and repression has resulted in a state of hopelessness (Kidane, 2015).

The United Nations Refugee Agency, UNHCR, reported that in the first 10 months of 2014, the number of Eritrean asylum seekers arriving in Europe nearly tripled, from 13,000 the previous year to 37,000 (UNHCR, 2014). In 2014, around 5,000 Eritreans fled their country each month, making the small country of 6 million a top generator of refugees. After Syrians, Eritreans made up the largest group of those entering Europe to seek refuge. These include unaccompanied minors and vulnerable women, arriving by boats, surviving the dangerous journey across the Sahara Desert and then across the Mediterranean Sea (UNHCR, 2014; Hotline for Migrant Workers, 2011). The sheer magnitude of the numbers leaving Eritrea, and its implications for the country, as well as the risks that people take to leave, has left many observers asking why Eritreans are leaving their country in such a manner (e.g., BBC, 2015; Kingsley, 2015; O'Brien, 2015; Economist, 2013). Several explanations have been offered for the decline in the state of affairs in Eritrea; many lament how Eritrea has plummeted from a beacon of hope (Babu, Babu & Wilson, 2002; Kibreab, 2009) to the sorry state described in numerous human rights reports. The dismal state that Eritrea is in now is considered a key factor that is pushing hundreds of thousands of Eritreans out of their country, often taking unimaginable risks (Kibreab, 2015).

Despite its small size and population, Eritrea continues to be listed among the top refugee producing countries in the world today. In 2014 and 2015, roughly 40,000 Eritreans each year made the extremely hazardous Mediterranean crossing to arrive in Italy (Lanni, 2016). Many people remain in refugee camps and live as urban refugees in neighbouring countries. According to UNHCR, in 2016 alone, 52,000 people escaped Eritrea, and, by 2018, it was estimated that about 12% of the population had been pushed out of the country, many escaping the prolonged national service (Human Rights Watch, 2018). The mass violation of human rights, government-induced poverty, and resulting exodus of refugees continue – despite the peace deal with Ethiopia and easing of international sanctions in 2018 (Selassie & Van Reisen, 2019).

Unfortunately, despite the violation of human rights and deteriorating conditions in Eritrea, refugee receiving countries, typically in Western Europe, continue to develop policies focused on limiting the number of refugees (Danish Immigration Services Report, 2014; UK Home Office, 2015a, 2015b). These policies are based on mitigating the economic incentives ('pull factors') that are drawing poor people from across the world, including from Eritrea, to Europe. This research was mainly conducted among Eritrean refugees across several contexts, including in refugee camps where resources are scarce and support is limited. The population in these camps is highly mobile, often taking risks to cross dangerous borders under hazardous conditions, and many end up losing their lives in the process. The UN COI report (UN Human Rights Council, 2015, p. 6) states: "In desperation, they [Eritrean refugees] resort to deadly escape routes through deserts and neighbouring war-torn countries and across dangerous seas in search of safety. They risk capture, torture and death at the hands of ruthless human traffickers".

The routes out of the first points of exit (the refugee camps across the borders) have changed over the years, in response to various policies aimed at making it hard for refugees to travel further in search of better prospects; however, the flow of desperate Eritrean migrants continues, resulting only in changes to the routes taken and the associated risks. The 'desperate situation' in the refugee camps is the reason given to explain why people continue to move on from the camps, in hope of finding better conditions (Brhane, 2016). Here it must be noted that while the search for prospects is understandable given the living conditions in the camps, the acceptance of the risks involved in undertaking the onward journey (which are well known to the refugees) cannot be fully explained without considering factors that play a role in the decision-making process. Indeed the UN COI report (Human Rights Council, 2015, p. 6) states: "To ascribe their decision to leave solely to economic reasons is to ignore the dire situation of human rights in Eritrea and the very real suffering of its people. Eritreans are fleeing severe human rights violations in their country and are in need of international protection".

An understanding of how trauma works leads to the conceptualisation that the traumatic experiences suffered by Eritreans have affected their ability to rationally assess the opportunities available to them in the various locations they find themselves in after their initial flight and, hence, they continue their perilous search for safety and a better opportunity to rebuild their lives (Van Reisen, Smits & Wirtz, 2019). Understanding this would facilitate the provision of better protection to Eritrean refugees in the camps in neighbouring countries, as well as other groups of vulnerable refugees who take similar risks in their desperate search for safety and prospects.

As well as an academic endeavour, this was a personal journey for myself, as a former refugee from Eritrea and a mental health professional with many years of experience working with refugees. For me, this research was an opportunity to understand, and hopefully explain, a phenomenon that has led to the death of many migrants. In addition, I am concerned that this gap in our understanding may have led to flawed policies on migration.

An attempt was made to understand the implications of trauma involved in the refugee-making process and then to address this trauma in order to explore the implications for refugees' assessments of their prospects ahead of their migration decisions. This required being able to develop an approach that is both effective and accessible in the circumstances in which refugees find themselves. Such an opportunity presented itself in the form of work among severely traumatised populations in Northern Uganda (detailed in chapters 6 and 7). This opportunity allowed for the development of a trauma support approach for communities that have been affected by severe trauma at the individual and collective levels, and the testing of this approach in a relatively settled community in Uganda, prior to further development of the approach to suit highly-mobile refugees from Eritrea.

1.3 Problem statement

The migration of refugees is often considered solely through the lens of political violence and its consequences. Such violence is considered a 'push factor', causing people to flow to destination countries, where they are provided with a level of protection, as well as economic opportunities, which are construed as 'pull factors'. Unfortunately, there seems to be a tendency to downplay the traumatic implications of conflict and political violence and overemphasise the 'economic incentives' that are pulling refugees away from their so called 'poor' countries, resulting in phrases such as 'economic refugees' and 'bogus refugees' (Zimmerman, 2011).

The push and pull model is one of the oldest models of migration (Ravenstein, 1885; 1889). This model considers all migration to be caused by the economy, and theorists believe that they can predict the level of migration from one geographical place to another based on the distance, population size and differences in economic

11

opportunities between the area of emigration and destination. In this model, migration decisions are determined using 'plus' and 'minus' analysis (Lee, 1966; Passaris, 1989). The first comprehensive attempt to understand and describe why people migrate was conducted by Ravenstein (1885; 1889) in a series of papers for the Royal Statistical Society. He studied the population data of the United Kingdom (Ravenstein, 1885), Europe and North America (Ravenstein, 1889) and published the results in *The Laws of Migration*.

The laws identified in this work are insightful and seemed to be valid beyond the United Kingdom, where they were first proposed, in the 19th century. The work provided an insight into various aspects of migration, such as rural-urban migration, counter-migration and female migration. Ravenstein also offered explanations for migration; for example, migration is produced by overpopulation, underdeveloped resources, persecutory laws, unfair taxation, an inhospitable climate, or unfavourable social surroundings (Ravenstein, 1889). While successful at enabling us to make sense of the patterns of human movement using statistical data, the laws and analysis proposed do not take the individuality of the migrant fully into account. Indeed Ravenstein himself admits, "I am perfectly aware that our laws of population, and economic laws generally, have not the rigidity of physical laws, as they are continually being interfered with by human agency" (Ravenstein, 1889, p. 241).

Based on Ravenstein's work, Lee (1966) developed the 'push-pull theory of migration', which is based on the basic principle that migrants are 'pushed' to move from their origins and 'pulled' to their destinations. Lee (1966) classifies all causative factors of migration into four categories: issues in the area of origin; issues related to the destination; any obstacles; and individual factors. In each category, it is assumed that there are countless factors that attract people to a place, as well as repel people from a place. Migration happens when push factors in the place of origin and pull factors in the destination are strong enough to overcome the obstacles to moving. The theory has been developed into a mathematical form (Dorigo & Tobler 1983) and empirical studies distinguish many factors that impact on migration decisions, such as income (Banerjee & Ray, 1991; Borjas, Bronars & Trejo, 1992; Roback, 1982, 1988), job satisfaction

(Banerjee & Ray, 1991), amenities (Roback, 1988), education (Borjas *et al.*, 1992), and climate (Roback, 1982). While Lee accepts that the push-pull factors are different for each individual, migrants' decision-making processes have not been fully explored. For instance, do migrants actively make decisions about a preferred destination, or are they passively led to the said destination?

Lee (1966) assumes that migration is essentially active, by arguing that migrants rationally weigh push-pull factors, but he acknowledges that a considerable proportion of migration seems 'irrational'. One explanation offered for such irrational decisions is said to be 'mental disorder':

> *The decision to migrate, therefore, is never completely rational, and for some persons the rational component is much less than the irrational. We must expect, therefore, to find many exceptions to our generalizations since transient emotions, mental disorder, and accidental occurrences account for a considerable proportion of the total migrations.* (Lee, 1966, p. 51)

This research proposes that one such disorder causing irrational migration decisions could be individual and collective trauma. In trauma, information about fear becomes highly activated, affecting the storing encoding and retrieval of information. Such a situation may diminish the individual's ability to accurately process non-threat related information, this could lead to attentional bias resulting in a focus on perceived threats in the environment (Chemtob, Roitblat, Hamada, Carlson & Twentyman, 1988). Threat arousal may, therefore, predispose an individual to interpret even innocuous stimuli as threatening, skewing rational decisions.

As described above, the risks entailed in the migration routes that many Eritrean refugees are choosing do not fit into a balanced equation, such as the one offered by the rational decisions outlined in the push and pull model (see Figure 1.1). Indeed the number of deaths and abductions on route, as well as the difficulties in obtaining asylum in destinations in Europe, makes the risks taken when deciding to continue moving far from rational.

Figure 1.1. Push and pull model of migration (© Selam Kidane)

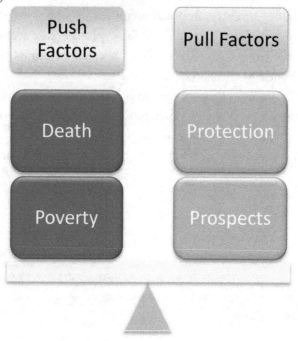

Figure 1.1 shows a balance between the factors considered when assessing the benefits of migration. However, in reality, there is a large list of factors that contribute to the migration decision, but it is unclear how these factors interact with each other and/or combine together (Skeldon, 1990) to trigger movement. In contrast to a perfectly balanced situation, the migration out of Eritrea, and then onwards from refugee camps in neighbouring countries, has a very skewed balance with numerous risks that make the decision to journey through the Sahara Desert and across the Mediterranean Sea to Europe an unsound one for those whose quest is protection and better prospects. Figure 1.2 shows the imbalance in the risks and benefits of migration for refugees.

Figure 1.2. Risks and benefits of migration (© Selam Kidane)

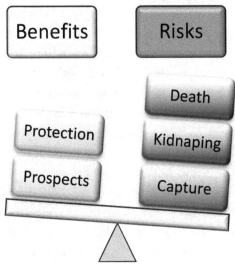

In addition, while an analysis of refugee producing situations would indicate that the level of general displacement (e.g., Eritreans moving to refugee camps in neighbouring Ethiopia or Sudan) generally corresponds with the level of violence in the country of origin (Suhrke, 1995), this does not explain the decision to either settle in the camps and wait for circumstances to change, or keep moving in search of better protection and prospects, especially when considering the enormous risks taken to do so, which often outweigh the potential benefits of migration.

Generally speaking, although risk is prevalent throughout migration, it is poorly theorised and the complex multi-faceted relationship between risk and migration has not been explicitly analysed. The views and perspectives of individual refugees are also largely overlooked (Williams & Baláž, 2012), and there seems to be no consensus on whether migrants are actively shaping their migration or passively allowing the inevitable to happen (Horbaty, Gollp, Daita & Carballo, 2006). This is an important consideration, as the intricacy of the route, the number of negotiations, the arrangements and the organisation taking place indicate that there is a level of active engagement and, hence, the impact of a refugee's traumatic experiences on their ability to make a 'rational' assessment of risks and benefits becomes a crucial factor in understanding migration.

Indeed the push and pull model has been used extensively to explain the outflow of Eritrean refugees, with many descriptive analyses of the various political and socio-economic 'push' factors and the corresponding 'pull' factors, such as relatively easy asylum in Europe, which may have caused as many as 37,000 Eritreans to cross the Mediterranean Sea to Europe in the first 10 months of 2014 alone (UNHCR, 2014). While some of these refugees have found reasonable protection and better prospects in Europe, many have taken enormous risks to do so, bringing the benefits of the journey into question. Others have lost their lives along the way. In this context, the model falls short of explaining the number of people who continue to use the migration route through the Sahara Desert and across the Mediterranean Sea, despite the risks involved (Faist, 2000). The extortionate amounts of money demanded by smugglers, the risk of being abducted by human traffickers, the hazardous journey itself, and the existence of policies intent on keeping refugees out of destination countries all imbalance the equation described in the push and pull model. One of the problems with this model is that it is based on factors used to predict migration at an aggregate level (Foresight, 2011), while the individualised assessment of costs and benefits (e.g., family reunion at any cost) is not given much weight. Furthermore, the model does not explain why the same set of 'push factors' (e.g., poverty, persecution etc.) does not result in similar migration patterns in all areas of the world (or even for some communities from areas of high flow). Nor is there much consideration given to the psychological implications of extreme experiences on individuals and communities, which may result in PTSD or collective trauma.

However, we cannot always assume the prevalence of traumatic stress in refugees on the move. Summerfield (1995, 1996) highlights the need for caution when drawing conclusions about the prevalence of PTSD, as confounding variables in the chain of events leading to mental disorders, accompanied by vivid and painful memories of the past, can fall within the range of normal responses to adverse contexts. Nonetheless, there is evidence indicating a direct link between exposure to conflict and atrocities and symptoms ranging from anxiety to chronic PTSD spanning a period of up to 50 years (Pederson, 2002). Other studies of political conflict also reveal findings, indicating a high prevalence of symptoms. In Southern Lebanon, Farhood, Dimassi and Lehtinen (2006) reported that a third (29.3%) of an adult sample (n=256) met the criteria for PTSD. Among internally displaced Turkish Cypriots displaced during both the 1963 ethnic conflict and the 1974 Cyprus War, 20% showed symptoms of PTSD even 30 years after the event (Ergun, Cakici & Cakici, 2008). In a study on lifetime and current PTSD rates among Iranians, Hashemian *et al.* (2006) reported rates of 59% and 33%, respectively; these were people exposed to high-intensity warfare, including chemical weapons, during the Iran-Iraq War (1980–1988).

In the case of Eritrea, many credible reports into the human rights situation in the country (Amnesty International, 2004; Human Rights Watch, 2009), including, as mentioned above, the report of the COI (UN Human Rights Council, 2015), consistently outline the extreme political repression, including torture and inhumane treatment, perpetrated against ordinary citizens. The prevalence of torture, political violence and armed conflict, whether targeted towards an individual or the population at large, poses an immense threat to people on various levels (Modvig & Jaranson, 2004). There is ample evidence to suggest that, aside from resulting in physical injury or death, political violence, such as that perpetrated in Eritrea, constitutes a traumatic threat to the integrity of the self (Chapman & Garvin, 1999). Understanding the implications of such traumatic experiences is crucial to understand migration trajectories and provide support to refugees.

Most people exposed to trauma will experience stress responses such as avoidance, sleep disturbances, hyperarousal and hypervigilance and engage in behaviour akin to anticipation of ongoing risks (Chrousos & Gold, 1992; Tsigos & Chrousos, 2002). Repeated or constant activation of the stress response in the body and brain, known as allostatic load (McEwen, 2003), corresponding to post-traumatic stress, creates a state of fear, hopelessness and even horror in response to the threat of injury or death (Yehuda, 2002).

Nonetheless, the impact of political violence should not only be examined in terms of the impact of trauma on individual survivors, but should extend to the additional impact on the community and society at large, as well as to collective trauma relating to the disintegration of family and social networks. Collective trauma refers to the shared injuries to a population's sociocultural context (Saul, 2014). Trauma can be perceived as collective when people who have a sense of belonging to one another feel that they have been subjected to fearful and painful events, which have left a mark on their collective consciousness and memory. Here trauma is a social construct with an impact not only on the past (or present) identity of subjects, but also on their future identity (Pastor, 2004).

The decision of refugees to continue their migration trajectory, despite the risks and the mitigated benefits, could well be based on their appraisal of the ongoing risks (risk-appraisal) in their current location being affected by the level of traumatic stress they and their communities are experiencing. The psychology and research reference site IresearchNet defines the term 'risk appraisal' as "an evaluation of the chances that a future event may occur" (IresearchNet, 2021). The site also states that similar terms in use include risk assessment, risk perception, perceived likelihood of risk, and perception of becoming vulnerable. The risks being appraised might range from events of global significance (wars and disasters) to personally significant events (bereavement, illness). People's appraisal of risk, or their perception of the potential to avert risk, influences a wide variety of decisions and behaviours in many life domains (Slovic, MacGregor & Kraus, 1987).

The assessment of potential risks to avoid danger is an important life skill that, in normal circumstances, would constantly change in response to an understanding of the context and one's own ability to avert danger (Boyer, 2006). Risk perception/appraisal leads to judgments and evaluations of hazards that people are, or might be, exposed to. Such perceptions drive decisions about the acceptability of risk and are a core influencer of behaviour before, during and after a disaster (Rohrmann, 2008).

However, distortions in risk appraisal are a common feature of disorders such as PTSD. Such distortions often emanate from stress symptoms that amplify both the likelihood of negative events occurring in the future and the gravity of the negative consequences of these events (Warda & Bryant, 1998). In PTSD, risk assessment is hampered by an expectation that future experiences will have the same harmful outcome as the past experiences that caused the trauma, re-experiencing symptoms makes it impossible to move on, reinforcing the belief and leading to 'overgeneralisation', impairing a person's flexible evaluation of actual risk. The person suffering from PTSD becomes prone to rigidity of thought, adversely influencing their judgement of safety (Warda & Bryant, 1998) and leading to impaired decisions. It is, therefore, crucial to incorporate the interaction between trauma/collective trauma and decisions into discussions around the decision-making process of refugees considering their prospects in the areas that they have been forced into (e.g., refugee camps). Those working to support and settle refugees should consider healing trauma as a key issue impacting on the lives of refugees.

As we have seen above, applications of the popular push and pull model of migration overlook many contributory factors when attempting to explain refugee migration. This model focuses mainly on external factors and does not consider the experiences of refugees and the impact of these experiences on their decision-making process. This research aims to challenge the push and pull model by highlighting the impact of the traumatic experiences of members of two communities studies (in Northern Uganda and Eritrean refugees) and offer an alternative theory that captures the complex dynamics of trauma and its impact on the perceptions of protection and prospects of refugees and their communities. It explores the possibility of offering trauma support in order to reduce levels of PTSD and bring about a more positive outlook on the social and economic prospects of refugees, as they contemplate the extremely risky migrations that often cost them the very lives they are trying to save. Figure 1.3 outlines the complex relationship between traumatising push factors, traumatic stress and the appraisal of prospects by refugees.

**Figure 1.3. Relationship between trauma and migration (©
Selam Kidane)**

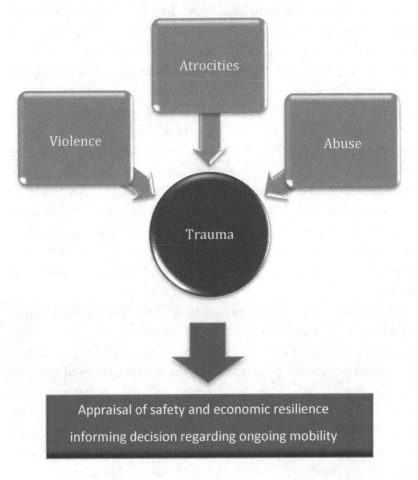

As also mentioned above, in addition to understanding individual
trauma it is vital to understand and address collective trauma. The
individual distress and persisting pain and suffering, including post-
traumatic stress and comorbid disorders such as depression, resulting
from mass disasters like war are well documented (e.g., Marsella,
Friedman, Gerrity & Surfield, 1996; Turner, Bowie, Dunn, Shapo &
Yule, 2003). However, much of this discussion focuses on individual
distress, ignoring the collective nature of such experiences. This
focus on individual trauma limits our ability to conceptualise the
problems and address them appropriately (Collier *et al.*, 2003;
Wessells & Monteiro, 2001).

1.4 Aim of the research

The aim of this research is to study the role of trauma in the consideration of safety and economic resilience by refugees during decisions about their migration trajectories. This was done by gaining an understanding of trauma, collective trauma and then trauma healing, and the implications of these on perceptions of safety and economic resilience.

Individual victims of atrocities such as torture may experience PTSD and, hence, would clearly benefit from individual intervention and support. However, this type of intervention does not address the structural context that enabled such atrocities to occur in the first place, nor does it address resultant problems, such as mistrust and the low social cohesion that often stems from the social, political and economic contexts that are incorporated into the collective consciousness, making the traumatic events become ingrained and inherent to the collective and, if left unattended, becoming cyclical (Johnson, 2006). Furthermore, without a broad and collective approach to trauma and healing, practitioners often fail to respond to the reality on the ground, when the most overwhelming concern for survivors is not past memories, as such, but the stress of daily living in situations where their social support networks have collapsed. Unlike individual trauma, which can be experienced by a small number of people, with most recovering within a given period of time, collective trauma does not refer to the symptoms of traumatic stress, but is an outcome that includes the response to traumatic events as well as the way these events are constructed into the beliefs, decisions, behaviours and narratives of the collective (Shamai, 2015), hence having the potential to impact on those who were not directly affected by the traumatic experiences themselves. This can include children who were not born at the time that the atrocities took place.

When considering trauma healing in refugee contexts, contextualising it at the collective level is crucial. This adaptation is in addition to the contextualisation in language and culture that many are becoming cognisant of (Dixon, Ahles & Marques, 2016; Bass *et al.*, 2013). Here, contextualisation also concerns the veracity of universal psychological interventions, often developed in Western contexts and focusing solely on individual trauma. As mentioned above, such interventions should be complemented by an understanding of collective cultures and the impacts of collective trauma. Collective cultures and, hence, collective trauma shape the context of the traumatic experiences and so should inform the approach taken to address traumatic stress.

Focusing on individual trauma, to the exclusion of the collective nature of traumatic experiences and impacts, de-contextualises the collective suffering in post-conflict communities. This leaves the very context of the suffering and, hence, the social and historical fabric that enabled the suffering and has now become the prevalent context, out of the healing process and can lead to further atrocities (Lykes, 2001; Van Reisen & Mawere, 2017). Moreover, failing to heal the networks and relationships hampers the recovery of those who are already suffering from PTSD and other mental health problems, by reducing the level and quality of support they are able to access within their community. A wider focus that locates trauma in the community, as well as in individuals who are suffering symptoms of traumatic stress, will give practitioners the opportunity to focus on the community-wide potential to effect healing (Bonanno, 2004; Kidane, 2015).

In addition, there needs to be a consideration of delivery approaches. This includes the consideration of language and culture, as well as availability, in a context of high mobility and low resources. Despite advances in research, theory, policy and models of treatment and the wide range of organisations responsible for providing mental health support to refugees, the inescapable reality is that most refugees with mental health problems will never receive the appropriate care, as a result of scarce resources and the inequitable distribution of mental health services (Silove, Ventevogel & Rees, 2017). Understanding trauma and its implications for decisions to move or settle will enable those working with refugees to develop, plan and deliver better policies, strategies and support for protecting them. Understanding the implications of healing trauma is crucial in the development and delivery of contextualised trauma support, within the context of resource limitations in most refugee settlements.

Part of the problem with resources is sourcing an adequately trained workforce to implement psychological interventions in low-resource refugee settings. The World Health Organization (WHO) has developed a self-help guide as a way of overcoming this challenge (Epping-Jordan *et al.*, 2016). WHO's Self-Help Plus (SH+) is based on acceptance and commitment therapy, a third-wave cognitive behavioural therapy that focuses on enhancing psychological flexibility. An adapted version was audio recorded in five sessions with an accompanying manual and delivered to Ugandan refugee in South Sudan. The trial found that the intervention was effective in reducing psychological distress in refugees (Hayes, Luoma, Bond, Masuda & Lillis, 2006).

The idea of a self-help guides solves an element of the problem (human resources), however, in addition to resources there are concerns about mobility and, while the delivery on audio is a helpful adaptation, it still does not make the intervention as mobile as the refugees are, unless delivered using information and communication technology (ICT). This research, thus, focuses on that next step of development, with particular reference to the delivery of trauma support via mobile phones, which have become a trusted and integral part of the lives of refugees scattered across many geographical areas, keeping families in contact and transferring cash and information across various locations. Based on this, a six-week, self-help trauma support for individuals and communities, called Trauma Recovery Understanding Self-Help Therapy (TRUST), was developed, which addresses both individual and collective trauma simultaneously.

1.5 Theoretical approach to trauma healing

PTSD is an anxiety disorder that impacts on cognitive processes fundamental to decision making. These disruptions could lead to poor choices, as a result of the erroneous analysis of the risks, rewards and consequences of various options. Decision-making is a complex process that should (under normal circumstances) involve clarity of options and an ability to envisage the potential benefits of outcomes – and this is often done against a backdrop of doubts and dilemmas about choices and options, elevating stress. PTSD exaggerates this stress, impairing the process (Rosenthal, 2012).

A study looking at the relevant neuronal pathways responsible for impaired decision-making capacity (Park, Wood, Bondi, Del Arco & Moghaddam, 2016) pinpointed the specific neuronal mechanisms in the prefrontal cortex (PFC) that explains the process. The study sought to determine the impact of a sustained anxiety state on the PFC neural processing on behaviour that involved cognitive flexibility. It found that anxiety results from debilitated ability to accurately encode and make effective choices based on this information. It was concluded that anxiety leads to bad decision making – specifically to risky decisions with little or no benefit, especially in situations of conflict or distress Decisions made under contexts of distress were found to correlate with the unclamping of very specific PFC neurons.

It is, therefore, crucial to understand the impact of trauma on refugees making the decisions to continue their migration journey, often at great risk and sometimes for little benefit. The push and pull model may explain one element of the migration trajectory, i.e., being pushed out of one's home to somewhere else, but it does not explain the ongoing migration, often involving immense risk, which has become a well-established pattern for many Eritrean refugees in camps across the border. This research looks at trauma as an intermediary in ongoing migration and, hence, attempts to fill the gaps in the push and pull model of migration.

1.6 Research questions and design

1.6.1 Research questions

The overarching research question to be answered by this study is as follows:

Main research question: *To what extent does trauma affect the appraisal of social economic resilience and explain decisions regarding the ongoing migration of refugees? And, are low resource trauma treatment programmes delivered using ICT effective in enhancing refugees' perceptions of safety and socio-economic resilience?*

This general research question is answered using the following sub questions:

Q.1   What is the level of post-traumatic stress (PTS) among refugees from Eritrea?

Q.2   Can levels of PTS affect the processing of information regarding safety and socio-economic resilience during decision making regarding ongoing trajectories?

Q.3   What are the trusted communication channels of refugees and is the prevalence of ICT and social media among Eritrean refugees such that it could play a role in the provision of trauma interventions?

Q.4   Is it possible to lower levels of PTS and enhance socio-economic resilience by delivering a short self-help trauma intervention in a high trauma/low resource context?

Q.5   Will a short self-help trauma intervention delivered using ICT have an impact on reducing PTS and enhancing resilience in the high trauma and low resource contexts of young Eritrean refugees? What are the key elements of such a short self-help trauma intervention in a high trauma/low resource context for it to impact on social economic resilience?

1.6.2 Research design

This study consisted of several components, each answering a specific research question, enabling us to build a fuller understanding of the role of trauma in migration trajectories in the digital era. To this end, five related studies are included in the research. These studies fall into three different categories: descriptive, design and feasibility.

Study 1: The first study was **descriptive** and focused on identifying levels of trauma and a viable method of measuring it. It was carried out among Eritrean refugee communities in Tel Aviv (Israel), Kampala (Uganda), and Tigray region (northern Ethiopia), as well as among Eritreans inside Eritrea affected by the migration crisis. The study was explorative in nature and conducted using the Impact of Events Scale-Revised (IES-R), using snowball sampling to gather participants.

Study 2: The second study was also **descriptive** and involved a questionnaire-based survey of ICTs used by Eritrean refugees in Khartoum (Sudan), Addis Ababa (Ethiopia) and refugee camps in northern Ethiopia. This study explored the prevalence of, and attitude towards, ICTs as a trusted medium of communication among refugees. Again, snowball sampling was used and a questionnaire developed for the purpose.

Study 3: The third study looked at **design** and included an extensive review of trauma healing, particularly in emergencies and among victims of mass trauma. It resulted in the design of a six-week programme of self-help trauma support for individuals and communities – Trauma Recovery Understanding Self-Help Therapy (TRUST) – suited to low resource communities.

Study 4: The fourth study looked at **feasibility** and tested the delivery of the TRUST intervention on the ground among internally displaced women traumatised by the civil war in Uganda (1980–1986) and atrocities perpetrated by the Lord's Resistance Army (LRA) in Northern Uganda. Conducting pre-post intervention experiments using the Impact of Event Scale (IES), Social and Economic Resilience Scale (SER), and individual and focus group interviews, the study sought to understand the effectiveness of TRUST.

Study 5: In the fifth study, which also looked at **feasibility**, the deliverability of TRUST via ICT in refugee camps in Ethiopia was examined using three psychometric tests. These tests were specifically adapted to fit the realities of a refugee camp (Impact of Events Scale-Short [IES-S], Social and Economic Resilience Scale-Short [SER-S] and Internet Social Capital Scale [ISCS]).

While the primary population of focus in this thesis is Eritrean refugees, due to similarities in the nature and impact of trauma, as well as the limited resources available for trauma support, displaced people in Northern Uganda were also included to inform the development of the trauma intervention, as detailed in the relevant chapters below.

1.7 Study instruments, locations, and collaboration

The research consisted of five elements, each answering one of the five sub research questions. The studies were carried out in various locations with different research populations, which were purposively selected in response to the context of the respective location and the aim of the research. The main research locations for Eritrean refugees were Tel Aviv (Israel) and the refugee camps in Tigray (Ethiopia). These locations were selected for their large concentration of Eritrean refugees. Eritrean refugees were also studied in Khartoum and Addis Ababa. In addition, as mentioned previously, there was an opportunity to work among traumatised women in Northern Uganda and this led to the development of TRUST, a trauma support programme for high trauma/low resource contexts. Table 1.1 shows which study addressed which research question, the instrument used (IES-R, SER etc.), the location where the study was carried out, the nationality of the participants, and how the findings research informed the next step in the research process.

Table 1.1. Study, question addressed, location and main finding

Study	Sub question and instrument	Location	Nationality of participants	Headline finding
1.	Q.1 What is the level of PTS among refugees from Eritrea? Q.2 Can levels of PTS affect the processing of information regarding safety and socio-economic resilience during decision making regarding ongoing trajectories? Instrument: IES-R	Eritrea Uganda Ethiopia Israel	Eritrean	PTSD among Eritrean refugees in different settings is high, as measured by the IES-R.
2.	Q.3 What are the trusted communication channels of refugees and is the prevalence of ICT and social media among Eritrean refugees such that it could play a role in the provision of trauma interventions? Instrument: Questionnaire	Ethiopia Sudan	Eritrean	ICTs are widely used to exchange information across Eritrean refugee communities.
3.	Q.4 Is it possible to lower levels of PTS and enhance socio-economic resilience	Uganda	Ugandan	TRUST is effective in reducing levels of trauma and enhancing

	by delivering a short self-help trauma intervention in a high trauma/low resource context? Instruments: IES-R, SER, interviews and observations			socio-economic resilience, as measured by the IES-R and SER, and supported by interviews.
4.	Q.5 (part b) What are the key elements of a short self-help trauma intervention in a high trauma/low resource context for it to impact on social economic resilience? Instrument: Literature review	Ethiopia	Eritrean	A difference was found between delivering just psycho-education (2 videos) and the full programme (6 videos) as part of TRUST, which was found to be more effective.
5.	Q.5 (part a) Will a short self-help trauma intervention delivered using ICT have an impact on reducing PTS and enhancing resilience in the high trauma and low resource contexts of young Eritrean refugees? Instruments: IES-S, SER-S, ISCS, interviews and observations	Ethiopia	Eritrean	TRUST can be delivered using ICT and is effective in reducing levels of trauma (individual as well as collective), as measured by IES and ISCS, and enhancing social and economic resilience.

1.8 Research collaborations

This research was part of two major projects funded by the Netherlands Organisation for Scientific Research (NWO), led by Professor Mirjam van Reisen:

- Causes and dynamics of mixed unskilled migrants trafficked within the Horn of Africa, a study that included Eritrea, Ethiopia and Sudan (Project number 08.400.159)
- Cost-benefit Analysis of Cash Transfer Programmes and Post Trauma Services for Economic Empowerment of Women in Uganda (Project number 08.390.001)

Relevant aspects of the findings have been reported in the following publications:

- Van Reisen, M., Kidane, S., & Reim, l. (2017). The trauma of survivors of Sinai trafficking. In Van Reisen, M., & Mawere, M. (eds), *Human Trafficking and Trauma in the Digital Era: The Ongoing Tragedy of the Trade in Refugees from Eritrea*. Bamenda, Cameroon: Langaa RPCIG, pp. 271–311.
- Van Reisen, M., & Kidane, S. (2017). Collective trauma from Sinai trafficking: A blow to the fabric of Eritrean society. In Van Reisen, M., & Mawere, M. (eds), *Human Trafficking and Trauma in the Digital Era: The Ongoing Tragedy of the Trade in Refugees from Eritrea*. Bamenda, Cameroon: Langaa RPCIG, pp. 317–340.
- Kidane, S., & Stokmans, M. (2018). *ICT-based psycho-social trauma relief in refugee camps in Ethiopia*. NWO Report. Tilburg: Tilburg University.
- Van Reisen, M., Stokmans, M., Nakazibwe, P., Vallejo, B., & Kidane, S. (2018b). *Livelihood-support and trauma relief in relation to social-economic resilience in Northern Uganda and northern Ethiopia*. Research Summary, NWO Report. Tilburg: Tilburg University.

In addition, the researcher had close collaborative links with Dr Primrose Nakazibwe, Rick Schoenmaeckers and Kristina Melicherova and their respective research projects. These collaborations resulted in the sharing of knowledge regarding locations in Eritrea and Uganda and populations of focus, as well as research instruments and methodologies, enhancing the depth of this research. Dr Nakazibwe's sustained focus on the post-conflict integration of women was key to focusing on economic resilience as an indicator of post-traumatic growth. Economic resilience was Kristina Melicherova's focus and the fact that her research was conducted in the same location as the current research was a confirmation of the veracity of focusing on resilience. Rick Schoenmaeckers' research, which focused on education, with an added dimension on the use of ICTs, bolstered understanding of the challenges and opportunities involved in using ICTs for addressing trauma and collective trauma among refugees.

1.9 Terminology

The central concepts used in this study are defined as follows.

1.9.1 Refugees

Refugees are persons seeking protection from political persecution or inhumane treatment in accordance with international law and the Refugee Convention (UN General Assembly, 1951). The primary and universal definition of a refugee that applies to states is contained in Article 1(A)(2) of this Convention, as amended by its 1967 Protocol, which defines a refugee as someone who:

> *[...] owing to well-founded fear of being persecuted for reasons of race, religion, nationality, membership of a particular social group or political opinion, is outside the country of his nationality and is unable or, owing to such fear, is unwilling to avail himself of the protection of that country; or who, not having a nationality and being outside the country of his former habitual residence, is unable or, owing to such fear, is unwilling to return to it.*

In the case of a person who has more than one nationality, the term "the country of his nationality" shall mean each of the countries of which he is a national, and a person shall not be deemed to be lacking the protection of the country of his nationality if, without any valid reason based on well-founded fear, he has not availed himself of the protection of one of the countries of which he is a national.

1.9.2 Trauma

Van der Kolk and Fisler (1995) define trauma as "an inescapably stressful event that overwhelms people's existing coping mechanisms". Trauma often comprises situations that pose considerable threat to life or integrity, diminishing a person's ability to cope. In order to cope, the person may dissociate during the event or may be affected in such a way that he/she is not "able to hold together the different elements of the event afterwards and 'integrate' them". This diminishes the ability of the traumatised individual to "think coherently about what happened or express and connect their feelings about the experience". Traumatic stress, thus, includes the individual distress and enduring pain and suffering, including PTSD and comorbid disorders, such as depression, caused by traumatic events such as war, torture and human rights violations (Marsella *et al.*, 1996; Turner *et al.*, 2003).

1.9.3 Collective trauma

'Collective trauma' encompasses psychological reactions to an extremely difficult event that affects whole societies, i.e., an event that is not "merely an historical fact and the recollection of a terrible event that happened to a group of people", but a tragedy "that is represented in the collective memory of the group. Like all forms of memory, it comprises not only a reproduction of the events, but also an ongoing reconstruction of the event in an attempt to make sense of it. Collective memory of trauma is different from individual memory, because collective memory persists beyond the lives of the direct survivors of the events and is remembered by group members who may be far removed from the traumatic events in time and space.

These subsequent generations of trauma survivors, who never witnessed the actual events, may remember the events differently than the direct survivors, and the construction of these past events may take a different shape and form from generation to generation" (Hirschberger, 2018, p. 1).

Collective trauma is defined here as: the impact of an experience, which becomes a keystone in the narrative of a group, their core belief system and their identity, both for the current generation and across generations. Collective trauma involves a "socially-constructed process" with "an impact on the identity of the group and its individual members" (Kidane & Van Reisen, 2017).

1.9.4 Socio-economic resilience

In a paper on social protection in health care and socio-economic resilience in highly vulnerable and traumatised communities in Uganda, Van Reisen *et al.* (2018b) offer a helpful definition of socio-economic resilience that is relevant here. The definition departs from the concept of ecological resilience (Gunderson, 2000), and focuses on the concept of social resilience, which is defined by Adger, Kelly, Winkels, Huy, and Locke (2002, p. 358) as the "ability of a community to withstand external shocks and stresses without significant upheaval". Resilience, therefore, is a concept framed within the socio-political context surrounding the community. Social resilience imports elements from the concept of community resilience used in humanitarian, resilience, and disaster theories (Norris, Stevens, Pfefferbaum, Wyche & Pfefferbaum, 2008; Patton & Johnston, 2001).

Community resilience refers to how communities are able to cope with, recover from, or adapt to hazards (Bergstrand, Larch & Yotov, 2015; Patton & Johnston, 2001). Accordingly, resilience requires a high level of functioning in the community, including a sense of community, feelings of efficacy, and coping strategies (Bergstrand *et al.*, 2015; Norris *et al.*, 2008).

Norris *et al.* (2008, p. 128) define community resilience within the context of disasters as "… [a] potentially traumatic event that is collectively experienced, has an acute onset, and is time delimited…".

In this context, disasters include episodes of mass violence, such as the ones addressed in this study (*ibid.*, p. 128). Norris *et al.* (2008) highlight four inter-related adaptive capacities required for the functioning of community resilience: economic; social capital; information and communication; and community competence.

The other side of community resilience is economic resilience, an important concept that is analysed using a variety of indicators and methods relating to a community's ability to foresee, adapt to, and leverage changing conditions to its advantage. In this research, socio-economic resilience, therefore, imports elements from social/community and economic resilience to give a comprehensive overview of resilience. However, there is a limitation to the above definition, as the definition is at the community level, whereas the research focused on individual perceptions of socio-economic resilience.

1.9.5 ICT

The term information and communication technology (ICT) refers to technologies enabling access to information using telecommunications, including the Internet, wireless networks, cell phones, and other communication mediums. Technological advances have provided us with a wide range of new communication opportunities. For example, people can now exchange communication with those in different places in real-time using technologies such as instant messaging, Voice over Internet Protocol (VoIP), and video-conferencing. Social networking websites like Facebook have enabled socialisation across the globe, creating a virtual 'global village'. All of this makes it important for us to study ICT in connection with its effects on society (Christensson, 2010).

1.10 Ethical considerations

This research involved a particularly vulnerable population, warranting special considerations to ensure that they were not taken advantage of in any way and that their privacy and confidentiality were not compromised at any point in the research process. There were three critical ethical principles followed in conducting this research. Firstly, it was important to uphold professional integrity in designing, conducting and reporting on the research. The second principle was respect for the rights of all involved in the research, including upholding their dignity at every stage of the process. The final principle involved protecting those involved from any physical or psychological harm. Below I discuss the practical implications of these principles and how they were upheld throughout the research process.

1.10.1 Professional integrity

research was designed, conducted and its results reported with uncompromising commitment to remaining unbiased and objective, and avoiding making value-based judgements for or against any entity. This principle also extended to analysing and understanding the data and, in particular, being clear about the limitations of the population and, hence, not making any generalised conclusions about 'all refugees' or even about 'all Eritrean refugees' or 'Ugandan IDPs'. Maintaining this principle meant that all conclusions needed to be supported by findings.

As part of maintaining professional integrity there was also a need to be clear about professional boundaries and, in particular, to understanding this in light of the expectations of participants who live under the most precarious circumstances. All researchers, including the local research assistants, had to be careful about not having unrealistic expectations in terms of their ability to highlight (advocate for) the various needs arising in the research locations. This was quite challenging, as both the expectations of the refugee participants as well as the urge to do more by the researchers were high. However, in accordance with the principle above, the objective was to understand, and not resolve, the situation.

The other aspect of this principle was to understand the researchers' own limitations and seek help when needed to fill any gaps created by the limitations in ability or experience. To this end, extensive use was made of language resource people, research supervisors and fellow researchers to ensure that the integrity of the research was maintained, especially in the analysis of statistical data, the development and adaptation of research instruments, and the development of conceptual frameworks.

1.10.2 Respect for the rights and dignity of all participants

In view of the particular vulnerability of the research participants, respect for their rights and dignity was a serious consideration that had to be upheld without compromising the relevant principles relating to consent, privacy and acknowledgement of the contribution of participants. Free and informed consent was sought from all participants in the study. This was done through briefings given to participants, after which the participants were given a letter that had a section for them to sign and give their consent. Ample time was given during the briefings for people to ask questions and they were told that they could withdraw their consent at any point in the process.

Participants were told why data was being collected and how data would be stored and published. Data was anonymised, through coding and the secure storing of names separately from the rest of the data, so the data could not be linked without decoding it. During interviews, participants were informed of the confidential nature of the interviews and afforded adequate privacy. Given that much of the research was carried out in refugee camps and crowded refugee settings, this was not always easy to provide, but the utmost care was taken to ensure as much privacy as the situation allowed.

The other important consideration was the importance of adequately recognising the contributions made by participants. This would, under normal circumstances, be a straightforward common sense issue; however, given the severe material deprivation in the context, it was important to considers the appropriateness of any gesture. To this end, in Uganda and Ethiopia, all participants (in the feasibility study) were reimbursed for any expenses incurred or anticipated. In Tel Aviv and with Eritrean refugees in Kampala (for the trauma survey), it was sufficient to thank participants and share ideas on promoting good mental health. Similarly, in the ICT survey, participants were thanked for their participation and there was no remuneration involved.

All research assistants who carried out work in contacting potential participants, making arrangements for data collection and supporting participants were appropriately remunerated and their expenses covered.

1.10.3 Wellbeing of participants

This principle involved ensuring, as far as possible, the physical, social and psychological wellbeing of all those who took part in the research. This involved ensuring confidentiality and mitigating any adverse impacts during and after data collection. As mentioned above, every effort was taken to protect the confidentiality and ensure the anonymity of participants. Accordingly, all names and any identifying features have been disguised and data is stored in a way that protects the subjects of the data, in compliance with the rules of Tilburg University.

Research participants were encouraged to ask questions to gain confidence in, and feel secure with, the research team. Participation in focus group discussions was by open invitation to all participants who took part in the individual interviews and care was taken to use a format that was easy going and encouraged participants to engage in a free flow of exchanges without constraint. The research was conducted in community venues that participants were familiar with.

The biggest risk was one that is endemic to researching trauma, namely, the vulnerability of participants to re-traumatisation in a context where additional mental health support is non-existent. This made it imperative for the researcher to ensure that there was ample awareness of the risks and preparation for any engagement with participants, taking time to be fully aware of the needs that might arise and the strategies for dealing with these. To this end, each study in the research was conducted with great empathy and the researcher (a fully-trained mental health professional) gave as much support as possible and worked in collaboration with organisations on the ground to maximise the support available (within the inherent restrictions). Some aspects of the research were designed with this consideration central to their development (see Chapter 8).

All requirements in Tilburg University's guidelines, including on data processing and storage, were adhered to, in accordance with the recommendations made by the Ethical Committee of the Tilburg School of Humanities and Digital Sciences.

1.11 Scientific and societal relevance

The concept of holistic refugee protection and durable solutions has been around since 1945, in response to the unprecedented forced displacement of people in Europe following Nazi aggression in World War II (Rothman & Ronk, 2015). Despite the commitment then and the 1951 UN Refugee Convention, and its 1967 Protocol, the magnitude and complexity of the challenge of providing adequate and durable protection for refugees persists. One of the challenges has come from the rise in the number of people being displaced. This has created an atmosphere in which many refugees are unable to settle and rebuild their lives, which is particularly problematic for refugees whose emotional status has been overwhelmed by traumatic experiences and who are prone to make decisions based on fight-flight response and informed by their traumatised cognition.

Moreover, even when they are available, psychological treatments used in refugee rehabilitation programmes are often not based on a consistent theory, and evidence on their effectiveness is lacking (Başoğlu et al., 2006). There are diverging opinions about whether to use standard treatment protocols such as Eye Movement Desensitisation Reprocessing (EMDR) therapy or if treatment should be adapted to incorporate the restoration of coping skills and resources (Laban, Hurulean & Attia, 2009; National Institute for Clinical Excellence [NICE], 2005). NICE (2005) recommends treatments initially focusing on addressing day-to-day problem solving and coping skills. However, the lack of evidence-based treatment options can make therapists uncertain about appropriate interventions. The aim of the current research is to develop and test an intervention designed especially for traumatised refugees on the move to enable them to cope with daily living problems.

Understanding migration by explaining the role of trauma in analysis by refugees of the pluses and minuses of moving further, including the risks involved, is also relevant. The push and pull theory of migration assumes a rational analysis, even though it recognises that there are exceptions to this. However, for the highly traumatised individuals and communities under consideration here, mental health processes do not merely give rise to an occasional irrational decision, but could be key to explaining the acceptance of the risks entailed in the entire trajectory.

1.12 Conclusion

Answering the question of why refugees take the risks they do requires us to understand the refugee-making process, starting with the cognitive processes of individual refugees, the impact of trauma on the individual and their community, and the impact of these on the implementation of policies that govern refugee protection. These are mammoth considerations – more than one research can fully address. This research looked at one tiny stream that links the traumatic experiences of refugees to their migration trajectories.

Unlike the African fable at the start of this chapter about the monkey who fell out of its tree into a bush of thorns, there is no easy, straightforward answer to the question of how one can help refugees, within the limits imposed by insufficient resources. Rather, this exploration seeks to enhance understanding, building on what we already know about the experiences that lead people to leave their country and the implications of these for their perceptions of protection and prospects in the locations to which they have been pushed. To this end, the five studies involved in this research established that TRUST, a short self-help therapy delivered to refugees via ICT, can reduce PTS. It is anticipated that this would enable the survivors of traumatic experiences to have enough cognitive capacity to appropriately consider their social and economic resilience where they currently are, as they contemplate the merits of potential ongoing journeys.

For me, answering these questions is more than a mere academic endeavour, it is a personal quest that has come to organise my thinking and activities. I ask these questions, alongside everyone else, every time I hear of a boat full of migrants drowned, or of young people abducted, sold and re-sold in the desert; I also ask every time a refrigerated lorry, with human 'cargo' is stopped on the streets of Europe. However, unlike the majority of people I share these questions with, the quest for answers does not leave me as easily when the headlines disappear. This quest became an urge that was eventually the organising force behind this research and the many hours of work that went into it.

Chapter 2

The significance of psychological trauma in the care and protection of refugees: A framework

No. 92...
I wonder what she called you?
Your precious mama...
Maybe she called you Berhan?... my light
Or did she call you Haben?... my pride
She may have called you Qisanet... rest
Or were you Awet? Victory...
Tell me, little one, did she name you after her hope?
Or her aspirations...her dream?
Did she name you after the brother she lost?
Or after her father long gone?
Did she name you after the desert she crossed
Or the land she left behind...?
Maybe she named you for the land you were to inherit?
Tell me, little one, what did your precious mother call you?
For I can't bear you being called number 92...

On 3 October 2013, the world awoke to the news that a boat carrying migrants from Misrata in Libya had sunk off the Italian island of Lampedusa. Nearly all the migrants were from Eritrea and the Italian Coast Guard rescued 155 bewildered survivors. On 12 October the officially confirmed death toll was reported as 359, but with some bodies still missing the death toll is now estimated at more than 360. The close-knit Eritrean community was devastated, nearly everyone was in shock and numb for days. Among the deaths were mothers with their children and a pregnant woman who gave birth to her baby boy as she drowned. I wrote the poem above as a tribute to the children who passed away, whose parents dreamt of a better future for them, against miscalculated odds. I still carry the pain of that disaster somewhere inside me; it fuels the urge that drove this research.

In this chapter, I discuss the theoretical framework for my research. As highlighted in the previous chapter, the issue of refugee migration cannot be fully discussed without taking into consideration the impact of trauma on the appraisal of safety and social and economic resilience by refugees during decisions regarding their ongoing trajectory. Here it should be clear that 'decisions' made by refugees on the move should not be confused with choice. Choice involves the presence of power and the opportunity to consider options, while decision refers to making up one's mind.

In this chapter I will outline how the traumatised brain processes danger differently, as a result of hypervigilance. I will also discuss the fact that, more often than not, the mass traumatisation entailed in the refugee-making process causes not only individual trauma (or PTS), but collective traumatises whole communities. Further consideration will also be given to the impact of trauma on socio-economic resilience, both in terms of the way trauma affects how refugees regard their resilience as well as their ability to build (or rebuild) their social and economic resilience.

The central consideration of this research relates to developing a trauma intervention that can be delivered to refugees to enable the reduction of trauma levels (both collective and individual) and enhance refugees' perception of their social and economic resilience. Given the fact that refugees often have little or no means of earning more than the donations they receive from refugee support agencies and family, it is in fact their perceived, rather than their actual, income (or prospect of income that changes) that is relevant here. In other words it is their self-efficacy and sense of agency that is anticipated to change in the course of the intervention. The Impact of Events Scale (IES-S and IES-R), Internet Social Capital Scale (ISCS), and Social and Economic Resilience Scale (SER) – the tools used to measure trauma, collective trauma and socio-economic resilience – are discussed in Chapter 3.

The conceptual framework illustrated in Figure 2.1 shows the relationship between traumatic stress (used as an indicator of individual trauma), social capital (used to indicate collective trauma) and socio-economic resilience (used as an indicator of perceptions of social and economic resilience) in the pre- and post-intervention phases. Pre-intervention, all three variables of concern are independent of each other, however, as the intervention is a trauma support intervention, post-intervention levels of trauma become a mediating variable that ultimately impacts on social capital (collective trauma) and social and economic resilience, as a result of changes in self-efficacy and agency (as opposed to changes in income levels or in the organisation of society).

Figure 2.1. Conceptual framework

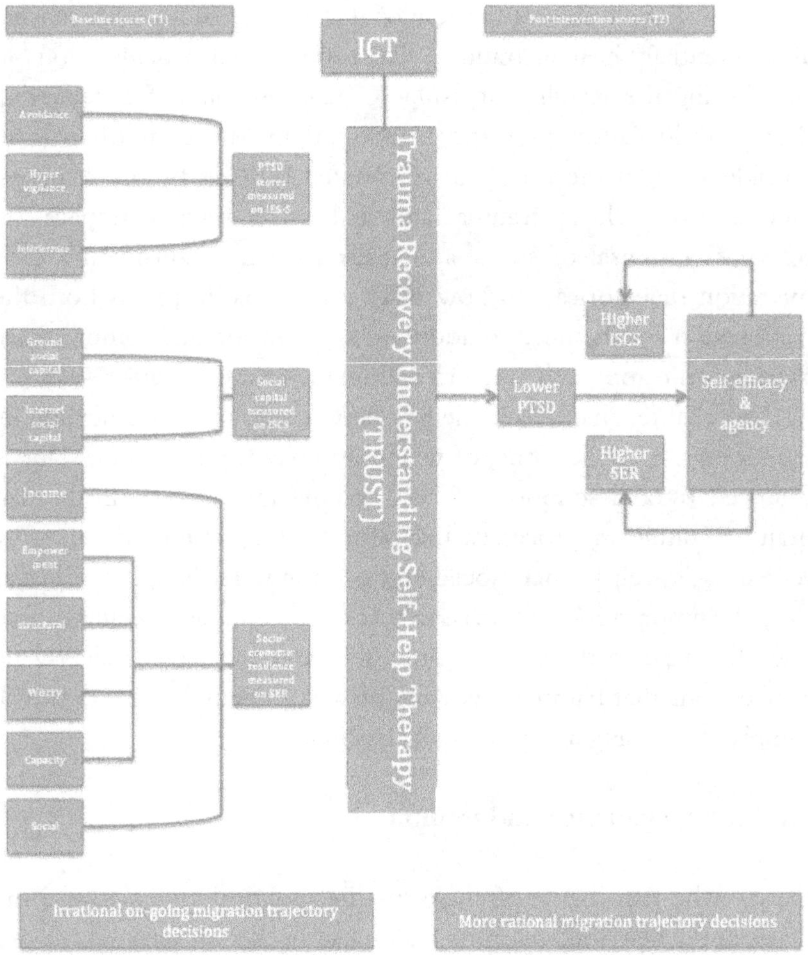

This chapter will, therefore, start by discussing trauma as a consequence of modern-day conflict. As we have seen in previous sections, the experiences under discussion are not limited to individuals, but impact on wider communities and often include societal narratives and culture as a whole. Therefore, I will discuss both individual and collective trauma and their consequences.

This research has taken the prevalence of ICT, particularly the use of social media and mobile phones, as an important context for the lives of refugees on the move in the digital era. I, therefore, also discuss ICT, focusing on the role of ICT in relation to both causing and potentially healing trauma. These are crucial considerations in establishing the viability of using ICT as a medium for delivering therapy in low resource settings and, perhaps more importantly, in consideration of the trust that is invested in ICTs by the refugees. Understanding how trauma and collective trauma impact on refugees' appraisal of safety and resilience when considering their migration trajectories and how ICTs play a role in this is both the justification for the need to address trauma in refugee communities, as well as the approach taken to addressing trauma in this research.

This chapter first makes the link between political conflict and its psychological implications, of which traumatic stress is one. This is followed by a description of how trauma impacts on the human brain, resulting in processes that affect the appraisal of safety by refugees, as well as their social and economic resilience. Following this, the implications of mass trauma are outlined, detailing how collective trauma damages communities and can have society-wide implications that hamper recovery. Finally, I detail the role that ICT can play in causing and potentially healing trauma.

2.1 Political violence and trauma

Despite the fact that it often seems that political violence, and the devastation that follows in its wake, has been ever present on our screens since the end of the Cold War, the trend in armed conflict has been downward. That is until recent years, when we have again seen an upsurge. This upsurge is marked by a change in the nature of the conflicts: today the predominant form of conflict is internal to the state, with a significant rise in civil conflicts and political violence (Gates, Nygård, Strand & Urdal, 2016).

Here political violence is defined as "violence that is perpetrated by one set or group of people on another set or group of people who were often [but not always] strangers to each other before the conflict began" (Cairns, 1996, p. 10). These are often political conflicts involving citizens fighting internally. The defining feature of intra-state conflict is the fact that civilians (including children) become, in many instances, the main combatants, as well as the main casualties (Watts *et al.*, 2017). Societies ravaged by conflict that embroils civilians suffer massive loss of human life, as well as economic, political and social disintegration. The vulnerable, including women and children, suffer immensely; they are often killed in their millions and are more likely to be physically injured and psychologically scarred.

One of the tragedies of current day conflict is the prevalence of sexual violence, often perpetrated to create a profound sense of humiliation and disorder (Meger, 2010). Sexual violence, including sexual slavery, is now regarded as a weapon of war, used to humiliate and ostracise women and girls, resulting in societal fragmentation (Sirleaf & Rehn, 2002). Sadly, there is a significant upward trend in the incidence of wartime rape (Cohen, Green & Wood, 2013) and, more specifically, there is an emerging trend of using sexual violence to induce the displacement of populations, often for the control of resources and/or strategic locations (UN Secretary General, 2013).

Torture and inhumane treatment are the other weapons of choice to inculcate fear as part of political violence. Irrespective of what specific form of torture is used, it always involves psychological suffering with the aim of terrorising the population into obedience and destroying those who are considered to be an 'internal enemy' (Pesutic, 1989). Another trend that is concerning is the targeting of children for abuse, which ranges from rape and other forms of sexual violence to the recruitment of children as soldiers. This trend includes attacking schools and hospitals (UN Secretary General, 2013, 2014).

Other cruelties perpetrated include the desecration of dead bodies and extending victimhood to friends and family members of the primary victim (co-victimisation). Ultimately, political violence reshapes not only the individual victim, but entire societies by undermining their value system (Kordon, Edelman, Lagos, Nicoletti & Bozzolo, 1988). These and many other targeted attacks on civilians during political conflicts, big and small, create large numbers of displaced people. In fact, the steady rise in the number of IDPs per conflict indicates that displacement is becoming a well-practised, deliberate tactic (Kaldor, 2014; Hampton, 2014), that causes human suffering, but is also a means of continuing the inter-group hostility, incubating the causes of further conflict (Doyle & Sambanis, 2006).

2.2 Individual trauma

"The word 'trauma' comes from the Latin word for 'wound'. Traumatic experiences can wound the body, mind, spirit, and relationships with others" (Eades, 2013). It is the sense of being overwhelmed and shocked in response to extreme events that poses a significant threat to the safety of victims and their loved ones. Many people exposed to traumatic experiences show post-traumatic reactions in the initial period following the event, however, these reactions usually remit spontaneously within a month or so after the event, depending on a number of risk and resilience factors (Rothbaum, Foa, Riggs, Murdock & Walsh, 1992; Ogden, Pain & Fisher, 2006; Orcutt, Erickson & Wolfe, 2004). If reactions persist then they might meet the criteria for a diagnosis of post-traumatic stress disorder (PTSD). The fifth edition of the Diagnostic and Statistical Manual of Mental Disorders (DSM-V) defines PTSD "as comprised of four clusters of symptoms including intrusive and recurrent memories of the trauma, avoidance of trauma related stimuli, numbing and/or negative changes in mood or cognitions pertaining to the trauma, and changes in reactivity and arousal" (American Psychiatric Association, 2013).

The scale of atrocities, displacement and dislocation entailed in the refugee-making process is producing a large number of people with a range of mental illnesses resulting from the extremely traumatic situations that they are fleeing. Muscat (2004) draws attention to the large-scale mental illness in post-conflict developing countries as deriving from the widespread physical and emotional trauma, fear, destruction of communities and institutions, betrayal and loss of trust, and social and cultural degradation that characterises the conflicts, highlighting the enormous challenges to any health care system, especially to a system embroiled in devastation to the point of disintegration.

Longitudinal studies have revealed that the suffering that follows mass violence includes PTSD and depression with comorbidities associated with high rates of physical disability (Mollica *et al.*,1999), which often result in premature death (Mollica, 2000). In addition there are many other problems with long-term mental health and impaired psychosocial functioning that persist in post-conflict settings (Bramsen & Van der Ploeg, 1999; Yehuda, Schmeidler, Wainberg, Binder-Brynes & Duvdevani, 1998).

Studies of asylum seekers have shown that they suffer high rates of mental distress, with symptoms such as depression, anxiety, demoralisation, stress, fear, pain and PTSD (Silove & Steel, 1998; Gerritsen *et al.*, 2006; Laban, Gernaat, Komproe, Van der Tweel & De Jong, 2005). Mental distress is found to be linked to their experiences of torture and political violence, which continues to interfere with their adjustment and reintegration into society, even when they are physically safe and no longer in immediate danger (Silove, Ekblad & Mollica, 2000).

Torture, which is often consciously used in political repression, has been found to cause PTSD, together with other anxiety disorders and depression (Saxena, Levav, Maulik & Saraceno, 2003). These psychological symptoms are persistent and simultaneously damage the victim's self-esteem as well as their trust in their fellow human beings, leading to many experiencing changes to their identity (Barudy, 1989). Studies of refugee populations indicate levels of depression and PTSD ranging from 40 to 70% (Baingana *et al.*, 2003); while this rate could be compounded by displacement, it also indicates the possibility that a significant proportion of post-conflict communities are debilitated by psychiatric illnesses or severe psychological reactions to trauma (Silove *et al.*, 2000a).

WHO estimates that in armed conflicts 10% of those who experience traumatic events will succumb to mental health problems, while 10% will develop behaviour that affects their functioning. Reported difficulties include depression, anxiety, insomnia and psychosomatic problems such as back pain or stomach aches (Saraceno & Saxena, 2004).

2.2.1 Trauma and the human brain

Trauma can cause changes to the brain and a comprehensive understanding of trauma and its physiological underpinnings is crucial in any attempt to address its impacts. The human body and mind's normal operational stance is within a resilient zone, where stress might be present, but is accounted for and balanced by the release experienced in attaining set goals. There is a set of important and predictable responses to stress and threat (Perry, 2002).

The human brain is organised into three sections – human brain, mammalian brain and reptilian brain – and is connected to the body in a way that enables the automatic triggering of a physical escape plan in the event of emergency; this system is operated from the oldest part of the brain (the animal brain) (MacLean, 1990). This concept of the 'triune brain', in which each tier serves a different function related to cognitive, emotional and body regulation, is useful in understanding the implications of hypo-arousal and hyperarousal during a traumatic event (see Figure 2.2). Accordingly, the brain is a system of conscious and unconscious components working in unison within the resilient zone. Over activity in one part of the brain causes disharmony in the whole system. Over arousal in the brainstem and cerebellum (or reptilian brain) can shut down the activities of the other two layers, reducing the functioning of the fight, flight, freeze mechanism afforded by the reptilian brain. This is normal brain functioning. However, when the actions taken fail to resolve the stress and the brain fails to resume normal functioning it becomes the site of unresolved trauma. Unresolved trauma affects a person in a way that results in the reconfiguration of the nervous system. This happens when the process that triggers the reaction that enables the body to run, hide or freeze also prevents our conscious mind (or higher brain) from averting the impending danger. If the emergency mode succeeds in averting danger the brain is then able to regain internal equilibrium and gradually begin to operate as normal. However, if the response triggered does not result in successful escape or aversion – if, for example, the person is prevented from taking effective action – the brain will continue to fire stress reactions (and chemicals associated with them), sending signals to the body to escape a threat that may no longer exist (Van der Kolk, 2014).

Post-traumatic stress disorder is, therefore, when the brain fails to attain its former multi-layered functioning and is stuck in the dysfunction of the overwhelmed system and reconfigures in that manner (Van der Kolk, 2014).

As the human brain's main function is to ensure survival, survival is always given precedence. Sensory information that enters the brain is channelled via the thalamus (in the reptilian brain) to the amygdala (in the limbic/mammalian brain) (Cozolino, 2002; Van der Kolk, 2014). This pathway from the thalamus to the amygdala is very fast. The amygdala filters information coming in – if there is any threat or perceived threat, the hypothalamus is immediately activated in response, triggering the release of hormones (cortisol and adrenaline), preparing the body to mount a defence (Cozolino, 2002) and alerting the system to become highly aroused and ready (Siegel, 2001). Information is also relayed to the hippocampal and cortical circuits for additional processing that is then relayed back to the amygdala (LeDoux, 1996); this process is much slower and produces a more considered response, often encouraging the system to calm down.

In dangerous situations, higher brain functions are overwhelmed (Siegel, 2003). When the brain is focused on immediate survival (Cozolino, 2002), oxygen is diverted away from the brain to the body and hormones are released activating the body for the 'fight-flight-freeze' response (Van der Kolk, 2014). When a person can successfully avert the threat, employing the strategy described above, they are less likely to be traumatised by the experience (Herman, 1992).

Figure 2.2 Triune brain (Maclean, 1990)

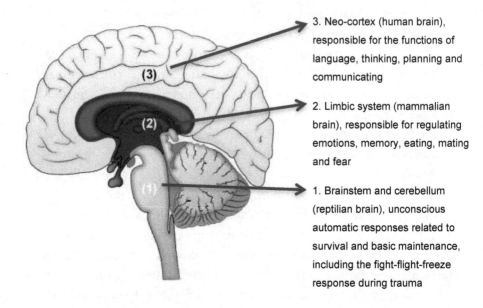

3. Neo-cortex (human brain), responsible for the functions of language, thinking, planning and communicating

2. Limbic system (mammalian brain), responsible for regulating emotions, memory, eating, mating and fear

1. Brainstem and cerebellum (reptilian brain), unconscious automatic responses related to survival and basic maintenance, including the fight-flight-freeze response during trauma

However, this overwhelmed status of the brain can also result in lack of integration and may lead to the dissociation that we often see in victims of trauma (Cozolino, 2002). If the active responses are unsuccessful in averting danger then the passive responses, such as dissociation, ensue. As Levine and Frederick (1997, p. 138) put it: "In trauma, dissociation seems to be the favoured means of enabling a person to endure experiences that can normally be beyond endurance". If the traumatic event is repeated or becomes ongoing then the activation is prolonged resulting in potential structural disintegration, which is often seen in situations of complex trauma, where trauma victims continue to act and react, often re-victimising themselves by being engaged in self-injuring behaviours such as self-harming. In some instances, victims resort to externalising the trauma by victimising others (Van der Kolk & McFarlane, 1996).

It is believed that this vicious cycle is formed by the creation of neural pathways or the wiring and firing of neurons in such a way that the person continues to re-experience the traumatic event due to the inability to modulate their aroused state (Siegel, 1999). This failure to recover from the normal effects of trauma to restore the system to its physiological homeostasis is effectively what PTSD is. PTSD results in a person experiencing fear, horror or helplessness following an event that causes threat of injury or death. Three distinct, but co-occurring, symptom clusters signify the disorder: interference, avoidance and hyperarousal. Symptoms must be severe, impairing functioning for at least a month. Sometimes PTSD symptoms are exacerbated by ineffective coping strategies, substance abuse, comorbid mood and anxiety disorders, inability to access social support, and stress-related medical conditions (Yehuda, 2002). Understanding these impacts of trauma on processes in the brain is essential when trying to unravel why people migrate, taking huge risks and moving from one source of danger to a potentially more dangerous situation.

Traumatised people become stuck and stop growing and developing as they are unable to integrate their traumatic experiences into daily life. Instead they continue to organise their lives as though the traumatic event is ongoing. Energy is focused on suppressing the inner chaos and attempting to maintain control over unbearable physiological reactions, rather than spontaneous involvement in their own lives (Van der Kolk, 2014). The significance of the imprints left by the traumatic experiences, which are often recorded so extensively, is seldom discussed and taken into consideration even less when developing strategies to deal with migration. When a brain system keeps being re-activated through unresolved trauma, it results in the fight-flight-freeze being triggered by even the slightest stimuli. This can lead to the making of incongruent and irrational decisions, based on erroneous assessments of safety and social economic resilience.

2.2.2 Trauma and socio-economic resilience

Despite war and political violence causing immediate immeasurable damage to civilians and their environment, more often than not, the effects of war and political violence continue to be counted merely as the number of causalities (Ugalde, Richards & Zwi, 1999). As devastating as loss of life is, it is only the 'tip of the iceberg' when it comes to the consequences of events that push refugees out of their homes. Diminished social and economic resilience in the form of poverty, malnutrition, economic decline and other devastative social consequences are often not well-documented, and this limits our understanding of conflict, which in turn limits the development of coherent and effective strategies for dealing with the associated problems (Murthy & Lakshminaryana, 2006).

Social and economic resilience measures the ability of an economy to minimise the impact of asset losses on wellbeing and is part of the ability to resist, absorb, accommodate and recover from asset loss in a timely and efficient manner (Hallegatte, Bangalore & Vogt-Schilb, 2016). A resilient community is a community with the ability to overcome the consequences of disasters, either by holding on to their pre-disaster social fabric or adapting to changes to survive (Gaillard, 2007). Hence, social and economic dysfunctions, caused and maintained by the trauma of conflict and political violence, should be an important feature of post-conflict developments, as should the organisation and provision of assistance to refugees.

As we have seen above, trauma affects a person in such a way that their preoccupation with averting danger (which may not be there any longer) impinges on their ongoing life and their ability to rebuild their livelihood. An example of a dysfunctional socio-economic behaviour that is detrimental to recovery is the situation in Rwanda, cited by Muscat (2004), where even 10 years after the genocide, farmers were observed to be neglecting the maintenance of the terracing that is essential for cultivation in the country's hilly environment and the replanting of coffee trees. Both of these behaviours are contrary to traditional pre-conflict practices and are believed to be the effects of depression over future uncertainty. Similarly, schools that were educating teenagers who went through the genocide in their formative years were reporting behavioural dysfunctions, pointing to lingering impacts on their social and economic prospects for many years after the conflict (*ibid.*, 2004).

Economic loss, in many conflict contexts, might prove too difficult to accurately estimate, as the loss of a labour force in rural self-employed contexts is not easily measured. Moreover, international humanitarian assistance, which is often a feature of such contexts, can create a situation where mental ill-health attracts support and, hence, might delay recovery, creating dependency, while undermining confidence and self-reliance (Muscat, 2004). The interaction between mental health and social and economic wellbeing in post-conflict contexts is not simple; on the one hand, mental ill-health affects work and production-related behaviour as well as productivity and, on the other hand, poor economic conditions and bad prospects hamper psychological recovery.

In addition, collective trauma is known to affect communities in ways that can be complex and difficult to understand. This has been the case in some of the worst politically violent contexts, and we need to understand these extraordinary and complex situations (Murthy & Lakshminaryana, 2006). For instance, Manz (2002) observed some Guatemalan communities apparently possessing remarkable resilience and the ability to revive their economic viability and gradually heal the wounds of their genocidal experience in the early 1980s. However, these post-conflict adaptations could also represent a significant structural change in the community and the relationships between its members. Ledgerwood, Ebihara and Mortland (1994) presented perspectives from the village of Svay in Cambodia, where the apparent resilience of the villagers after the Khmer Rouge atrocities in the 1960s was in fact a selfish and self-interested behaviour, making the village they observed very different, in many ways, to its pre-conflict societal structure.

Stressors, such as natural and man-made disasters, including war, political upheaval and repression, can be powerful events that impact on individuals, families, and communities alike (Weisaeth, 1992). These traumatic impacts can have wide-ranging consequences that extend across the life span of individuals; however, individual responses to trauma vary widely. Understanding the differences in reactions and their interaction with the broader social context, including material resources, is important, as it enables us to identify factors influencing adjustment after traumatic injury to aid the development of the assessment and treatment of the psychological impairment that may follow traumatic events.

The conservation of resources (COR) theory was developed as a general stress theory to help explain why certain circumstances are stressful and the process of people's reactions to stressful circumstances (Hobfoll, 1989). According to COR theory, stress is a result of actual loss of resources or threat of loss of resources and then failure to gain resources following significant resource investment. When a significant proportion of resources are used to offset the stress that occurred, it inevitably means that there are fewer resources available to combat further stresses. This often means that resources are simply not available when a person is vulnerable and needs them the most, creating a loss spiral, decreasing both the person's resource reservoir and their coping efforts. Accordingly, having resources at one's disposal can buffer against future loss and create a situation of potential gain (regain) (Hobfoll, 1989).

Understanding the complex impact of lingering psychological problems on post-conflict socio-economic recovery is also crucial. The above examples outline how persistent psychological debilitations have considerable implications for social and economic resilience. When these are further impacted on due to the devastated social and economic fibre of the society, the ramifications can prove insurmountable, if considerable support is not available. Therefore, there is an urgent need to understand these impacts and address them adequately to affect the post-conflict healing of individuals and their communities. The need to provide mental health support for populations in war and conflict situations, as part of the relief, rehabilitation and reconstruction process, is evident; however, our understanding of the psychological consequences that should drive the development of emergent interventions seems to be lagging.

The concept of community-wide resilience is based on the inherent competence and connectedness of all human beings and can be defined as: "A community's capacity, hope and faith to withstand major trauma and loss, overcome adversity and to prevail, usually with increased resources, competence and connectedness" (Landau & Saul, 2004, p. 286). Based on studies of communities exposed to mass violence, Norris and colleagues developed a framework with four variables for community resilience (Norris & Stevens, 2008; Norris *et al.*, 2002a; Norris, Friedman & Watson, 2002b).

At the individual and family level, socio and economic resilience relates to factors and processes that exclude people from production and consumption opportunities that support the wellbeing of individuals and households, often preventing the continuity of income generation and access to contingency funds for recovery. Hence, resilience can be understood as the characteristics and capabilities that help re-connect people to such opportunities or create conditions for developing new opportunities that are crucial for enhancing their capacity to cope with and facilitate adaptation (Lo, Xu, Chan & Su, 2016).

This is similar to the concept of socio-economic standing (SES) – the access to collectively desired resources (Oakes & Rossi, 2003). These resources, be they material or other, enable individuals and groups to thrive; hence, individuals aim to improve their SES, or the SES of their offspring, in order to improve their life chances. In this thesis, I do not directly refer to SES, as there are complexities that are beyond the scope of this research, but the concept is helpful in understanding social and economic resilience at the level of individuals and their families.

The process that results in people being dislocated and becoming refugees entails the loss of access to material resources and opportunities. In this sense, migration itself can be seen as an attempt to gain the lost resources, and resilience is, thus, the ability to regain access to such opportunities and make use of them to rebuild resources. The mental processes and behaviours involved in promoting personal assets and protecting an individual from the potential negative effect is, in essence, what we refer to when we talk about resilience (Fletcher & Sarkar, 2012). In this research, I sought to understand social and economic resilience by looking at the processes and behaviour involved in promoting personal assets and protecting an individual from the potential negative effects of stressors (*ibid.*). These were incorporated into the SER tool as the subscales: 'capability', 'empowerment', 'worriedness', 'social embeddedness', 'trust in the system' and 'income'.

2.2.3 Trauma, information processing, decision making and risk appraisal

Decisions, especially decisions about the best options in an emergency context, are almost always made under stress, and there is research that reveals that stress alters decision making (Starcke & Brand, 2012). One reason cited for this is the connection to the changes at the neuronal level, mentioned above. The brain regions associated with decision making are sensitive to stress induced changes (Lupien *et al.*, 2007).

However, studies are not consistent on the exact neuronal process. Some studies have revealed that in PTSD there is increased metabolic rate in the amygdala during emotional rest as well as during emotional challenge (Bremner *et al.*, 2005; Semple *et al.*, 2000) and the medial and prefrontal cortex showed decreased metabolism under the same conditions (Hou *et al.*, 2007; Semple *et al.*, 2000); however, these results have not been consistent in all studies, and some have found contrary results (see Astur *et al.*, 2005; Bremner, 1999; Molina *et al.*, 2010). It seems that when the activities of the amygdala cannot be regulated by the activities of the prefrontal cortex this can lead to deficiencies in emotion regulation and impaired resolution of traumatic events. While, in general, decision-making deficits are not core-symptoms of PTSD, the structural functioning of changes in the brain suggest that decision-making abilities may also be altered (Starcke & Brand, 2012).

Researchers have also found that traumatic experiences have an effect on the victim's cognitive processes, as functioning, including cognitive appraisals adopted in response to danger, may have negative effects on decision-making abilities (Lerner & Kennedy, 2000). Researchers who focused on the cognitive processes and consequences of PTSD contend that, once activated, the perception of current threat is accompanied by intrusions and re-experiencing and other symptoms of arousal that affect the appraisal of the threat, leading to maladaptive behavioural strategies and cognitive processes (Ehlers & Clark, 2000). A specific strategy that has a direct relationship with the experiences of flight and migration is what is known as 'safety behaviour'. This is the set of actions and behaviours

56

individuals engage in to prevent, or at least lower, anticipated further catastrophes. These also involve belief that, without these preventive actions, the feared catastrophic consequences would indeed (Salkovskis, 1996). From this perspective the need to keep moving, whatever the risk, can be seen as a preventive action against further calamity, induced by a strategy developed in response to PTSD, as opposed to a considered decision based on the pros and cons of the action.

Another example of a maladaptive cognitive process, that has been correlated with chronic PTSD, and that can influence the appraisal and decision making of traumatised people, is mental defeat. This refers to a perceived loss of psychological autonomy accompanied by a sense of not being human (Ehlers et al., 2002; Dunmore, Clark & Ehlers, 1999). Mental defeat leads PTSD sufferers to interpret their experiences as evidence for a negative view of themselves, that they are not a worthy person (Ehlers & Clark, 2000), which is a classic depressive state (negative affect). Negative affect plays an important role in cognitive processes, and even mild positive affect is recognised today as an important influence on thinking (Sen, 1993; Baron, 2008). Estrada, Isen, and Young (1997) conducted an extensive study that demonstrated "that positive affect generally leads people to be gracious, generous, and kind to others, to be socially responsible and to take the other's perspective into consideration (while not losing sight of their own perspective)". More crucially for the discussion at hand, they found that "decision makers and problem solvers in whom positive affect has been induced are more flexible, open, and innovative, as well as more careful and thorough in addressing interesting or important issues". Moreover, their cognitive capacity remains at an optimum level with the level of their motivation and systematic processing intact. They seem to be more motivated, thoughtful, organised and clear-headed than those with negative affect.

This finding is echoed in many studies that have shown that affective feelings can exert substantial influence on judgement (Schwarz & Clore, 2007; Cohen, Pham & Andrae, 2008; Isen, 2001; Pham, 2004). People regard feelings as important information that they can use to evaluate their current situation (Schwarz & Clore,

2007). This can include their assessment of safety and perceptions of socio-economic resilience. Strong negative feelings indicate that the current situation might be unsafe and even dangerous and can lead a person to focus on negative information that backs up these feelings. This effect will only be countered if a person realises the link between negative feelings and associated negative emotions (Schwarz, 2012). Un-countered, negative moods have a more general negative impact than emotions (Schwarz, 2012), and may lead refugees with PTSD to perceive fewer opportunities in their current situation.

In particular, it has been shown that the influence of feelings typically increases in situations where the ability to process information is reduced by various factors including cognitive load (Shiv & Fedorikhin, 1999). The neurological impacts of trauma (i.e., the reduced functioning of the cortex) can also reduce the ability to process information and results in feelings becoming substituted for substantive information, which would require more cognitive resources to process (Avnet, Tuan, Pham & Stephen, 2012).

Ultimately, decision making is a complex process that requires the ability to recognise and evaluate the probability and consequences of each alternative available to the decider. The diminished cognitive capacity entailed in PTSD, which limits the brain from processing fight-flight-freeze reactions, the negative strategies adopted as a response, and the negative affect resulting from the wrong assessment of self can severely hamper the decision-making process of refugees. This is an important consideration, as it indicates the capacity to make assessments of prospects and safety, as well as the ability to process information regarding the capacity to influence outcomes for safety and prospects. There have been a lot of efforts to raise the awareness of refugees regarding the dangers of onward migration, as well as the opportunities for training and other livelihood support initiatives in the refugee camps. However, without an understanding of the impact of trauma on the ability of refugees to process this information it is almost impossible for these efforts to achieve the desired goals. This could be one of the reasons why refugees are taking enormous risks to engage in ongoing or secondary migration.

Indeed, studies have tried to identify if symptoms of PTSD are risk factors for increased risk-taking behaviour (lack of appropriate risk appraisal) (Ben-Zur & Zeinder, 2009; Rheingold, Acierno & Resnick, 2004; Tull, Weiss & McDermount, 2016). In contrast, Augsburger and Elbert (2017), in pioneering research to assess risk behaviour on displaced individuals with extremely high levels of trauma, found that high risk-taking behaviour was predicted by little or no exposure to organised violence, such as war and torture. Here it was concluded that the association between risk-taking behaviour and traumatic stress might depend on the specific risk. However, the researchers also concluded that, as there is no research regarding culturally different concepts of risk behaviour, the differences in education and societal values might be the difference impacting on engagement in risk behaviour. A 2017 study by Hamburg University, Germany, involving risk taking, trust and traumatisation among Syrian refugees in Jordan, found that the degree of traumatisation had some effects on behaviour with regards to risk-taking games and it is thought that the behaviour is driven by having experienced the loss of close relatives in Syria and by having spent some time in refugee camps in Jordan. However, the research also found that compared to their Jordanian peers, Syrian refugee students were not different in their risk-taking behaviour when the risks tested for were not specific to leaving or staying in the camp (El-Bialy, Nicklisch & Voigt, 2017). While there is little by way of research to conclusively establish a firm link between traumatic stress and the type of risks we see refugees such as Eritrean refugees in Ethiopia or Sudan taking, we are beginning to identify the possibility of a link between risky decisions and trauma in refugees.

As mentioned previously, modern-day conflicts are characterised by the impact on civilians who become victims not just by getting caught in the crossfire, but by actually becoming a target of attack, either in an effort to demoralise and punish those fighting or to deliberately 'cleanse' them from a place for political or economic gain. It is believed that the element of betrayal in these events makes traumatisation more likely (Van der Kolk et al., 2007) and recovery complicated (Salter, 1995). Without intervention, victims of such traumatic experiences can continue to live their lives as if they are still in danger – weeks, months, years or even decades after the experience. This is particularly the case for victims, including refugees, of events that were of 'human design' (American Psychiatric Association, 2000). The assistance given to refugees will be seriously hampered and fall short of providing the protection needed if it continues to lack insight into the inner turmoil that refugees are trying to escape from.

2.2.4 Self-efficacy and trauma

Perceived self-efficacy (PSE) relates to people's ability to have aspirations for themselves, as well as how hard they try to achieve their goals (Bandura, 1977). Specifically, here it refers to the refugees' belief about what they can achieve if they try hard and are persistent, using what is available to them (the opposite of what often happens when refugees fail to recognise social and economic opportunities, because they fail to recognise their ability to make good use of them due to their impaired cognition from trauma). PSE relates to people's belief in their ability to influence the events affecting their lives. This is the foundation of motivation, performance, and accomplishment, as well as emotional wellbeing (Bandura, 1997, 2006). Those who do not believe they can produce a desired result through their actions have little incentive to perform activities or persevere in the face of difficulties. A strong sense of self-efficacy enhances human accomplishment and personal wellbeing. The reason why it is important to discuss self-efficacy here is that it plays a central role in enabling refugees to believe in their ability to rebuild their life where they are. However, post-traumatic stress causes a sense of helplessness that undermines self-efficacy. Hence, it is anticipated that reduced levels of trauma would result in enhanced self-efficacy, which would in turn result in increased socio-economic resilience.

People who are certain about their capabilities approach difficult tasks as challenges to be mastered. They take great interest and become deeply involved in their activities, setting themselves challenging goals, and are able to recover from failure without much distress, approaching even threatening situations with the assurance that they can exercise control over them. On the other hand, people who doubt their capabilities avoid difficult tasks, have low aspirations and show weak commitment to their goals. They are slow to recover their sense of efficacy following failure or setback, losing even more faith in their capabilities and succumbing to stress and depression. A sense of self-efficacy is central to human agency, reinforcing the core belief in the power to produce desired effects by one's actions and creating incentives to act and persevere in the face of difficulties (Bandura, 1997).

Reaction to traumatic stress and coping with threatening situations is affected by a person's sense of self-efficacy on several levels (Bandura, 1997). Firstly, it is determined by appraisal of the initial stress response to a traumatic event and, hence, it determines the viable coping options available (Bandura, 1997). Secondly, self-efficacy results in better coping: self-efficacy affects post-traumatic event adaptation/growth due to differences in the motivation to fully utilise effective coping strategies – higher levels of self-efficacy result in increased efforts when faced with setbacks (Bandura, 1997).

Helplessness is a key factor in trauma; this can have a detrimental effect on self-efficacy creating a motivational deficit, which can be mitigated or otherwise by the level of self-efficacy that the individual started with. High levels of self-efficacy are reported to result in fewer traumatic symptoms while low self-efficacy is reported to being related to more traumatic stress symptoms (Benight & Harper, 2002; Johansen, Wahl, Eilertsen & Weisaeth, 2007). It was also found that these differences persist over time, determining long-term adjustment and recovery (Benight & Harper, 2002; Heinrichs *et al.*, 2005; Johansen *et al.*, 2007), and self-efficacy also determines the acuteness (or otherwise) of the symptoms experienced (Benight & Harper, 2002).

Self-efficacy (an individual's belief in their ability to manage unexpected events and to produce desired effects from a given activity) is considered to be a protective factor for PTSD (Bandura, 1997), as it enables people to consider anxiety and stress symptoms as controllable and temporary (Leganger, Kraft & Røysamb, 2000). Accordingly, the self-help trauma intervention TRUST was developed to enable people to regain control over trauma stress symptoms and, thereby, enhance their self-efficacy; this was, in turn, expected to improved their perception of community connectedness (social capital) and social and economic resilience.

2.3 Collective trauma

This section looks at trauma at the community/societal level. As emphasised previously, collective trauma can affect even those who are not suffering from traumatic stress themselves, as a result of coping strategies that emanate from the traumatic experience that leads to the acceptance and reinforcement of the maladaptive coping strategies, which can become entrenched and hard to shift.

2.3.1 Understanding collective trauma and its implications for refugees on the move

In addition to causing individual trauma, the experiences that lead to the refugee-making process often affect more than the individual. They can have an impact on entire families and communities (Van Reisen & Kidane, 2017). Ultimately, this collective suffering and resultant collective trauma is grounded in the social and historical context that led to the atrocities (Lykes, 2001), creating a vicious cycle of victimisation. In recognition of the significance of collective trauma in the lives of refugees on the move, I discuss its implications in relation to the situation when entire communities are dealing with traumatic stress. I also address the impacts of collective trauma on social bonds, as well as the implications of this for culture and identity at the societal level, but first I start by outlining the concept.

2.3.2 What is collective trauma?

In the 1970s Kai Erikson developed and described the concept of collective trauma, firstly looking into individual psychological trauma and defining it as "the state or condition produced by a stress or blow that may produce disordered feelings or behaviour" in a person (Erikson, 1995, p. 184) and then extending that to the community level: "Sometimes the tissues of community can be damaged in much the same way as the tissues of the mind and body" (Erikson, 1995, p. 185). The definition of collective trauma actually comes from Erikson's (1976, pp. 153–154) earlier work, where it was stated: "By collective trauma ... I mean a blow to the basic tissues of social life that damages the bonds attaching people together and impairs the prevailing sense of communality". Accordingly, collective trauma is said to:

> [...] work its way slowly and even insidiously into the awareness of those who suffer from it, so it does not have the quality of suddenness normally associated with 'trauma'. But it is a form of shock all the same, a gradual realisation that the community no longer exists as an effective source of support and that an important part of the self has disappeared. 'I' continue to exist, though damaged and maybe even permanently changed. 'You' continue to exist, though distant and hard to relate to. But 'we' no longer exist as a connected pair or as linked cells in a larger communal body. (Erikson, 1976, p. 154)

As Erikson (1995, p. 185) later clarified, trauma can also create community. He stated that even when "the tissues of a community" are not damaged, "traumatic wounds inflicted on individuals can combine to create a mood, an ethos, a group culture, that is different from (and more than) the sum of the private wounds that make it up", detailing how the sense of difference that people often experience after enduring traumatic experiences can unify and draw similarly situated individuals together in a group. With a new feeling of being distinct or set apart and perhaps not fully understood by those who have not undergone the same experiences, "estrangement becomes the basis for commonality" (Erikson, 1995, p. 186). In this sense trauma contains the centripetal and centrifugal dimensions setting apart a person who has experienced the traumatic event and then pulling them towards those who are better able to relate to them (Erikson, 1995). However, the communality in estrangement is not limited to those who were present during the disaster, but affects all those who are part of that "damaged social organism", the community that endured the blow to the system (Erikson, 1995, p. 188).

Building on the work of Erikson (1976), sociologists have provided a definition of trauma in the social sense, moving the discussion beyond the psychological and neurological aspects described in previous sections (Alexander, 2004). Taken together, collective trauma is defined as the result of an event involving multiple persons who simultaneously experience, witness or are confronted with actual death or threat of it, often due to war, political violence, terrorist attacks or natural disasters (Landau, Mittal & Wieling, 2008), causing emotional and psychological wounds over an individual's lifespan and across generations, as well as impacting on community-wide structures and processes. Unlike individual trauma, which can be experienced by a small percentage of people, with most recovering within a given period of time, collective trauma does not refer to the symptoms of traumatic stress, but is an outcome that includes social responses to a traumatic event as well as the way it is constructed into the beliefs, decisions, behaviours and, ultimately, the narratives of the collective (Shamai, 2015).

2.3.3 Individual trauma in the context of collective trauma

Calamitous man-made and natural events are powerful events that impact on individuals, their families, and even entire communities (Weisaeth, 1992). In addition to loss of life and resources during traumatic events, displacement entails the loss of a sense of place and belonging, as well as material wealth and position in the community from which the person is displaced. When the loss is collective, the ability of people to collaborate and support each other to overcome the loss is curtailed, removing the buffer against further loss. The resources that can be accessed from the community are stretched or depleted altogether, detrimentally affecting the potential for recovering resources (Hobfoll, 1988).

More often than not, traumatic loss also includes traumatic loss of life and, in the case of mass traumatisation, often the loss of many lives. Researchers are becoming increasingly aware of the interconnectedness of trauma has with loss as well as grief (Figley, 1998; Lattanzi-Licht & Doka, 2003; Litz & Gray, 2004; Neimeyer, 2005). Moreover, an untimely, sudden and violent death is known to be one of the most common sources of trauma (Norris *et al.*, 2002a, 2002b). The loss of many lives can, thus, become a devastating factor that compounds the impact of the traumatic event on those who survive.

In addition, the loss can include 'ambiguous loss', which refers to the physical absence yet psychological presence of a person. In the aftermath of a disaster, communities are often exposed to searches for missing people (Boss, 2007) that can last many months or even years. This uncertainty is common in communities facing collective trauma. When death (loss) is certain, a space is created for mourning and closure, but in cases of ambiguous loss the mourning process becomes complex and may lead to symptoms of PTSD, such as anxiety, guilt and intrusive memories, as well as difficulty making decisions, particularly regarding life choices. Refugee communities are indeed blighted by people who have lost contact and are unaccounted for, and this becomes yet another source of stress that contributes to the trauma caused by all the other types of loss discussed above. When a significant proportion of a community is affected by loss (including ambiguous loss) due to conflict or disaster, the loss becomes collective and evokes collective pain, anxiety, depression and guilt, which has implications for how the collective (sometimes an entire nation) copes with problems (Possick, Sadeh & Shamai, 2008).

The situation often makes suitable grieving conditions impossible and rituals and processes that enable families to receive support from extended family, friends, neighbours, and religious and community institutions fail to be activated, leaving individuals and families to detach from painful emotions. They can appear to be coping, causing unresolved mourning, but the pain of loss can resurface unexpectedly at different times and in different ways. Such pain may be expressed in the form of guilt, shame or blame of others, including family members (Aarts & Op den Velde, 1996; Levi, 1986), fragmenting communities and even individual families.

Loss is not always limited to loss of life, integrity, health or property; it can include loss of belief and identity, which are collective losses that result from unanswered questions, including 'why us?'. These can contribute to the disorientation endemic to collective trauma, where formerly held beliefs and explanations fall short of explaining the extreme event. The experiences of Serbs following the war in the former Yugoslavia, the perception of Jewish children following the Holocaust, as well as the experiences of African Americans traumatised by the slave trade, illustrate the impacts of losing identity and the implications of such loss as a collective trauma (Shamai, 2015). This situation can lead to damaged identity, which can be expressed through anger towards other collectives or subgroups within the collective, destroying social bonds. In many cases, the damage remains in the subconscious and is transmitted to subsequent generations (Brave Heart, 2004).

The damage to people's perceptions about themselves (their ability to protect themselves and their community) and about the collective's ability to recover and avert further catastrophes can linger for years, making the world seem like an unsafe place. This can impact on cognition and behaviour, as well as the sense of collective worth or trust in others (Janoff-Bulman, 1985, 1989, 1992). This gives an indication of the frame of mind that many refugees carry with them as they move from place to place, making decisions informed by this sense of disorientation and lack of trust in the collective.

A community is the wide range of social arrangements, further than the intimate private sphere of home and family, but not extending to the wider and impersonal institutions . it is the "interlocking social networks of neighbourhood, kinship and friendship" (Crow & Allen, 1994, p. 1). This sense of belonging and cooperation results in ways of dealing with challenges as a group (Wegner, 2000), and, inevitably, traumatic events that result in collective trauma weaken the confidence in the collective's ability to protect its members and, hence, weaken the bond (Adger, 2000; Kimhi & Shamai, 2004).

Studies also indicate that man-made trauma (such as accidents and technological failures, as well as war and terrorist attacks) are more likely to result in collective trauma than natural disasters (Norris *et al.*, 2002a, 2002b). A possible explanation could be the inevitability and, hence, relative acceptability of natural disasters. Another explanation is the sense of betrayal involved in man-made traumatic events (Gampel, 1988; Solomon, 2013; Schuster *et al.*, 2001). Either way, this makes such experiences more traumatic than those caused by natural disasters that the same community may have faced and overcome. Collective trauma impacts on a society by damaging the interrelated systems within it; that is to say that the large number of people affected by trauma and traumatic stress will impact on how the society is organised and operates, while these changes will go on to affect more people and may have further detrimental impacts on those who are already suffering as a result of PTSD and other comorbid symptoms. Figure 2.3 demonstrates the systemic impacts of trauma, which cause disruption across many spheres and to many interconnected people, disrupting those connections and processes.

Figure 2.3. The interrelated impact of collective trauma (adapted from Shamai, 2015)

In reference to refugees, and particularly mass migration, the main difficulties are loss of community-wide problem solving skills and

resources and loss of continuity (hence, discontinuity), cutting off the inherent competencies contained in the community's history, culture and traditional rituals. Both of these are described below.

2.3.4 Diminished problem-solving skills

Norris *et al.* (2008) assert that war and terror reduce a community's ability to function as a unit and cause individuals to perceive their community as significantly less functional. In addition to individual pain, there are social processes developed in the immediate aftermath of the events that impact on the whole community. These processes are often characterised by in-community over-cohesiveness and homogeneity (over-identification with each other to the exclusion of those considered not to have been affected, i.e., the community in estrangement), resulting in monolithic thinking that does not allow for differences of opinion or conflict (Shamai, 2015). In the short-term, these processes may serve the community by bringing people closer together, empathising with each other; however, the long-term readjustment and reestablishment of resources by accessing outside help could be hampered to a degree that affects community functioning as well as community resilience (Lahad & Ben Nesher, 2005).

Therefore, the level of collective trauma, in many respects, affects community resilience. Community resilience includes the ability of a community to absorb the turbulence created by traumatic experiences, recover effectively, and attain a higher level of functioning in doing so. An important aspect of community resilience is "the capacity to rebound from adversity, strengthened and more resourceful. It is an active social process of endurance, self-righting and growth in response to crisis and challenges" (Walsh, 2006, p. 4).

Walsh (2007) identified three key social processes that facilitate community resilience, and these are clearly sensitive to the effects of collective trauma: (1) shared belief systems (referring to a positive outlook, transcendence and spirituality that enable a community to making meaning of traumatic loss experiences); (2) organisational patterns (referring to the availability of economic and institutional resources and the connectedness and flexibility of the community to engage the resources as appropriate); and (3) communication and problem solving (referring to open emotional expression and collaborative problem solving across members of the community).

These are crucial considerations when thinking about the reality of refugees on the move and the consequences of the causes of mass migration, beyond individuals and individual families, and, in particular, the inability to generate and implement problem solving ideas, as the community becomes saturated by problems and unable to generate new ideas, having been cut off during the traumatic response (e.g., estrangement, as described above). It is not too farfetched to see that migrating further and further away might be one of the 'solutions' adopted during the traumatic event, and never revised, making the community blind to other solutions, including ideas suggested by those considered to be 'others', i.e., people not impacted by the traumatic events. This is a combination of the effects of 'community in estrangement', which excludes others who are perceived as outside those sharing the pain, and the depleted capability of those who are included, limiting the range of problem-solving abilities within the traumatised community.

2.3.5 Discontinuity

Another consequence of collective trauma, particularly the kind of trauma that results in mass migration, is the discontinuity it causes along the pathways that create continuity across the past, present and future, as a result of which people may lose access to the inherent competence, resilience, strength and resources that their families and tribes had accessed and utilised across time (Landau-Stanton, 1990). When communities are able to access their resilience by accessing their history and narrative, they can reconnect their current status, knowing where they had come from in relation to their current position. This helps them to make informed choices about what to keep and draw on from their past and what to leave behind, and to plan where to go and how to get there (Landau & Saul, 2004). Even without migration, collective trauma can cause such discontinuity that it changes the order of things; however, migration makes the cut-off both physically and psychologically, depriving refugees of the wisdom and information contained in the fabric of their culture and heritage. As a result, migration makes people prone to decisions based on instincts informed by their overwhelmed system, rather than core values and principles that would usually provide a guide.

Following their studies of communities exposed to mass violence, Norris and colleagues developed a framework with four variables for community resilience (Norris & Stevens, 2008; Norris *et al.*, 2002b): (1) economic development (to enable people to withstand the devastation and continue to remain within the norms of their social values social capital); (2) community-wide network and a sense of belonging (to enable people to meet the many emergent needs of the situation); (3) reliable and dependable communication (to enable people to arrive at a community-wide narrative); and (4) community-wide competence (enabling the community to develop collective problem-solving and decision-making skills that empower the community to cope with challenges) (Norris & Stevens, 2008).

Removed from realistic means of developing community-wide resources that reduce future vulnerabilities, deprived of meaningful involvement in rebuilding their communities including their own relationships, and deprived of trusted sources of information to reconstruct their narratives, refugee communities are left to continue in the traumatised system that hampers their recovery and makes them perpetually vulnerable. Most situations that cause the mass migration of refugees are man-made, result in individual and collective trauma that affects both the state of the individual (emotional and cognitive state) and the state of the community (social structures, social bonds or social capital, and shared values). These disruptions not only make it difficult for individual victims to heal, but may also end up generating additional individual and collective trauma.

The benefits of social connections and cooperation and shared values engaged to attain collective goals are devastated in a situation of mass trauma, are the very things that are described as social capital (Schuller, Baron & Field, 2000). Putnam (2000, p. 19) defines social capital as "connections among individuals – social networks and the norms of reciprocity and trustworthiness that arise from them". The availability of social capital can give a good indication of the wellbeing of a community (Somasundaram, 2014). I have, thus, taken social capital as an indicator of the level of collective trauma in the research.

2.4 The relevance of ICT in trauma and collective trauma

In addition to issues of identity and belonging, similarity and difference, inclusion and exclusion, place and time, the concept of a community should include processes important to the community including change and modernisation, as well as a definitive spatial and social context (Bell & Newby, 1971; Cater & Jones, 1989; Crow & Allen, 1994; Johnston, 2000; Silk, 1999). In the case of Eritrean refugees, it is important to include the introduction of information and communication technology, and, in particular, the mobile phone and, more specifically, smartphones, in the discussion of refugee's current migration trajectories. This follows observations that mobile phones are used extensively in maintaining links among families and friends scattered along exile routes and places. Mobile phones are also used to obtain information about ongoing journeys. However, the role of mobile phones is not necessarily always positive.

The harmonisation of technology combined with powerful computing and low-cost handsets, has enabled the explosive growth of the mass mobile market on a global scale. While this is generally regarded as a common good, it may also be a mediator of new threats to societies. For instance, in the context of human trafficking for ransom, which has resulted in the abduction, hostage taking, and torture of thousands of Eritrean refugees crossing the Sinai desert on route to Israel (Van Reisen, Estefanos & Rijken, 2014), traffickers used ICT to facilitate intelligence gathering, for negotiations about the routes, including those with local security authorities, and to effect transactions and the payment of ransoms. These technologies are accessible, available, affordable and easy to use, without the need for any technical training or education. They also, to a large extent, allow the user's identity to remain hidden. It is difficult to imagine contemporary human trafficking for ransom and smuggling operations being realised without the use of ICTs for communication and mobile money transfers (Van Reisen *et al.*, 2017). In addition,

Van Reisen and Gerrima (2016) contend that the impact of ICT is more profound and acts at a deeper level, allowing people to share tragic circumstances all over the globe, contributing to collective trauma.

Van Oortmerssen (2015) argues that while ICT is often regarded as an enabling technology, it is also a disruptive technology: innovations such as automation and digital platforms mean many people are losing their jobs on the one hand, while on the other hand jobs that did not exist before are being created. ICT is challenging existing institutions, like our legal system, and causing the emergence of new types of criminal behaviour, such as cybercrime. In addition, as well as enabling people to challenge the adverse behaviour of leaders, as was seen during the Arab Spring, social media and the Internet can be used by dictators to find protestors and suppress activities that threaten their position of power.

2.4.1 The role of ICT in causing trauma

In addition to their technological use for smuggling, human trafficking, hostage taking and ransom collecting, mobile phones have also been exploited as a way of traumatising people by communicating distressing messages from victims of human trafficking in a bid to extract ransom money from their distraught friends and family. The power of ICT to remotely control and influence the emotions, attitudes and behaviour of people is enormous and unprecedented in the history of humanity. The hostage takers effectively exploit this element to their advantage. Family members, relatives and friends of the victims are made to communicate with the victims while they are being tortured to encourage them to pay the ransom (Van Reisen *et al.*, 2012, 2014, 2017).

Human trafficking for ransom is essentially the abduction of human beings (e.g., Eritrean refugees on the way to Israel), holding them hostage, and torturing them until their family and friends pay a ransom for their release. To induce the collection of the said ransom, traffickers rely on technology to expose the family to the trauma of the torture by making them listen and watch the agony and humiliation of their loved ones as they beg and plead for their release (Van Reisen *et al.*, 2014). Technology has enabled the traffickers to traumatise the victim's entire network of family and friends, transcending time and space, as some of the calls from the torture camps are played on social media and through satellite radio broadcasts from the diaspora, impacting on almost every Eritrean. This has created a situation of mass trauma and enabled the extortion of unimaginable sums of ransom money (Van Reisen *et al.*, 2017).

If the refugee's friends and families in Eritrea and the diaspora were unable to access the large sums demanded, they had to involve their extended network, even making public appeals on community radio and social media, to maximise their chance of collecting the ransom demanded. This was coupled with the efforts of activists and journalists, who sought to gain public support, thereby using community radio and social media to widen the pool of people exposed to the extremely distressing material of people being heinously tortured and suffering physical and psychological pain (Kidane & Van Reisen, 2017). This situation turned the traumatic experience into a mass trauma involving a network of people linked directly and indirectly to the primary victim (Van Reisen *et al.*, 2017). The deliberate act of torturing thousands of Eritreans, many coming from the same region and even the same village (as groups of people who know and trust each other often flee together) has led to a classic situation of collective trauma, with enough impact to become a keystone in the group's narrative, set of beliefs and identity, both for the current generation and subsequent generations. Many Eritrean families and communities, and the nation itself, have been blighted by the trauma ensuing from human trafficking in the Sinai.

In addition to collective trauma, individuals can be exposed to secondary trauma. Secondary trauma is trauma that occurs indirectly and is defined as: "Learning about unexpected or violent death, serious harm, or threat of death or injury experienced by a family member or other close associates" (American Psychiatric Association, 2000, p. 463). In the Diagnostic and Statistical Manual of Mental Disorders 4th Edition (DSM-IV), classifications of what constitutes a traumatic event also suggest that knowledge of a traumatic event can be traumatising (American Psychiatric

Association, 2000). Over the years, researchers have started to elaborate on this and have identified that individuals can be traumatised without being physically harmed or threatened, by learning about the traumatic event (Figley, 1995a, 1995b; Steed & Bicknell, 2001). Some even argue that those indirectly exposed to trauma can exhibit the same symptoms as direct victims (Figley, 1995a, 1995b). Figley defines Secondary traumatic stress is defined as "natural, consequent behaviours and emotions resulting from knowledge about a traumatising event experienced by a significant other". Symptoms are often produced in response to exposure to details of traumatic events experienced by others (Hensel, Ruiz, Finne & Dewa, 2015).

Desperate to raise the impossibly high ransoms demanded by the traffickers, friends and families of victims, activists and journalists have inadvertently increased the number of those traumatised by the torture of the primary victims. The narrative of Eritreans as people who beat many odds to establish their nation through a bitter independence struggle has suffered great damage because of the collective trauma resulting from Sinai trafficking (Kidane & Van Reisen, 2017). An entire generation of Eritreans born and raised after Eritrea's independence has come to only ever see and hear of themselves as victims of atrocities and unwanted refugees (Van Reisen *et al.*, 2017).

2.4.2 The potential of ICT for healing trauma

Conversely, ICT has also been used to support many successful psychological interventions. E-therapy, psychotechnologies, psychotherapy 2.0, teletherapy, mediated technology, i-therapy, online therapy and many other expressions have been used to describe the opportunity to work therapeutically in the digital world. ICT offers new ways of working, with the potential to reach many new clients, addressing concerns over the availability and cost of therapy (Wieiz, 2014).

The evidence for the effectiveness of computer-based therapy has been growing. A study, comparing a six-session, computer-based version of cognitive behavioural therapy (CBT) with therapist-administered CBT and a waiting list control group (Selmi *et al.*, 1990), found that both treatment groups were significantly improved. In a similar study, patients at a community mental health centre who were waiting for CBT were offered an opportunity to use computerised CBT (Van den Berg, Shapiro, Bickerstaffe & Cavanagh, 2004). This study also demonstrated improvements.

Reger and Gahm (2009) found that Internet or computer-based CBT was superior to waiting list and placebos, and equal to therapist-delivered treatment of anxiety. Similarly, Ebert *et al.* (2015) found evidence for the efficacy of computer-assisted CBT for anxiety and depression in youth. Indicating that such intervention may have good prospects, as alternative when face-to-face treatment is not feasible. There are other examples of the positive role of technology in psychotherapy, including the use of virtual reality to treat PTSD (Kaplan, 2005), as well as the use of websites with online screening instruments for depression and anxiety, indicating the potentially ground-breaking implications of the technology.

More pertinent to the current study, Internet-based treatments have been proposed as a good fit for delivery in the treatment of anxiety disorders, especially PTSD. The use of ICT could potentially address some logistical impediments, including geographic and resource constraints, enabling those in remote areas to gain access to specialised services (Cukor Spitalnick, Difede, Rizzo & Rothbaum, 2009). In addition, delivery via ICT gives the additional benefit of enabling individuals to avoid stigmatisation related to accessing mental health treatment, as well as offering an opportunity for people with anxiety related difficulties that makes travel and social interactions of traditional therapy difficult (Cukor *et al.*, 2009). In an analysis of Internet and computer-based treatments for anxiety disorders, Reger and Gahm (2009) concluded that "although there is preliminary support for the use of ICT for PTSD, there is limited data to substantiate its use at this time", indicating that, at the time of their study, the delivery approach was still relatively novel and required development.

A review of e-mental health literature in 2014 found applications addressing four areas of mental health service delivery, namely: provision of relevant information; screening, assessment, and monitoring; intervention; and social support. It identified the potential that e-mental health has to address the gap between the needs and capacity for provision of conventional treatment. The review also identified better accessibility, cost effectiveness (although start-up and research and development costs are necessary), flexibility in standardisation and potentials for personalisation, interactivity, and consumer engagement as particular strengths of the approach (Lal & Adair, 2014).

The latest development in the delivery of mental health support via ICT has been mobile technology for mental health (mobile MH), which offers portability for access and is more cost effective than desktop computers, which were used previously. Furthermore, with mobile technology there is the potential of providing real-time feedback. Two areas of mobile MH that have grown exponentially are mobile MH Apps and social networking (Hilty, Chan, Hwang, Wong & Bauer, 2017). Mobile MH has helped people by enhancing coping strategies, empowerment and self-efficacy (Ferreira-Lay & Miller, 2008). Users have reported a reduction in levels of anxiety and isolation, enhanced connectedness, and an enhanced ability to make decisions on health-related behaviour (Morahan-Martin, 2004; Murray et al., 2003; Hu, Kung, Rummans, Clark & Lapid 2015).

More research is required to assess the outcomes of mobile MH, compared to in-person care options and other technology-based services. In addition, there are dilemmas associated with the various Apps and the fact that there is currently no framework for the development, evaluation and regulation of Apps, which has led to a chaotic mix of Apps with varying degrees of effectiveness and dangers. There are also serious ethical considerations regarding security and safe use. The industry could benefit from the creation and adoption of standards by an international interdisciplinary consortium to enable the technology to become more widely used (Hilty et al., 2017).

Owning and using a smartphone when you are a refugee on the move is not a luxury, but a necessity; it is crucial for staying connected to family members and receiving information and resources on the journey. During flight, information about routes, destinations and facilitations is crucial, and so refugees are very much invested in staying connected with each other, despite the technological challenges. Maintaining links with people with information while in the refugee camps and across borders is also crucial and can often only be achieved through social media on a smartphone. This research, thus, extends the technological and therapeutic advances that are beginning to have an impact on the better delivery of mental health services to refugees, who are already using the technology and adapting it to their needs. However, even though connectivity and affordable technology are crucial in this day and age, many refugees in camps or on the move are not as connected as they need to be (Schoenmaeckers, 2018).

2.4.3 The challenges of connectivity

Internet and mobile communication are transforming our world, making information readily available and offering abundant ways to stay connected with friends, family and colleagues via social media. However, refugees are often excluded from this information and connectivity superhighway, because the places where they live lack digital networks or being connected is beyond their financial means (UNHCR, 2016). UNHCR's research found that only 17% of rural refugees live in areas with 3G coverage, compared to 29% of the global rural population, while 20% of rural refugees have no mobile coverage at all, which is double the proportion of the global rural population without coverage. This was despite the fact that refugees often spend up to a third of their disposable income on staying connected and connectivity can significantly improve their safety and security.

A 2017 Harvard University Survey of mobile phones, mental health and privacy at a Syrian refugee camp in Greece revealed that mobile phone access was important to over 80% of refugees and that, accordingly, 94% of men and 67% of women owned a mobile phone, with 94% using WhatsApp and 78% using Facebook. In addition, the survey identified a link between depression (which affected 40% of refugees and 58% of women refugees) and mobile phone usage: each additional day an individual used a phone in the previous week was associated with a reduction in their probability of being depressed

(Latonero, Poole & Berens, 2018), indicating the benefits of connectivity for refugees.

In the Ethiopian refugee camps, where much of this research took place, Schoenmaeckers (2018) found that nearly everyone in the cohort of participants over the age of 15 years owned a mobile phone; however, connectivity in the camps was poor, with the exception of the time between midnight and seven in the morning, when there might be a good enough connection to access the Internet or make phone calls. To circumvent these difficulties in connectivity, the refugees used various strategies, like dialling 112 (an emergency support access number in Europe) repeatedly to get a few minutes-worth of strong enough connectivity. There are also applications that have proven helpful in gaining connectivity, like the Psiphon, which was originally designed to enable safer web surfing for people living in repressive regimes. When connected, people are able to access Facebook, Viber, Imo (a free video call App) and Facebook Messenger, as well as applications that allow them to play games and access poems and jokes (Schoenmaeckers, 2018). Despite technological challenges, mobile phones seem to play a key role in refugee communities, connecting people, and alleviating isolation and information deprivation.

The literature is clear that refugees flee from situations that expose them to individual and collective trauma, and the level of post-trauma stress in individuals and their communities hampers recovery, sometimes trapping people in a cycle of diminished resilience, vulnerability, impaired cognitive skills and problem solving skills, and diminished social capital. In addition, it is also clear that ICT is having an impact on refugee trajectories: adding to the pain and trauma (as they are able to see and hear the misfortunes that have befallen their family and friends), but also reducing trauma by allowing refugees to stay connected. ICT could indeed be a versatile and mobile mental health support delivery instrument that empowers people, enabling them to choose the time and place in which they access support. However, issues of connectivity can potentially prevent refugees from fully benefitting from the use of technology in this way.

Conflict and political violence can have devastative implications, both at the individual and collective levels, which can affect the cognitive capacity of victims, leading them to make decisions based on impaired information processing mechanisms. In addition, the collective nature of the traumatic events resulting in collective trauma means that individuals suffer doubly from their own symptoms and from living in communities where the societal fabric has been dealt a devastating blow, cutting them off from social support and resources that would have been protective and built their resilience. Instead such individuals are often caught in a downward spiral of loss. This is the backdrop against which many members of refugee communities are trying to manage their ongoing trajectories. We have also seen that ICT can play a role in both causing and healing trauma. These are the aspects of the research that connect what we already know about the context of migration trajectories in the digital era to the subject of the current research, exploring the impact of an intervention to heal trauma using the extremely limited resources available in these communities.

2.5 Conclusion

In answering the question pertaining to the role that individual and collective trauma might play in migration trajectories, and whether ICT is aiding or mitigating this, this chapter has outlined the potential of ICT to cause and heal trauma. Clearly the experiences of war and political violence, as well as having to flee one's own country, constitute stressors that could result in traumatic stress for many individuals. Traumatic stress and collective trauma impact adversely on a person's ability to appraise safety, as well as their social and economic resilience. Trauma changes processes of cognition, making the victim less able to regard situations as positive, causing people to believe that they are more vulnerable and less resilient than they actually are, and this can impact on the quality of the decisions that refugees make during their migration trajectories. Moreover, the nature of the atrocities entailed in political violence also means that the impact can extend beyond those who are primary victims to those in their immediate and wider circles in the form of collective trauma, which can have intergenerational implications, affecting wider society. In the today's digital era, refugees and migrants, much like the rest of society, are greatly affected by ICTs, which play both positive and negative roles: causing and extending the reach of traumatic experiences as well as helping refugees stay connected and informed and potentially facilitating the healing of trauma.

Pulling all of this together leads us to the conclusion that discussing migration, particularly refugee migration, in terms of push-and-pull factors, without looking at the impact of trauma on trajectories, leaves out much of the reality, as we have come to understand it. This includes the realities of individual and collective trauma as well as the role of ICT in causing and potentially healing trauma. Hence, this research proposes an alternative and seeks to provide a fuller explanation of refugee trajectories in the digital era.

Yohanna was the young pregnant mother who gave birth as she sank during the Lampedusa disaster in 2013 (mentioned at the start of this chapter). Her plight sent a shock wave through the international community, refugee community and diaspora – it touched a nerve with everyone who heard the story. I too wondered what her thought process might have been. Whether or not she had consulted her mother? If she discussed anything with a trusted elder? If she knew of the dangers, as the disaster was not the first such disaster? Six months after the Lampedusa disaster, when the media hype had died down, I found that I was still asking the question, why? I couldn't stop thinking about the steps that led Yohanna to that fateful journey.

Ode to Yohanna's Baby

In
The small cramped quarters
A lone light bulb dangling above
A baby was born
Her bright intelligent eyes wide open

On
The dusty streets
Where food was as scarce as hope
A girl grew up
With rich vivid dreams

At
The sparse unconvincing classroom
With few books and one tired teacher
A student shone bright
A glorious rising star

In
The smelly dingy barracks
Where anguished cries go unheard
A young woman was raped
Countless times

In
The embrace of a devoted companion
Where a promise is dearer than life
An unlikely glint sparkled
Love uninvited

On
The vast dark sea
His mother feebly fighting to stay afloat
A baby boy was born
No one saw his eyes
Open briefly
Then shut

Selam Kidane

At the bottom of the poem I had written this note: Six months ago today I learnt what despair meant... 366 young Eritreans died and the world watched the whole thing... that hurt, but knowing it might happen again fills me with anger... not the righteous anger that makes one rise up and kick something, but the desperate type that makes me want to tear my hair out... the feeling of having so many desperate questions and not a single answer... RIP Yohanna and Baby, I hope there is no desperate anger on the other side.

Chapter 3

Research design and methods

When one tries to explain the phenomena of the ongoing migration trajectory of a refugee community from within it, what one soon becomes very aware of is the need to find the right approach to telling the story. Without a coherent approach, Yohanna and the 366 people who died with her become an anecdotal detail in an impossibly difficult story that people will push aside, because it is too hard to understand. As a mental health professional trained in healing trauma, this was the direction I would naturally use, as an approach that sought to understand the thought processes and their implications. Whether or not I have managed to relate the situation aptly and do justice to the reality is something that the reader will have to answer, but I myself am grateful to all those who helped me find a framework for organising my thoughts and investigating and presenting the phenomena in the way I have been able to.

This chapter outlines the design of the research and the methodological approaches employed in collecting the data. The main emphasis here was to find a reliable methodological approach that captures the various elements of the research and still maintains its integrity. The chapter begins with the design of the research, followed by its methodology, including the instruments that were developed and adapted for use. This is followed by the methods used to collect the qualitative and quantitative data and the sampling approaches used[1].

The research consisted of five interrelated, but distinct, studies: (1) describing the prevalence of trauma and (2) the role of ICT, followed by (3) the designing of a trauma intervention approach, (4)

---

[1] This and subsequent sections contain direct quotes from: Van Reisen, M., Stokmans, M., Kidane, S., Melicherova, K., & Schoenmaeckers, R. (2018a). *Causes and dynamics of mixed unskilled migrants trafficked within the Horn region. A study including Eritrea, Ethiopia and Sudan.* Synthesis Report. Tilburg: Tilburg University. I was one of the main authors of that report and have used parts of it here with the permission of the other authors.

testing the effectiveness of the approach on reducing trauma levels and, finally, (5) using the approach to enhance social and economic resilience. Accordingly, a mixed method design was used, consisting of interviews, focus group discussions, observations and surveys. Table 3.1 outlines the research methodology for each study in the research.

Table 3.1. Research methodology

Study	Research sub question	Design, methodology, sampling and instruments used
1.	Q.1 What is the level of PTS among refugees from Eritrea? Q.2 Can levels of PTS affect the processing of information regarding safety and socio-economic resilience during decision making regarding ongoing trajectories?	Design: Descriptive survey design Instrument: IES-R Data collection method: Psychometric questionnaire Sampling: Snowballing and convenience sampling
2.	Q.3 What are the trusted communication channels of refugees and is the prevalence of ICT and social media among Eritrean refugees such that it could play a role in the provision of trauma interventions?	Design: Descriptive survey design Instrument: Questionnaire (See Appendix 1) Data collection method: Interviews Sampling: Snowballing and convenience sampling
3.	Q.5b What are the key elements of a short self-help trauma intervention in a high trauma/low resource context for it to impact on social economic resilience?	Design: Design study (development) Desk research

4.	Q.4 Is it possible to lower levels of PTS and enhance socio-economic resilience by delivering a short self-help trauma intervention in a high trauma/low resource context?	Design: Feasibility study Instruments: IES-R and SER, topic lists for interviews and observations Data collection method: Psychometric questionnaire, focus groups, research team observations Sampling: Snowballing and purposive sampling
5.	Q.5a Will a short self-help trauma intervention delivered using ICT have an impact on reducing PTS and enhancing resilience in the high trauma and low resource contexts of young Eritrean refugees?	Design: Feasibility study Instruments: IES-S, SER-S and ISCS (see appendixes 2, 3 & 4), topic list for interviews and observations Data collection method: Psychometric questionnaire, individual interviews, focus groups, research team observations Sampling: Snowballing and purposive sampling

3.1 Research methodology

The research used a mixed methods approach resulting in both qualitative and quantitative data. Mixed methods is an emergent methodology for research that involves the systemic integration of qualitative and quantitative data within a single research design. Such integration permits the more complete and synergetic use of data to give a more comprehensive understanding than would have been afforded by either approach on its own (Wisdom & Creswell, 2013). In the following sections I focus on the overall methodological approach and then discuss the construction and validity of the various instruments that were used to gather the data.

Both qualitative and quantitative data were gathered for this research to explain findings more fully and provide a more comprehensive understanding. This mixed methods approach overcame, to some extent, the shortcomings of each approach. For example, the Impact of Events Scale-Revised (IES-R), used in the feasibility study in Uganda, was producing results that were contrary to the observations and reports emerging from the interviews (i.e. participants were reporting lower levels of PTSD symptoms, while their IES-R scores were high). Those involved in conducting the interviews suggested that this might be due to the fact that they were actually becoming more aware of the various symptoms and were able to name and report them better. The clarity that was provided by the qualitative data removed concerns over potential bias. However, the approach was not without its difficulties; the collection of qualitative data was resource intensive, both in terms of the data collection stage as well as in the analysis.

As this research involved participants who were perhaps not familiar with psychometric approaches, there were various advantages envisaged in the use of a mixed methods approach for overcoming any gaps involved in a single method. Indeed, the following aspects were realised by using a mixed methods approach:

- **Triangulation:** The researcher used mixed methods to converge, corroborate and validate results from the quantitative data by using the interviews with individuals and focus group discussions, both in Uganda and Ethiopia.

- **Complementarity:** The mixed methods approach was useful in elaborating on the findings of the statistical data by relating it to the lived experiences of participants. In Uganda, for instance, the interviews and focus group data were crucial in enabling further illustrations of the kinds of experiences that resulted in traumatic stress, which, in turn, enabled the researcher to understand what a reduction in the level of trauma looked like and, hence, attest to the effectiveness of the intervention. This would not have been possible without the qualitative approach being used to clarify the results of the quantitative data. Similarly in Ethiopia the changes in the thought processes of participants were illustrated using their responses during focus group discussions.

- **Expansion:** In addition to illustrating findings, the mixed methods approach enabled the scope of the elements of the study to be expanded, resulting in more comprehensive results. This was particularly the case in the survey into ICT, in which, while the quantitative data looked at the experiences of participants (refugees and their peers in the region), the qualitative data (focus groups) addressed the infrastructure and policy concerns related to the prevalence and accessibility of ICT in the context.

3.2 Quantitative research design

The research was conducted in five distinct, but interrelated, studies; however, all studies had one thing in common – they all focused on Eritrean refugees. One study looked at the delivery of the trauma intervention among internally displaced women who had experienced extreme trauma during the civil war in Uganda. As such there were three distinct designs implemented: descriptive survey, design study and feasibility study.

3.2.1 Descriptive surveys

The first two studies were descriptive surveys, aimed at establishing the prevalence of trauma in refugee communities and the significance of ICT, particularly smartphones and social media use. Survey was the preferred method because it allowed the situation to be described in a large population across different locations.

The first study explored the prevalence of PTSD among Eritrean refugees (detailed in Chapter 4), using the IES-R among members of various Eritrean refugee communities in Tel Aviv, Kampala, the Tigray region in Northern Ethiopia and inside Eritrea. All respondents, except those inside Eritrea, were surveyed by the researcher using the IES-R, but explaining terms and concepts in Tigrigna. The scores were calculated in accordance with the guidelines designed by the developers of the scale.

Similarly, the second study aimed to identify the prevalence of ICT using a survey (as detailed in Chapter 5). For this study a questionnaire was developed in English (see Appendix 1) and translated into Tigrigna and Arabic. As will be described in Chapter 5, the survey was part of a wider study into building resilience against human trafficking among refugee youth and youth in their host community. For the purposes of the present study, only the relevant sections dealing with the prevalence of smartphones and social media usage are discussed.

3.2.2 Design study

The third study (outlined in Chapter 6), focused on the development of a trauma intervention taking into account all the constraints involved in working with refugees on the move. In addition to language and culture, the contextualisation encompassed the incorporation of the collective nature of the experiences and, hence, the intervention aimed to treat PTSD and collective trauma simultaneously. This study resulted in the development of a six-week intervention called TRUST.

3.2.3 Feasibility studies

As mentioned above, the last two studies were experiments to ascertain the effectiveness of an intervention in a real-life context, which is reflected in their design. These studies explored the effectiveness of the TRUST intervention in the real-life settings of rural Northern Uganda and two refugee camps in the Tigray region of northern Ethiopia. For this, an experimental set-up was developed that enabled the effect of the intervention on trauma levels and perceptions of social and economic resilience to be determined.

In a true experimental approach all variables are controlled and, consequently, causal conclusions can be drawn; however, in the real-life context of these studies such an artificially controlled design was not possible, as it would have reduced the real effects of the intervention within the real-life situation and its ecological validity. A real-life set-up, such as the one used for this research, responds well to the increasing demand for research to be beneficial to society. The problem identified by many policymakers and practitioners who are interested in evidence-based decision making, is that research tends to be carried out in a sterile experimental set-up, which precludes understanding of what may be expected of an intervention in a real-life situation. It is, therefore, necessary to consider the advantages and possibilities of studying interventions in a real-life context. This does not mean that the effectiveness of an intervention cannot be studied (Snow, Morrill & Anderson, 2003). However, it does mean that one should be thorough and meticulous when carrying out such research, by committing oneself to sensitivity (or responsiveness) to the research situation at hand and applying different research methods (triangulation) in order to have data to verify and validate the results of the testing of the effect of the intervention (in the specific situation).

One possibility is to elaborate a natural design (Shadish, Cook & Campbell, 2002) in which all-important key variables may not be known. Such a design demands specific requirements of a study, such as that it be responsive to what is taking place in the environment and that all contextual specifics taking place before, during, and after the intervention or treatment is applied be carefully documented. In such a case it is clear under what conditions the intervention did or did not work. By doing similar research in another situation, one gains an understanding of the effectiveness of (variations in) the intervention, given the characteristics of the situation at hand. This was the case for the two feasibility studies, in which TRUST was implemented in two different contexts, producing results along the same trend of reducing trauma levels and enhancing social and economic resilience.

The suggestion to attend closely to the research situation in its real-life context is counterintuitive to traditional positivistic empirical research. This traditional approach prescribes that a researcher behaves as an objective (outsider) observer, who does not interfere with the research situation and who is interested in finding general laws. This argument can be countered by considering the reality of the situation in which the researcher is conducting the research. He or she is working in a specific social context with human beings whose values and sensibilities need to be seriously considered, from both the perspective of research ethics and human rights. Thus, the point is that the researcher gathers specific information, which necessarily and unavoidably makes him/her a part of the social reality in which the intervention is taking place (Burawoy, 1998).

This research was conducted in real-life settings, more specifically, mainly rural areas, in which researchers are an extraordinary phenomenon. People have expectations of what a researcher is doing and how to approach them. Moreover, the researcher has to approach and interact with local authorities, participants and non-participants in the research according to proper (local) social norms. Consequentially, the researcher is not an objective, outsider (observer), but an engaged participant who is trying to discover an appropriate way to improve the social situation for a particular group of people. According to positivistic logic, such an expectation concerning the research itself should not exist. However, in reality, the social situation is present and cannot be ignored. Therefore, epistemologically, it is sounder to acknowledge the effects of the social embedding of the research, rather than artificially deny the existence of the specific social interaction of the real-life experiment with its environment.

By researching the effect of an intervention for a defined group (internally displaced Ugandan women in Northern Uganda, and Eritrean refugees in Ethiopia), one helps this specific group (and, therefore, not another group), even though the findings of the research can potentially be applicable, in part or entirely, in similar contexts elsewhere. This choice can trigger envy; for instance, the men in the study community in Northern Uganda (spouses, fathers, and sons) asked to be included in the intervention. Such a reaction by a community indicates that conducting research is not an objective, neutral act that can be located outside the social situation in which the intervention takes place, but an integral part of the social situation. In this study, the wider community and the participants of the different research groups were all given access to the trauma support intervention programme. Local radio broadcasting about the programme was sought to provide broader benefits from the intervention to the community as a whole after the research was completed, so as not to interfere with the experimental set up of the study. Similarly, in Ethiopia, all participants were given access to the entire intervention (if they wanted it) upon completion of the research. A similar approach of using radio broadcasting to inform a broad audience about research findings was successful in Uganda (Neema, Kroon, Van Der Aa & Draulans, 2018).

Participants were allocated to one of the research groups and their data was collected pre- and post-intervention using the instruments described below:

- In the Uganda study, participants were purposefully divided into the following groups, with half of them receiving TRUST as an intervention for PTSD: (1) participants who received social protection, (2) participants who received social protection and counselling, [2] (3) participants who received counselling, and (4) a control group of participants who received no assistance.

---

[2] This counselling programme was offered by a non-governmental organisation (NGO) and is different to the kind of support provided by TRUST. More details can be found in Van Reisen et al. (2018b).

- In the Ethiopia study, participants were randomly assigned to receive a short or a full version of the TRUST intervention. As some of the participants also received livelihood support, four groups were established: (1) participants who received a short version of the TRUST intervention and livelihood support, (2) participants who received the full version of TRUST and livelihood support (3) participants who received just the short version of TRUST, and (4) participants who received just the full version of TRUST.

The surveys and experiments discussed thus far were all supplemented by interviews and observations to triangulate the results. These are described in section 3.4. The specific design of each study is outlined fully in the respective chapters; here it suffices to say that this was a research employing various designs and methods, as will be described below.

3.3 Research instruments

In this section, I discuss the research instruments used in my studies. First, I deal with the development and statistical properties of the quantitative instruments (IES-R/S and SER) used in the questionnaire into trauma detailed in Chapter 4, as well as the pre- and post-intervention data gathered using these instruments, in Chapters 6 and 7. Following this I briefly go into the questionnaire for the survey on the use of social media, detailed in Chapter 5 (see also Table 3.1 above).

As mentioned previously, this research enjoyed many collaborations and, as such, there were significant contributions made by fellow researchers, both in the development of instruments, as well as in the statistical analysis of results. Dr Primrose Nakazibwe developed the SER instrument for a study that looked at the cost-benefit of cash transfer programmes and post-trauma services for the economic empowerment of women in Uganda (2016–2018). The SER instrument was subsequently adapted by the current researcher for the Ethiopia study, taking into account the context of a refugee camp where the availability of resources and opportunities is different to that in Uganda. Similarly, Dr Mia Stokmans analysed all the statistical data on the reliability of the instruments and helped in the development of the short version of the IES as well as adaptations made to the SER.

3.3.1 Impact of Events Scale-Revised

Trauma was operationalised by means of the IES-R. The IES-R is the most widely used self-reported measure of PTSD. The scale was developed in 1979, as a short self-reporting measure for assessing the degree of symptomatic response to a specific traumatic experience that took place in the previous seven days (Horowitz, Wilner & Alvarez, 1979). Its development draws on the understanding of the traumatic stress responses of intrusion and avoidance as the primary domain of measurement.

In the initial report (Horowitz, Wilner & Alvarez, 1979), data supported the existence of homogeneous clusters of intrusion and avoidance, as measured by Cronbach alpha (0.79 for intrusion and 0.82 for avoidance). The correlation between subscales was small, allowing for the independence of the subscales (explaining 18% of the variance). Test-retest reliability was satisfactory too (with coefficients of 0.87 for intrusion and 0.79 for avoidance).

Later, Zilberg, Weiss and Horowitz (1982) conducted a comprehensive replication and cross-validation of the psychometric characteristics of the scale and its conceptual model. The result revealed that all items were endorsed frequently (44% to 89% of the pooled sample), suggesting that the content of experience following traumatic events, as represented in the IES item pool, was similar across the different types of events and different populations (e.g., patients and non-patients). A decade later, Sundin and Horowitz (2002) presented a summary of 18 studies on the correlation between a variety of other measures of symptoms and intrusion and avoidance. The correlations with general symptoms were larger than the average relationship between the two subscales.

However, the IES was still an incomplete assessment of PTSD, as it did not track the responses to the domain of hyperarousal, to overcome this the new version was developed starting with data from a longitudinal study of responses by emergency service personnel to traumatic events including a major earthquake, researchers developed a new revised version of the scale, called the Impact of Events Scale-Revised, by adding a set of seven additional items to tap hyperarousal (Weiss, Marmar, Metzler & Ronfeldt, 1995). These additional items, which were interspaced with the existing items and the splitting of one double-barrelled question, brought the IES-R in line with Diagnostic and Statistical Manual of Mental Disorders (DSM-IV) criteria. Crucially, the revised version was developed with a view to maintaining compatibility with the original, the instruction on the one-week timeframe was maintained, as was the original scoring scheme. The internal consistency of the three subscales, the pattern of item-total correlations, test-retest stability, and communality of the inter-item correlations were all satisfactory (Weiss *et al.*, 1997). In addition, in response to the experience of respondents frequent answering questions with the response 'sometimes' and 'often', respondents were asked to report on the degree of distress, rather than the frequency of symptoms; this modified the format of the response.

The IES-R was used in the survey that assessed trauma in Eritrean communities, as well as in assessing the impact of the intervention on trauma in Northern Uganda. The IES-R consists of three subscales: intrusion (8 items), avoidance (8 items) and hyperarousal (6 items). The scale values of the items include 0 (not at all), 1 (a little bit), 2 (moderately), 3 (quite a bit) and 4 (extremely). Two ways of scoring IES-R can be used, and both have their benefits in relation to the specific application of the scale. To obtain the three subscale scores (avoidance, hyperarousal, intrusion): calculate the mean of the subscale items; this gives separate scores for each subscale and more detailed analysis of the impacts of an intervention, for instance, while the total score can be calculated using the mean of all non-missing items. It is possible to calculated for the subscales of intrusion, avoidance, and hyperarousal. For this the authors suggest using means rather than the summed scores for the three subscales to allow comparison with the Symptom Checklist 90-Revised (SCL-90-R; Derogatis & Lazarus 1994). As the maximum mean score for the subscales is '4', the maximum 'total mean' IES-R score is 12. Lower scores are indicative of lower symptoms. A total IES-R score of 33 or over, from a theoretical maximum of 88, signifies the likely presence of PTSD (Weisset al., 1995).

In order to explore the effect of different modes of social support on the IES-R, the statistical properties of scale items are first described. The scale is analysed separately for the pre- and post-intervention. In order to obtain some idea of its reliability, an item analysis is conducted for each of the subscales, which consists of inter-item correlations and the internal consistency of the scale (Cronbach's alpha). Then the correlations between the items and the scales are identified; the correlation of the item with its own scale (with the item removed) and with the other IES-R scales is explored. In the ideal case, an item is correlated higher with its own scale than with the other scales. Finally, correlations between the subscales are reported. It is not possible to give test-retest reliability statistics due to the fact that the different modes of social support have different impacts on the reported trauma.

Below is the statistical analysis of the scale's reliability based on the feasibility study in Uganda.

3.3.1.1 Statistics of items in IES-R subscales

The IES-R was proven to be a statistically strong enough instrument for use in this research, based on the analysis of its use in Uganda. The mean, standard deviation and percentage of missing cases for each item in the intrusion, avoidance and hyperarousal scale, pre- and post-intervention, are detailed in Van Reisen, Nakazibwe, Stokmans, Vallejo and Kidane (2018) and the results indicate that the standard deviation for all of the items, in both the pre- and post-test settings, was 1 or above. This is substantial for a 5-point scale and indicates that the items are able to record differences in the level of post-traumatic stress across respondents.

In addition, the percentage of missing values for most items indicated that only a few respondents missed items, and often missed only one item in the total scale. This suggests that the items were appropriate given the population at hand. Furthermore, the distribution of the scale's values approximates normal distribution (skewness and kurtosis are between -1 and 1, except for the skewness of intrusion, the skewness of hyperarousal in the post-intervention and the kurtosis of intrusion in the post-intervention stage, which are all higher than 1).

Finally, Cronbach's alpha test indicates that all items in a specific scale correlate quite well with one another. A closer look at the inter-item correlations revealed that most items correlate sufficiently with their own subscale (corrected item total correlations are all above 0.35), with items having a rather high correlation with the other scales (above about 0.5) and some items having an even higher correlation with the other subscales than with items in their own scale, indicating that the subscales are intertwined, correlating substantially.

3.3.1.2 Construction and reliability of IES-S

The length of the IES-R turned out to be problematic in both the survey of Eritrean communities and the Uganda study. As a result, it was decided to develop a shorter version that would be more user-friendly. To guarantee the validity of this short version, the three constructs of the IES-R (intrusion, avoidance and hyperarousal) were all included (as suggested by Thoresen *et al.*, 2010). In order to decide which items of the IES-R are most indicative for each subscale, inter-item correlations were examined, as reported in the Uganda study (Van Reisen *et al.*, 2018b), as well as the face validity of the items to be selected (answering the question whether or not these items are relevant for refugees in a camp). By selecting (at least) two items of a subscale with the highest corrected item total correlations, as reported in the Uganda study, seven items were identified for the short version of the IES-R (Table 3.2).

Table 3.2. Items of IES-S

Subscale	Items	Corrected item total correlation in Uganda study
Intrusion	Other things kept making me think about it.	0.87
	I had waves of strong feelings about it.	0.87
Avoidance	I stayed away from reminders of it.	0.77
	I tried not to talk about it.	0.75
Hyperarousal	I had trouble falling asleep.	0.89
	I had trouble concentrating.	0.88
	Reminders of it caused me to have physical reactions, such as sweating, trouble breathing, nausea, or a pounding heart.	0.88

To explore the statistical properties of this short version of the IES, an item-analysis was conducted, which consists of the statistics of the items (mean and standard deviation; there was no item non-response) and the internal consistency of the scale (Cronbach's alpha). The results suggest that the scale construction was successful, as can be seen in tables 3.3 and 3.4.

Table 3.3. Mean and standard deviation of IES-Short items

	Mean		Standard deviation	
	Pre-test	Post-test	Pre-test	Post-test
Other things kept making me think about it.	3.583	3.085	1.4985	1.4418
I had waves of strong feelings about it.	3.359	2.936	1.5266	1.4051
I stayed away from reminders of it.	3.825	2.574	1.3535	1.4027
I tried not to talk about it.	3.417	2.649	1.5116	1.4421
I had trouble falling asleep.	2.777	2.521	1.4137	1.4348
I had trouble concentrating.	3.068	2.404	1.5033	1.4242
Reminders of it caused me to have physical reactions, such as sweating, trouble breathing, nausea, or a pounding heart.	3.000	2.628	1.5780	1.5861

Table 3.3 also indicates that in the pre-test the level of post-traumatic stress is higher than in the post-test (post-intervention) stage; all items have an average score above 2.5, which is regarded as the cut-off point for high trauma (1.5 if the scale goes from 0–4; see Creamer, Bell & Failla, 2003). In the post-test, where the level of post-traumatic stress seems lower, the values of both avoidance and hyperarousal are about 2.5 and only the items on the intrusion score remain high at about 3. The standard deviation of all the items is above 1, and almost 1.5. This is significant for a 5-point scale, indicating that the level of post-traumatic stress reported varies a lot across the respondents in both the pre- and post-test.

Table 3.4 details the internal consistency of the scale, showing the corrected item-total correlations and Cronbach's alpha. The IES-S correlates quite well with the scale (all item-total correlations are above 0.35) and gives good internal consistency (pre-test: Cronbach's alpha = 0,887; post-test: Cronbach's alpha = 0,873).

Table 3.4. Internal consistency of IES-S

Cronbach's alpha: first wave = 0.887; second wave = 0.873	Corrected item – total correlation	
	Pre-test	Post-test
Other things kept making me think about it.	0.669	0.693
I had waves of strong feelings about it.	0.786	0.701
I stayed away from reminders of it.	0.742	0.534
I tried not to talk about it.	0.652	0.0758
I had trouble falling asleep.	0.572	0.654
I had trouble concentrating.	0.661	0.646
Reminders of it caused me to have physical reactions, such as sweating, trouble breathing, nausea, or a pounding heart.	0.679	0.580

It can thus be concluded that the IES-S developed was a reliable measurement of PTSD using similar items as the IES-R, but allowing for brevity of work in more mobile communities. Table 3.5 summarises the key statistics of IES-S scores pre- and post-test.

Table 3.5. Key statistics of IES-S

	Mean	Standard deviation	Skewness	Kurtosis	Items in the scale
T1	3.29	1.15	-0.48	-0.67	7
T2	2.68	1.09	0.18	-1.04	7

3.3.2 Social and Economic Resilience Scale

The Social and Economic Resilience (SER) instrument, was developed and first used in the Uganda study to measure the participants' own perceptions of their socio-economic resilience and its statistical veracity is fully described in the report of the project (Van Reisen *et al.*, 2018b). Below, I will first outline the main statistical features to demonstrate its veracity as a basis for the scale's use in developing a shorter more relevant version for the Ethiopia study. After that, the development and statistical properties of a shorter version of the instrument, referred to as SER-Short (or SER-S), will be detailed.

The SER consists of Likert scales in six domains: social embeddedness (5 items), capability (6 items), income (13 items), empowerment (12 items), trust in the system (2 items), and worriedness (10 items). The scale values of the items range from 1 (strongly disagree), 2 (disagree), 3 (neutral), 4 (agree), to 5 (strongly agree). Most statements are stated positively (a high score indicates a positive mindset), with the exception of the subscale worriedness, where a high score indicates more worry. To explore the reliability of the scale, an item-analysis was conducted on each of the scales, which consists of the statistics of the items and the internal consistency of the scale (Cronbach's alpha). Furthermore, the correlations between the items and the scales were examined.

The statistical analyses revealed that SER was a reliable instrument with internal consistency and good correlation across items. Table 3.6 presents the characteristics of the scale, revealing that all subscales are normally distributed (skewness and kurtosis are within the range -1 to 1) and seem to have a smaller standard deviation in the post-test, as compared to the pre-test data set. Full details of this, including Cronbach's alpha for each subscale, are detailed in the complete report (Van Reisen *et al.*, 2018b).

Table 3.6. SER characteristics of the subscales, first and second wave

	Scale	Cronbach's alpha	No. items	Average (range 1–5)	Standard deviation	Skewness	Kurtosis	Missing
T1	Social embeddedness	0.707	5	3.96	0.56	-0.17	-0.06	0
	Capability	0.894	6	2.67	0.91	0.35	-0.25	0
	Income	0.916	13	2.99	0.74	0.14	0.001	0
	Empowerment	0.882	12	3.13	0.77	0.25	-0.26	0
	Trust in the system	0.832	2	3.10	1.16	-0.29	-0.60	0
	Worriedness	0.764	8	3.55	0.66	-0.37	0.05	0
T2	Social embeddedness	0.748	4	4.08	0.56	-0.91	1.59	0
	Capability	0.845	6	3.12	0.72	-0.35	-0.31	0
	Income	0.874	11	3.59	0.59	-0.96	1.69	0
	Empowerment	0.822	8	3.82	0.53	-0.55	2.21	0
	Trust in the system	0.585	2	3.70	0.68	-0.64	0.35	0
	Worriedness	0.799	8	3.48	0.71	-0.42	0.13	0

3.3.2.1 Development of SER-S

As described above, the SER-S scale was based on the SER-tool used in the Uganda study and designed to measure the perception of each participant of their socio-economic resilience. Due to the ICT context, as well as the fact that the participants were living in a refugee camp, we needed a shorter and slightly-adjusted version of the SER scale. To guarantee the validity of this short version, the six constructs of the SER instrument (social embeddedness, capability, income, empowerment, trust in the system and worriedness) were all included in the short version, but items were selected according to their strength and relevance.

Item selection was based on the inter-item correlations, as reported in the Uganda study. However, some items that were considered appropriate in the previous study were not relevant in the current context of refugees in a camp (for example, items related to earning income). These items were adjusted based on an intimate knowledge of the context and an understanding of the cultural and linguistic nuances.

Accordingly, three items with the highest corrected item-total score were selected from each subscale and the wording adjusted to make them more relevant to the current context. In the Uganda study, the 'trust in the system' subscale comprised only two items, so we added one item. Furthermore, the 'worriedness' scale is a very important indicator of resilience and, hence, five items were selected. The income items used in the Uganda study rely heavily on financial income and economic opportunities. As these themes are not relevant in refugee camps (see also Melicherova, 2018), items indicative of the improvement of income or economic resources were formulated. The items used in the SER-S are shown in Table 3.7.

Table 3.7. SER-S items

Item	Questions	Corrected item-total correlation in Uganda study (new items indicated)
Income	I am able to meet my financial needs.	New
	I am able to save money.	0.551
	I will have good means of earning money in the next six months.	New
	I am able to survive in times hardship.	0.542
Empowerment	I am able to get more time for productive activities.	0.709
	I am able make my own decisions.	0.636
	I feel improvement in my self-worth.	0.689
Worriedness	I am worried that conflict/war may erupt again.	0.431
	I am worried that I will fail to provide for myself and/or my family.	0.545
	I am worried that support organisations will not treat me fairly.	New
	I am worried my physical or emotional health will deteriorate.	New
	I am worried that I may not have enough money to meet my needs.	0.583
	I am worried about my safety in the camp.	New
Capability	I feel I can get information about anything I want.	0.714
	I have acquired new skills to improve my life.	0.750
	I feel change in the amount of knowledge I hold.	0.769

Similarly to the full SER scale, the SER-S scale values of the items include 1 (strongly disagree), 2 (disagree), 3 (neutral), 4 (agree) and 5 (strongly agree), with most statements being stated positively (high score indicates a positive mindset), except for the subscale for worriedness, for which a high score indicates more worry.

3.3.2.2 Statistical properties of SER-S

The statistical tests carried out on the results generated from the SER-S are detailed in Table 3.8, where an item analysis and the internal consistency of the scale (Cronbach's alpha) indicate that, as expected, respondents reported no change (or negative change) in their income levels, but regarded their prospects as better in the post-test. Similarly, 'empowerment' and 'capability' scores increased in the post-test data. In the pre-test, all items scored about neutral (3) and in the post-test all items score above 3 and two items even above 3.5. For the 'social embeddedness' subscale (Table 3.8), the same trend can be observed: in the pre-test all items scored slightly above neutral (3), and in the post-test all items scored about 3.5 and one item scored 4. On the other hand, the subscale for 'worriedness' did not show the same trend; here a diffused picture emerges. In the pre- and post-test, the items that are about personal worry are lower (above neutral) and those about social or situational worry are higher (below neutral). Furthermore, the amount of worry reported in the post-test is smaller than in the pre-test.

Table 3.8. Mean and standard deviation of SER-S items (pre-test: n=103; post-test: n=95)

	Mean		Standard deviation	
	Pre-test	Post-test	Pre-test	Post-test
Income				
I am able to meet my financial needs.	2.447	2.457	1.2889	1.3089
I am able to save money.	1.437	1.368	1.0726	0.8998
I will have good means of earning money in the next six months.	2.272	2.663	1.2695	1.5953
I am able to survive in times of hardship.	3.388	3.883	1.0312	1.1250
Empowerment				
I am able to get more time for productive activities.	2.835	3.389	1.3798	1.5457
I am able make my own decisions.	3.427	3.758	1.0252	1.2003
I feel improvement in my self-worth.	2.893	3.484	1.3129	1.3198
Trust in the system				
I feel I am able to exercise my rights.	3.437	3.832	1.1772	1.2936
I am able to access support services I need easily.	2.961	3.389	1.1875	1.3706
I understand organisations offering support services in the refugee camp work.	3.068	3.705	1.2777	1.3596
Worriedness				
I am worried that conflict/war may erupt again.	1.835	1.611	1.0010	1.1041

I am worried that I will fail to provide for myself and/or my family.	4.417	4.189	0.9854	1.2573
I am worried that support organisations will not treat me fairly.	2.757	2.516	1.2404	1.3358
I am worried my physical or emotional health will deteriorate .	3.282	3.253	1.3962	1.4438
I am worried that I may not have enough money to meet my needs.	3.650	3.253	1.2184	1.5843
I am worried about my safety in the camp.	2.126	1.937	1.2421	1.2532
Capability				
I feel I can get information about anything I want.	3.379	3.789	1.1725	1.2874
I have acquired new skills to improve my life.	2.563	3.284	1.4119	1.5344
I feel change in the amount of knowledge I hold.	2.854	3.453	1.3314	1.4715
Social embeddedness				
I feel my relationship with the rest of the community has improved.	3.738	4.095	1.0661	1.1492
I feel my contact with the leadership in the camp has improved.	3.505	3.663	0.8731	1.0975
I feel I trust my community.	3.233	3.411	1.1393	1.3248

In the pre- and post-test, the standard deviation for most items was about 1, which is substantial for a 5-point scale. It indicates that the items are able to capture differences in the level of social and economic resilience reported by respondents. This is especially true for 'empowerment' and 'capability'. The statistical analysis also revealed that none of the respondents missed an item. Consequently, I believe that the items are appropriate for eliciting this kind of information.

The results for the internal consistency of the scale are highlighted in Table 3.9, which presents the corrected item-total correlations and Cronbach's alpha. The results for this were mixed and at times poorer than anticipated, which led to some adjustments to strengthen the results as much as possible (see below).

Table 3.9. Internal consistency of SER-S

	Corrected item-total correlation	
	Pre-test	Post-test
Income, Cronbach's alpha: first wave 0.68; second wave 0.625		
I am able to meet my financial needs.	.610	.548
I am able to save money.	.475	.332
I will have good means of earning money in the next six months.	.535	.528
I am able to survive in times of hardship.	.249	.260
Empowerment, Cronbach's alpha: first wave 0.505; second wave 0.742		
I am able to get more time for productive activities.	.312	.583
I am able make my own decisions.	.276	.488
I feel improvement in my self-worth.	.391	.656

	First wave	Second wave
Trust in the system, Cronbach's alpha: first wave 0.553; second wave 0.667		
I feel I am able to exercise my rights.	.391	.427
I am able to access support services I need easily.	.466	.545
I understand organisations offering support services in the refugee camp work.	.330	.468
Worriedness, Cronbach's alpha: first wave 0.584; second wave 0.632		
I am worried that conflict/war may erupt again.	.210	.001
I am worried that I will fail to provide for myself and/or my family.	.230	.386
I am worried that support organisations will not treat me fairly.	.174	.505
I am worried my physical or emotional health will deteriorate.	.488	.477
I am worried that I may not have enough money to meet my needs.	.446	.583
I am worried about my safety in the camp.	.379	.222
Capability, Cronbach's alpha: first wave 0.617; second wave 0.794		
I feel I can get information about anything I want.	.193	.447
I have acquired new skills to improve my life.	.577	.753
I feel change in the amount of knowledge I hold.	.552	.743
Social embeddedness, Cronbach's alpha: first wave 0.638; second wave 0.593		
I feel my relationship with the rest of the community has improved.	.601	.514
I feel my contact with the leadership in the camp has improved.	.488	.433
I feel I trust my community.	.301	.284

The 'income' scale was found to have questionable Cronbach's alphas in the pre- and post-test (between 0.6 and 0.7). In addition, the item-total correlations indicate that the item 'I am able to survive in times of hardship' correlates rather low with the rest of the scale in both the pre- and post-test data sets. When removing this item, Cronbach's alpha for the pre-test increases to 0.73, which is regarded as acceptable (between 0.7 and 0.8) and in the post-test Cronbach's alpha increases to 0.647, which is still questionable. Due to these findings, this item was removed from the scale.

Similarly, on the 'empowerment' scale, Table 3.10 reveals that Cronbach's alpha is rather poor (between 0.5 and 0.6) for the pre-test, but acceptable for the post-test (between 0.7 and 0.8). In the pre-test, all three items have a rather weak correlation with the rest of the scale (all item-total correlations are below 0.4). However, in the post-test all items have an acceptable item-total correlation (> 0.35). As a result of this analysis, all three items were kept in the scale.

The 'trust in the system' scale has poor internal consistency (Cronbach's alpha 0.553) in the pre-test and a questionable internal consistency in the post-test (Cronbach's alpha 0.667). In the pre-test, the item 'I understand organisations offering support services in the refugee camps work' has a low item-total correlation (< 0.35). However, removing this item did not improve Cronbach's alpha, hence, all three items were kept in the scale.

The 'worriedness' scale also has poor internal consistency (Cronbach's alpha 0.584) in the pre-test and a questionable internal consistency in the post-test (Cronbach's alpha 0.632). In the pre-test, there were three items with a rather low item-total correlation. Due to these findings, two items ('I am worried that conflict/war may erupt again' and 'I am worried about my safety in the camp') were removed from the scale. This resulted in a Cronbach's alpha of 0.50 in the pre-test, which is rather poor and an acceptable Cronbach's alpha of 0.73 in the post-test.

The internal consistency of the 'capability' scale was also questionable (Cronbach's alpha 0.617) in the pre-test and acceptable in the post-test (Cronbach's alpha 0.794). In the pre-test, the item 'I feel I can get information about anything I want' had a low item-total correlation (< 0.35); removing this item increased the internal consistency to 0.790, which is acceptable. Due to the fact that in the post-test this item has an acceptable item-total correlation (> 0.35), all three items were kept in the scale.

The final subscale, 'social embeddedness', had a Cronbach's alpha of 0.638 in the pre-test, which is questionable, and 0.593 in the post-test, which is regarded as poor. In the pre- and post-test, the item 'I feel I trust my community' had a low item-total correlation (< 0.35) and removing this item enhanced the internal consistency to an acceptable level of 0.762 in the pre-test, although the post-test consistency remained at a questionable level of 0.687 and, hence, this item was removed from the scale. A summary of the key statistics of the SER-S is given in Table 3.10.

Table 3.10. Summary of SER-S statistics

		Number of items included	Mean	Standard deviation	Skewness	Kurtosis
Income	Pre–test	4	2.05	0.98	0.858	-0.123
	Post–test	4	2.16	0.99	0.620	-0.480
Empowerment	Pre–test	3	3.05	0.88	-0.267	-0.640
	Post–test	3	3.54	1.11	-0.373	-0.905
Trust in the system	Pre–test	3	3.15	0.88	-0.370	-0.403
	Post–test	3	3.64	1.04	-0.502	-0.445
Worriedness	Pre–test	4	3.53	0.77	-0.344	-0.132
	Post–test	4	3.30	1.05	-0.074	-0.905
Capacity	Pre–test	3	2.93	0.98	-0.215	-0.691
	Post–test	3	3.51	1.21	-0.287	-1.061
Social embeddedness	Pre–test	2	3.62	0.87	-0.670	0.655
	Post–test	2	3.88	0.98	-0.708	-0.076

3.3.3 Internet Social Capital Scale

In this study it was important to measure social capital, as studies have been consistent in their findings that chronic civil war can deplete social capital (Kawachi & Subramanian, 2006; Wind & Komproe, 2012). Social capital includes community networks, relationships, civic engagement within norms of reciprocity and trust in others, which facilitates cooperation and coordination for mutual benefit (Cullen & Whiteford, 2001). Modern intra-state conflicts often deliberately destroy social capital in order to control communities. Given the communalities shared by social capital and collective trauma, loss of social capital has also been used to measure collective trauma (Somasundaram, 2014).

Social capital can be measured using the Internet Social Capital Scale (ISCS) (Williams, 2006). The scale was developed to measure social interaction in an era of online social networking. The ISCS was constructed in recognition of the fact that increasing levels of social interaction now occur online and happen in parallel and in conjunction with offline interaction. The concept of 'social capital' (Coleman, 1988) is used to establish a framework and develop question items within this framework to account for both online and offline social interactions. The ISCS consists of two underlying dimensions: online and offline. This necessitates two parallel scales: one for online use and one for offline use. Both scales consist of 11 items, as listed in tables 3.11 to 3.14. The scale values are from 1 to 5: 1 (strongly disagree), 2 (disagree), 3 (neutral), 4 (agree) and 5 (strongly agree). In general, high scores indicate a high level of social capital, however, two items are formulated negatively (items 3 and 9). These two items are recoded for the analysis. Some items were adjusted to ensure that they made sense in the refugee camp context; for example, where the item referred to 'last dollar' we included other materials such as last food or clothing, to capture other sorts of sharing.

3.3.3.1 Social capital online

Table 3.11 outlines the mean and standard deviation of the data gathered from the ISCS. The table shows that the pre-test standard deviation for all items is above 1, and approaching the value 1.5, while the post-test standard deviation for all items is above 1.5. This is substantial for a 5-point scale and indicates that the level of online social capital varies a lot among the respondents.

Table 3.11. Mean and standard deviation ISCS (online)

	Mean		Standard deviation	
	Pre-test	Post-test	Pre-test	Post-test
There are several people online I trust to help solve my personal problems.	3.155	3.436	1.5451	1.5832
There is someone online/offline I can turn to for advice about making very important decisions.	2.981	3.234	1.4818	1.6489
There is no one online/offline that I feel comfortable talking to about intimate personal problems (recoded).	2.214	2.766	1.4393	1.6683
When I feel lonely, there are several people online/offline I can talk to.	2.854	3.277	1.5618	1.6225
If I needed an emergency loan, I know someone online/offline I can turn to.	2.214	2.415	1.4393	1.5548
The people I interact with online/offline would recommend me to people in their network.	3.155	3.543	1.3192	1.5216
The people I interact with online/offline would be good job references for me.	2.903	3.415	1.5244	1.5409
The people I interact with online/offline would share their last dollar/food/clothing with me.	2.019	2.500	1.4001	1.6313
I do not know people online/offline well enough to help me get ahead (recoded).	2.204	3.085	1.1321	1.6439
The people I interact with online/offline would help me fight an injustice.	2.718	2.968	1.4580	1.5893
I have a good network of friends and family.	2.796	3.160	1.5362	1.5678

Table 3.12 outlines the internal consistency of the scale through the results of the corrected item-total correlations and Cronbach's alpha. In both the pre- and post-test, all items had good internal consistency (pre-test: Cronbach's alpha 0.899; post-test: Cronbach's alpha 0.960). In addition, each item of the online social capital scale correlates well with the scale (all item-total correlations are above 0.35).

Table 3.12. Internal consistency of ISCS (online)

Cronbach's alpha: pre-test 0.899; post-test 0.960	Corrected item-total correlation	
	Pre-test	Post-test
There are several people online I trust to help solve my personal problems.	0.741	0.869
There is someone online/offline I can turn to for advice about making very important decisions.	0.739	0.847
There is no one online/offline that I feel comfortable talking to about intimate personal problems (recoded).	0.479	0.777
When I feel lonely, there are several people online/offline I can talk to.	0.526	0.774
If I needed an emergency loan, I know someone online/offline I can turn to.	0.615	0.690
The people I interact with online/offline would recommend me to people in their network.	0.742	0.859
The people I interact with online/offline would be good job references for me.	0.725	0.853
The people I interact with online/offline would share their last dollar/food/clothing with me.	0.566	0.741
I do not know people online/offline well enough to help me get ahead (reversed).	0.406	0.787
The people I interact with online/offline would help me fight an injustice.	0.639	0.795
I have a good network of friends and family.	0.766	0.916

3.3.3.2 Social capital offline

Similar to the above analysis of the ISCS online, we carried out a series of analyses to examine the scale of social capital offline. Table 3.13 shows the mean and standard deviation of offline social capital. Results show that for the pre-test, about half of the offline social capital items score between 2.5 and 3. This suggests a neutral and slightly negative offline social capital, however, the picture is less clear when compared to the online social capital. In the post-test, all items of the offline social capital score are higher, with most scores above 3, indicating a neutral and slightly positive offline social capital.

For standard deviation, the scores for all items are above 1 and about half of them are about 1.5. This indicates that all items are able to capture differences in the level of offline social capital reported by respondents.

Table 3.13. Mean standard deviation of ISCS (offline)

	Mean		Standard deviation	
	Pre-test	Post-test	Pre-test	Post-test
There are several people online/offline I trust to help solve my personal problems.	3.049	3.585	1.3531	1.4548
There is someone online/offline I can turn to for advice about making very important decisions.	2.903	3.585	1.4178	1.4548
There is no one online/offline that I feel comfortable talking to about intimate personal problems (recoded).	2.427	3.011	1.4525	1.5828
When I feel lonely, there are several people online/offline I can talk to.	3.505	3.809	1.2436	1.3382
If I needed an emergency loan, I know someone online/offline I can turn to.	1.981	2.521	1.3059	1.6312
The people I interact with online/offline would recommend me to people in their network.	3.621	4.085	0.9406	1.1608
The people I interact with online/offline would be good job references for me.	3.019	4.000	1.2908	1.2181
The people I interact with online/offline would share their last dollar/food/clothing with me.	1.602	2.043	1.0510	1.4212
I do not know people online/offline well enough to help me get ahead (recoded).	2.456	3.106	1.2189	1.6426
The people I interact with online/offline would help me fight an injustice.	2.854	3.128	1.2634	1.5397
I have a good network of friends and family.	2.854	3.585	1.3461	1.4173

The internal consistency of the scale was examined through the corrected item-total correlations and Cronbach's alpha. The results are presented in Table 3.14.

Table 3.14. Internal consistency of ISCS (offline)

Cronbach's alpha: pre-test 0.792; post-test 0.922	Corrected item-total correlation	
	Pre-test	Post-test
There are several people online/offline I trust to help solve my personal problems.	0.564	0.704
There is someone online/offline I can turn to for advice about making very important decisions.	0.657	0.731
There is no one online/offline that I feel comfortable talking to about intimate personal problems (recoded).	0.450	0.619
When I feel lonely, there are several people online/offline I can talk to.	0.406	0.698
If I needed an emergency loan, I know someone online/offline I can turn to.	0.415	0.613
The people I interact with online/offline would recommend me to people in their network.	0.485	0.751
The people I interact with online/offline would be good job references for me.	0.392	0.738
The people I interact with online/offline would share their last dollar/food/clothing with me.	0.286	0.540
I do not know people online/offline well enough to help me get ahead (reversed).	0.188	0.744
The people I interact with online/offline would help me fight an injustice.	0.480	0.676
I have a good network of friends and family.	0.610	0.835

The results show that, in the pre-test, most of the items in offline social capital scale correlate quite well with the scale (all item-total correlations are above 0.35). There were two items whose correlation was not as strong as the rest, however, this did not affect the internal consistency of the scale. In the post-test, all items have an acceptable item-total correlation (above 0.35) and Cronbach's alpha indicates that the internal consistency of the scale is excellent (above 0.9).

In conclusion, the ISCS was an effective instrument for measuring social capital, with strong consistency and reliability across both the offline and online scales. Table 3.15 outlines the key statistical features of the scale.

Table 3.15. Key statistics of ISCS (online and offline)

	Wave	# of items	Mean	Standard deviation	Skewness	Kurtosis
Social capital online	Pre-test	11	2.64	1.01	-0.115	-0.990
	Post-test	11	3.07	1.35	-0.271	-1.261
Social capital offline	Pre-test	11	2.75	0.72	-0.302	-0.357
	Post-test	11	3.30	1.09	-0.303	-0.923

3.3.4 Survey of social media use

In addition to the psychometric tests discussed above, a survey questionnaire looking at social media usage was also developed for the purpose of the second study. The questionnaire was in Arabic and Tigrigna and conducted by native speakers of these languages (see Appendix 1). The questions focused on sources of information, medium and language for information, as well as content.

This survey was carried out in Khartoum (Kassala region of Sudan), Addis Ababa (Ethiopia) and Eritrean refugee camps (Tigray region of Ethiopia). The data in relevant sections of this wider survey was used in the second study. Questions covered the following topics:

- Radio listening habits and the medium used for listening
- Social media usage
- What people consider to be reliable sources of information
- The content of information exchanges (topics of discussions).

The questionnaire contained seven questions, most with three sub questions, including an open question.

For radio listening habits the survey combined an open question about the station frequented and details of how often (with a three choice closed answer) and language choice (Arabic, Tigrigna and Amharic, as well as a choice of other local or other international language). Following this, the questionnaire inquired about the mechanism used for listening to the radio, i.e., the Internet, smartphone, communal radio or a traditional radio.

Similarly, the questionnaire asked about social media usage, enquiring which social media platforms were in use (giving a choice of Facebook, Pal Talk, Viber, Skype, Twitter, none and other); in addition, a follow up question asked about the frequency of social media usage, giving a choice of often, rarely or never. The answers to these questions enabled us to establish the prevalence of mobile phones and the wide usage of social media.

3.4 Qualitative research design

As mentioned above, a mixed methods approach was used for this research and, in accordance, qualitative and quantitative data were combined. This was particularly the case in the feasibility studies in Uganda and Ethiopia, where individual interviews and focus group discussions were conducted, and observations considered (see Appendix 5 for a list of topics for the interviews and observation format). These will be discussed, together with the results, in more detail in the respective chapters, however, below I give a brief outline of the general process of how the interviews and focus groups were convened and conducted.

The qualitative data were used to gain an in-depth understanding of the interventions and how they were understood by participants, as well as their impression of the change that was (or was not) captured by the data. In a sense, this was an opportunity to look beneath the data and understand the impact of the intervention from the perspective of the participants. The three approaches that were used in this research were in-depth interviews, focus group discussions and observations.

3.4.1 Interviews

Each survey was conducted in an interview style, whereby, in addition to completing any of the questionnaires, participants were engaged in an open in-depth interview in which they talked about their experiences and the impacts of their experiences. This was the case for:

- All participants in the descriptive trauma survey among Eritrean refugee communities
- All participants in the descriptive ICT survey in Ethiopia and Sudan
- 27 participants from the Uganda feasibility study of TRUST
- All participants in the study into the feasibility study of TRUST delivered via ICT in refugee camps in Ethiopia

Detailed notes of these interviews were taken and these notes were then categorised thematically to elucidate the various issues emerging. Together, the statistical data and the interview data (as well as the focus group discussions) led to a more comprehensive interpretation of the information gathered from participants.

Interviews were particularly crucial in the interpretation of the Uganda data. As the limited time period between the intervention and the post-test, as well as some shortcomings in the statistical data, may have resulted in less clarity, in this case direct quotes were used to support or explain the findings of the statistical data (see Chapter 7).

3.4.2 Focus group discussions

In both of the feasibility studies (in Ethiopia and Uganda) there were focus group discussions (two in Ethiopia and one in Uganda). The groups were made up of willing participants who took part in the studies (i.e., accessed TRUST), with the researcher moderating the discussions and asking questions about their experiences of TRUST and its impact on their lives and communities. The data from the focus group discussions was used to supplement the interviews and the observations, as well as the statistical data from the various psychometric instruments discussed above.

As for the interviews, the notes taken during the focus group discussions were analysed to make a list of the ideas raised. In addition, group interactions and reactions were also included in the data gathered. These were used to highlight issues raised through other methods of data gathering and explain any gaps in the information collected.

3.4.3 Observations

Unstructured observations were conducted during interviews and focus groups without any specific pre-determined objective. Both the researcher and research assistants had intimate knowledge of the communities they were working with and this provided opportunities to observe the appearance and presentation of participants, as well as the general interaction across their respective communities. Observations were made without influencing or altering the activities and interaction of participants. The data generated was used to complement all other data to give a fuller explanation of the phenomena under investigation.

3.5 Sampling

As outlined in Table 3.1, a combination of sampling approaches was used, as the main emphasis was on shedding as much light as possible on the experiences and situation of the participants to help us understand the impact of trauma and trauma healing on socio-economic resilience. To this end a lot of emphasis was placed on identifying typicality and a snowball sampling approach used to identify cases of interest by sampling participants who had, generally, similar characteristics, starting with key contacts well situated in the various research contexts (Patton, 2002).

Convenience and purposive sampling approaches were used in combination with snowball sampling, taking into account the differences in context as well as the nature of the specific study. In the descriptive survey studies convenience sampling was used and participants were selected based on their availability and willingness to take part. In addition, participants were asked to suggest others and, hence, a combination of convenience sampling and snowball sampling was used. These were descriptive studies and between the participants and the locally-recruited assistants we were able to mitigate the bias that could have resulted from the approach (I will discuss the role of locally-recruited research assistants below). Participants were briefed on the purpose of the study and, hence, were able to suggest others who were able to elucidate points. As there were no incentives (reimbursements of costs, etc.), the selection of participants was not affected by this as a factor.

For the feasibility studies, a more strategic approach of purposive sampling was employed. Here we relied on the judgement of the research team when choosing participants. The approach involved identifying and selecting individuals or groups of individuals specifically relevant to the research subject (Cresswell & Plano Clark,

2011), as well as available and willing to participate (Bernard, 2002; Spradley, 1979). Availability was crucial, particularly in the final study, where the research was among highly-mobile communities in the Eritrean refugee camps in Ethiopia.

Members of the local research teams had substantive understanding of their context and their judgements could, thus, be relied on to obtain an information-rich and representative sample to comprehensively answer the research questions (Cresswell & Plano Clark, 2011). In addition, as these were explorations into some extremely difficult experiences, there needed to be an assessment of their willingness to participate, as well as their ability to reflect and communicate that reflection, while remaining as near to the theoretical norm (representativeness) of their respective community as possible (Allen, 1971).

In the final study, which was conducted in Ethiopia, local research assistants were recruited and briefed on the qualifications, then asked to draw a list of potential participants. The list was finalised during team-wide discussions. Similarly, in Uganda, selection criteria considered the needs of women for trauma support, and local research assistants made the selection based on this criteria. This selection procedure may have impacted on the results.

3.6 Conclusion

As the research is made up of various studies, it was important that the methodological approach for each study fitted the context of the participants and the research questions in that study. In terms of the ability to develop such an approach, the instruments developed, despite their limitations, were indeed able to capture the situation. In addition, the sampling approach overcame a potential bias and enabled the researchers to gain insight through the use of a mixed methods approach, combining both qualitative and quantitative methods. The main objective of the research was to examine the impact of trauma on socio-economic resilience and social capital and present a practical approach to addressing trauma to enhance socio-economic resilience and social capital in similar contexts (but not necessarily a universal intervention that could be standardised and applied in every situation). It was felt that this was adequately achieved by focusing on situational factors.

The mixed methods research approach enabled the collection and analysis of quantitative and qualitative data within the same study, resulting in an appropriate exploration of the intricately layered research questions. Quantitative methods were used to shed more light on the qualitative results, and vice versa. This enabled participants' voices to be prominent in sharing their experiences and enriching the data, adding to the veracity of the findings.

However, the approach was not without its challenges, particularly in relation to briefing the research assistants on both qualitative and quantitative approaches, as well as the purposive selection of participants, as both required an enhanced reliance on the research assistants' intimate knowledge of the context. This challenge was overcome by using the knowledge and understanding of the research assistants and supplementing it with enough flexibility in methodology, while maintaining the integrity of the tools selected. Consequently, the mixed method approach afforded both rich data and a flexible approach, while maintaining the integrity of the data collected.

I have spent many days and nights despairing about how I could tell the story of tens of thousands of my Eritrean compatriots in Tel Aviv who have survived the most harrowing experiences of human trafficking. I have pained over what I could do to be of some assistance to those stuck in desolate refugee camps in Ethiopia and I have struggled with my own feelings of hopelessness thinking about the enormity of the devastation. Finding something (however small) by way of an answer, as I have tried to do here, I am satisfied that I have come close to addressing my own desperate questions.

Chapter 4

Levels of traumatic stress among Eritrean refugees

"We are thinking like lizards!"

This quote is from a conversation with an Eritrean gentleman during a workshop in Gent in Belgium, where I was talking with the Eritrean community about the need to address traumatic stress. I mentioned how trauma confines the person to thinking from only the hind brain, also known as the 'reptilian brain'; my fellow conversant was fully cognisant of the implications of being preoccupied with a sense of danger, coming at any minute from any direction, and putting all mental energy towards averting a danger that probably only exists inside the traumatised brain. Living in our respective Eritrean communities, we were both familiar with the ill thought-out ongoing migration decisions that continue to devastate our communities, with one disaster after another. What the gentleman did not realise, and I was only starting to unravel, was the extent and level of traumatic stress in our community.

This chapter addresses the first two research sub questions: Q.1. What is the level of PTS among refugees from Eritrea? Q.2. Can levels of PTS affect the processing of information regarding safety and socio-economic resilience during decision making regarding ongoing trajectories? The main objective of this part of the research was to gain an understanding of the level of PTS among Eritrea refugees and to consider whether or not this could be reliably measured on an established trauma scale.

4.1 Introduction

The study presented in this chapter took place in the summer of 2015. It consisted of a survey into the prevalence of PTSD among refugees in Tel Aviv (Israel), Kampala (Uganda), and Tigray region (northern Ethiopia, as well as acquaintances of abductees in Asmara (Eritrea), and asked people to reflect on the impact of human trafficking in the Sinai. The survey was conducted using the English version of the IES-R and a translation in Tigrigna was used as guide to answer questions from participants (e.g., regarding the meaning of certain words and concepts). For this purpose, language resource colleagues translated the IES-R into Tigrigna, and then back into English to compare it with the original. The translation was adequate, although some of the terms were difficult to translate and, hence, the English version was used to ask the questions directly to participants, with explanations (not translations) in Tigrigna for those who were not proficient in English. As well as looking at the prevalence of trauma among refugees, the study addressed questions relating to the significance of trauma in decision making about migration trajectories, during which refugees have to assess the likelihood of finding protection and prospects.

4.2 Human trafficking in the Sinai

Between 2009 and 2013, thousands of Eritreans fell victim to human trafficking in the Sinai Peninsula. This new trade in human beings, in which smugglers and traffickers prayed on vulnerable migrants fleeing indefinite national service and persecution in their country, involved refugees being captured, tortured, held for ransom, sold and resold. This form of trafficking, which became known as Sinai trafficking, was a highly organised transnational crime (Van Reisen *et al.*, 2012, 2014). This situation became a cause of extreme traumatic stress for the thousands of victims, their friends and families, and, ultimately, entire communities. Human trafficking is but one of many causes of traumatic stress for Eritrean refugees, who are fleeing war, persecution and political violence in Eritrea.

The sole objective of human trafficking in the Sinai was to profit from the payment of ransoms. The extortion was achieved by forcing refugees held in captivity to contact family and friends by mobile phone, often while being tortured, to ask them to pay a ransom for their release. There was immense pressure on family and friends to pay the ransoms. Torture was the modus operandi and many victims died. Refugees were also threaten with the sale of their organs on the commercial organ market, and this is generally believed by the victims and their families to have taken place (even though there is no concrete proof available to date) (Van Reisen & Rijken, 2015).

Victims included both genders and spanned all ages, including very young children and even babies, some born in captivity, and elderly people (Van Reisen & Gerrima, 2016). Torture was executed for a prolonged period of time (often longer than one month and sometimes for over a year) and included electrocution, beating, hanging, burning, chaining, prolonged exposure to the sun, cruel acts, severe sexual violence, forced drug use, malnutrition, water deprivation, sleep deprivation, light deprivation and threat of killing (Van Reisen *et al.*, 2014). The exact number victims who died has not been established; however, estimates are that between 25,000 and 30,000 people passed through the Sinai as victims of human trafficking in the period between 2009 and 2013 and it is thought that 20 to 33% of the people held captive died as a result of the trafficking (Van Reisen *et al.*, 2014).

The majority of victims of Sinai trafficking were from Eritrea. Eritrean refugees were smuggled or trafficked from within Eritrea and the neighbouring countries, where they went to seek refuge, escaping political violence, persecution and indefinite national service in their country (UN Human Rights Council, 2015). The number of victims abducted and their families, as well as those who were desperately trying to raise awareness about what was happening, meant that a substantive proportion of the population either experienced the traumatic event (were a victim of human trafficking) or became intimately aware of the details of the event (secondary or collective trauma). The main objective of this study was to determine if the situation had indeed traumatised people to the extent of causing PTSD and if this could be reliably measured using a scale recognised for identifying PTSD.

4.3 Method

4.2.1 Research instrument

For this study the revised Impact of Events Scale (IES-R) was used, as described in Chapter 3. The scale is widely used as a relatable diagnostic indicator and consists of three subscales: intrusion (8 items), avoidance (8 items) and hyperarousal (6 items). The scale values of the items range from 0 (not at all), 1 (a little bit), 2 (moderately), 3 (quite a bit) to 4 (extremely). The sum of the mean for all items is an indication of the level of trauma (ranging from 0 to 88). This way of calculating the level of trauma is different to the method in which the maximum mean score for each of the three subscales is 4, therefore, the maximum total mean IES-R score is 12. Lower scores on the scale are better, i.e., refer to a lower level of trauma. A total IES-R score of 33 or over, from a theoretical maximum of 88, has been cited as the cut-off point for a preliminary diagnosis of PTSD. Various researchers have suggested the following cut-off points (see Table 4.1).

Table 4.1. IES-R diagnostic indications

Score	Diagnostic indications
24 or more	PTSD is a clinical concern. Those with scores this high who do not have full PTSD will have partial PTSD or at least some symptoms. (Asukai *et al.*, 2002)
33 or more	This represents a good cut-off point for a probable diagnosis of PTSD. (Creamer, Bell & Failla, 2003)
37 or more	This is high enough to suppress a person's immune system from functioning (even 10 years after an impact event). On the original IES, a comparable score would be approximately 39. (Kawamura, Yoshiharu & Nozomu, 2001)
44–75	Severe impact: capable of altering one's ability to function. (Reed, 2007)

Due to its effectiveness and simplicity, the IES-R has become the instrument of choice for many researchers worldwide. It has been translated to many languages including Chinese (Wu & Chan, 2003), French (Brunet, St Hilaire, Jehel & King, 2003), German (Maercker & Schüetzwohl, 1998), Japanese (Asukai *et al.*, 2002), Spanish

(Baguena, Villarroya & Belena, 2001) and Italian (Pietrantonio, De Gennaro, Paolo & Solano, 2003). There is also a Dutch version (Weiss, 2004) and a Bosnian version that has been used in a study comparing refugee and non-refugee populations (Hunt & Gakenyi, 2005). Veronese and Pepe (2013) used an adapted shorter version of the IES in Arabic, which was usually used with children to accurately measure vicarious trauma on professional social workers and emergency workers operating in war contexts.

In addition to its effectiveness in identifying levels of trauma, the IES-R has also been used to measure the effectiveness of interventions. For example, Zang et al. (2013) used the Chinese version of the IES-R (along with several other measures) to assess the efficacy of Narrative Exposure Therapy (NET) as a short-term treatment for PTSD for Chinese earthquake survivors. Similarly, Kim, Pae, Chae, Jun and Bahk (2005) used the IES-R and other scales to investigate the effectiveness of the antidepressant mirtazapine during a 24-week continuation treatment of patients with PTSD in Korea.

However, having drawn attention to the complexities of comprehensively assessing trauma in different cultures and contexts (e.g., war and disruption), Veronese and Pepe (2013) contend that while the response to trauma may be considered universal, there is a lack of univocal evidence regarding how best to assess and classify this response, especially in non-Western contexts (Giacaman, Abu-Rmeileh, Husseini, Saab & Boyce, 2007). This is because there is ample evidence to suggest that cultural differences modulate the emotional and behavioural distress responses to traumatic stress (Rahman, Iqbal, Bunn, Lovel & Harrington, 2004).

In addition, war and political violence affect wellbeing, not only at an individual level, but also at the collective and community levels (Giacaman et al., 2007). For instance, it was found that, in the Palestinian population, humiliation, lack of dignity, and the inability to operate freely and safely constitute forms of war trauma, hence, there is a need to include these dimensions in an exhaustive assessment of trauma (Giacaman et al., 2007; Veronese & Pepe, 2013). Nonetheless, despite the challenges mentioned above and others associated with the accuracy of language usage, as well as the limited and specific time frame specified in the instrument, IES-R offers the advantage of an effective, short and easily understandable measure of distress, ranging from normal stress response to PTSD, as experienced in the week preceding the test. In this research, the scale is not used to provide a diagnosis, but to indicate levels of symptoms of PTSD and give a snapshot of symptomatic status at the specific times of testing.

4.2.2 Procedure

Participants were asked to identify a specific stressful event related to human trafficking as a refugee and rate how much they were distressed or bothered by it during the past 7 to 10 days (e.g., 'Any reminders brought back feelings about it'). Items were rated on a 5-point scale ranging from 0 (not at all) to 4 (extremely). Item scores were summed to give the total score (ranging from 0 to 88). Subscales can also be calculated for intrusion, avoidance, and hyperarousal. However, here it was the total that was used, as it gave an easier cut-off point for the preliminary indication of PTSD.

4.2.3 Participants

The study was carried out among 9 Eritrean refugees in Kampala (Uganda), 21 in Asmara (Eritrea), 21 in Tigray (Ethiopia), and 39 in Tel Aviv (Israel). Using purposive (Patton, 2002) and snowball sampling techniques (Biernacki & Waldorf, 1981), a small group of participants known to the research assistants in each country were asked to identify other potential participants to take part in the survey. Of those interviewed, 65 had close friends and family members who had spent time in the Sinai as victims of human trafficking. The rest had followed events closely through social and traditional media; 35 were victims of Sinai trafficking and are now refugees in Tel Aviv (14) or in refugee camps in Tigray (21).

Except in Asmara, where the questionnaire had to be sent in together with the briefing to research assistants, and questions further clarified during telephone conversations, the researcher was present during the completion of all questionnaires and was on hand to explain details to participants. There were three centres in Tel Aviv, two camps in Ethiopia and one meeting point in Kampala where the IES-R was administered to participants, who were invited by locally-recruited research assistants in each location. In Asmara, the questionnaires were filled out by local research assistants, who collected data during one-to-one home visits.

4.4 Results

All participants, with the exception of one of the participants from Kampala, scored above the cut-off point of 24, indicating levels of traumatic stress that would be of clinical concern, with many scoring levels, above 44, a level deemed sufficient to impair functioning for significant periods of a sufferer's life (even 10 years after the event), although scores are higher for the primary victims of trafficking, i.e., abductees, scores are generally high across the board as indicated in Table 4.2.

Table 4.2. Total scores on IES-R

Asmara (non-abductees)	Kampala (non-abductees)	Tigray (abductees)	Tel Aviv (abductees)	Tel Aviv (non-abductees)
50	62	81	87	63
52	58	82	79	56
51	59	74	77	49
54	50	70	70	56
51	41	36	83	45
52	44	67	45	75
52	44	79	83	39
53	16	75	35	47
59	60	66	76	54
55		73	74	78
50		77	72	75
51		77	75	59
49		78	68	62
34		52	85	28
63		71		36
55		80		77
63		72		65
68		72		61
65		72		66
71		72		53
83		72		70
				74
				50
				42
				42

Many participants were found to be exhibiting PTSD symptoms that would be considered extreme, indicating high levels of distress, and these levels were not confined to former human trafficking abductees; similar levels of symptoms were found in many participants, indicating that symptoms of post-traumatic stress were also prevalent among friends, families, and members of abductees extended community, as well as in primary victims. This indicates a wide prevalence of not just PTSD, but collective trauma; in other words, human trafficking has become a collectively-shared traumatic event affecting not only those with direct experience as abductees, but a much wider group whose set of beliefs and identity may have shifted as a result.

All participants, who were identified as survivors of human trafficking in the Sinai scored above 33 on the IES-R, the point considered a 'good cut-off point' for probable PTSD (see Figure 4.1). Figure 4.1 charts the IES-R scores of people who were involved in Sinai trafficking as primary victims, who were directly tortured by the human traffickers. Of these, all but two (one in each group) scored well above 37, the score considered to be high enough to impact on functioning even 10 years after an impact event. Many scores were between 44 and 75, which is considered to have enough impact to alter functioning permanently. In addition, when looking at female survivors of Sinai trafficking, it appears that women had a higher average score than men. Among the participants of this study, the average score for women was around 5 points higher than the average score for men. All women scored above the threshold for severe impact (44) (defined as capable of permanently altering one's ability to function).

Figure 4.1. IES-R scores of survivors of Sinai trafficking

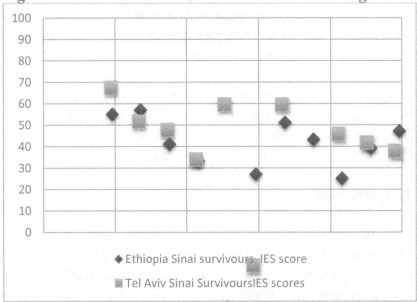

In the group not directly involved in human trafficking (as an abductee), only one participant in Kampala scored below the 'cut-off' point of 33 for probable PTSD (see Figure 4.2).

Figure 4.2. IES-R scores of Eritrean refugees (non-abductees)

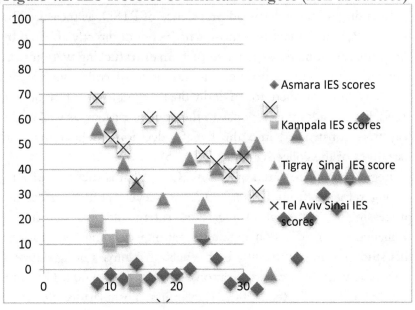

Although the scores for this group were generally lower than the scores obtained using the same scale for victims of Sinai human trafficking in Tel Aviv and refugee camps in Tigray in Ethiopia, they still constitute levels of trauma consistent with PTSD, with some indicating severe impact with long-term impairment of functioning (Reed, 2007). These scores signify that the traumatic impact of Sinai trafficking is far wider spread than merely among primary victims. The results are indicative of the prevalence of widespread and acute PTSD among members of Eritrean refugee communities.

4.5 Conclusion

From the above it can be concluded that the distressing experiences of Eritreans related to Sinai human trafficking have become a cause of extreme trauma and PTSD at the individual level, affecting not only those who were abducted and tortured, but also those who listened to or heard about the distress of others, either by mobile phone or on social media, because they were friends and family of the abductees trying to raise funds or simply members of the community exposed to the traumatic material through the various awareness raising and assistance campaigns.

In addition, the widespread prevalence of PTSD, as measured by the IES-R, and the fact that those who were not directly affected by the primary traumatic experience of human trafficking were just as traumatised as those who were, is indicative of collective trauma, which is not confined to an individual's symptoms of traumatic stress, but includes the response to the traumatic event, as well as the way it is constructed into the beliefs, decisions, behaviours, and narratives of the collective (Shamai, 2015).

Regarding our research questions (Q.1. What is the level of PTS among refugees from Eritrea? Q.2. Can levels of PTS affect the processing of information regarding safety and socio-economic resilience during decision making regarding ongoing trajectories?) this study found significantly high levels of trauma among refugees with potentially clinical implications (Asukai et al., 2002; Creamer, Bell & Failla, 2003; Reed, 2007; Kawamura, Yoshiharu & Nozomu, 2001), which, as established in the theoretical discussions on PTSD in Chapter 2, can cause structural changes in the functioning of the brain, affecting decision making (Starcke & Brand, 2012). Researchers have found an effect on cognitive processes and functioning, including the adaptive strategies adopted in response to danger, potentially having a negative effect on decision-making abilities (Lerner & Kennedy, 2000). This effect could be caused by the fact that the perception of the current threat is accompanied by intrusions and re-experiencing and other symptoms of arousal, affecting the appraisal of the threat and leading to maladaptive behavioural strategies and cognitive processes (Ehlers & Clark, 2000). For migrants on the move, 'safety behaviour' is particularly relevant. This refers to actions that individuals take to prevent or minimise anticipated further catastrophes; it involves the belief that the feared catastrophe will occur if one does not engage in preventative action (Salkovskis, 1996). From this perspective, the need to keep moving, whatever the risk, can be seen as being induced by a strategy developed in response to PTSD, as opposed to a considered decision based on the pros and cons of the ongoing migration, as suggested by the push and pull theory of migration.

The findings of the research clearly indicate that PTSD is prevalent among Eritrean refugees. The high levels found, together with the understanding of the implications of such high levels, is the problem that this research seeks to respond to. The challenge is to find a trauma support approach that responds to both the high levels of PTSD and the low levels of resources available to Eritrean refugee communities. ICT is an innovation that presents itself as amenable to use for trauma support and, hence, a more comprehensive understanding of its prevalence and current use is, thus, the subject of the next chapter.

Discovering that the devastation caused by the traumatic experiences, both to individuals and their respective communities, was neither imagined nor anecdotal was the start of the long and hard process of addressing the problem – healing trauma. I am primarily a frontline mental health practitioner and firmly believe in the benefits of psychotherapy. However, I am also aware of the resources required to effect a successful session, as well as the need for a certain level of stability for feasible therapeutic engagement. The context of Eritrean refugees makes this impossible, as the community is highly mobile. Furthermore, adequately trained mental health professionals who speak the language and are a cultural match for the community are virtually non-existent, making a feasible solution seem virtually impossible, or at least extremely difficult.

Chapter 5

The prevalence of ICT and social media in Eritrean refugee communities

"I still feel a shockwave every time the phone rings."

This is a comment from a conversation with a mother of a human trafficking victim who spent months listening to her son's voice across the desert on a cell phone. ICT in the form of a cheap mobile phone enabled ruthless human traffickers to find their way into her psyche and forced her and her family to sell everything they owned, including the family home where her son and his siblings grew up, to rescue him. The ransom money was transferred using the same technology. Ironically, I realised that it might be possible to also provide trauma healing through this technology.

This chapter seeks to answer the third research question: Q.3. What are the trusted communication channels of refugees and is the prevalence of ICT and social media among Eritrean refugees such that it could play a role in the provision of trauma interventions?

Despite the various reasons curtailing accessibility and connectivity, as mentioned in Chapter 2, the use of ICT and social media seemed to have potential for delivering trauma support and information to refugees. Using ICT and social media would certainly provide opportunities to address the kinds of PTSD levels highlighted in Chapter 4 in order to enable refugees to better assess danger and prospects during their migration trajectories. However, the potential of ICTs and the challenges of connectivity warrant a clearer understanding, prior to investing scarce resources. In addition, it is crucial to assess the attitude towards technology as a trusted medium among refugees. Hence, the objective of the study being discussed in this chapter is to ascertain the prevalence and status of ICTs and social media and also clarify the situation with respect to connectivity.

The research question was answered by looking closely at the results of a survey that was aimed at understanding how technology could be used to create resilience among young Eritrean refugees throughout the Horn of Africa in the context of human trafficking. The original study started with the objective of determining the radio usage habits of young refugees and their peers in host communities with a view to developing a radio broadcast project to inform young Eritrean refugees and young people from host communities of the risks of trafficking and possible alternatives. In this context, social media usage and the significance (trust) of information exchange across refugee communities was also examined. Here, only ICT and social media prevalence and use by Eritrean refugee youth as a trusted means of receiving information is considered.

5.1 Introduction

At the time of the research (2016), over 100,000 Eritreans were estimated to be living in refugee camps in northern Ethiopia and towns and cities throughout the country (Prandi, 2016). On the other side of the border, eastern Sudan hosted 112,283 Eritrean refugees, of whom 83,499 live in camps and 28,784 in urban areas (ICMC Europe, 2013). This is a highly-mobile community, with refugees often leaving camps and settlements to join family and friends in other migrant communities, or engaging in secondary migration across the Sahara Desert to Libya, then across the Mediterranian Sea to Europe. Many do not reach their final destination, and those who make it face an extremely traumatic journey and harsh reception, severely impacting on their ability to cope with their experiences and the demands of settling into their new home.

ICTs, particularly smartphones, appear to play a pivotal role in the lives of migrants and refugees in the region. However, despite the fact that ICT plays such a key role in enabling the flow of information between geographically-dispersed people, including a key role in facilitating human trafficking (Van Reisen *& Gerrima*, 2016), little has been done to use this technology to build and promote resilience and improve coping strategies among youth in Eritrean refugee communities. Nevertheless, it is clear that ICT has great potential for developing community resilience, both due to its ability to transcend barriers of accessibility and its versatility in responding to current concerns in real-time.

Using ICT, people can reconnect with each other, their history, and the wisdom of their faith and traditions, enabling them to make coherent choices about their future. This increased connection can go beyond enabling communities to simply cope with traumatic experiences and can potentially result in positive psychological changes or trauma healing. The creative engagement of a tool such as ICT could bring about post-traumatic growth, by enabling a community to successfully struggle against adversity (Tedeschi & Calhoun, 2004). In addition, ICT has the potential to enhance community resilience by giving people access to the wider world and enabling victims to raise awareness and obtain material and moral support. In our specific context, ICT has great potential to overcome the difficulties caused by lack of trained and qualified mental health practitioners to deliver trauma support. ICT could be used to deliver adaptable interventions, overcoming the challenges posed by the mobility of the community, as well as the dearth of adequate human resources. Table 5.1 sets out the four variables identified by Norris *et al.* (2002a, 2002b) and describes how ICT can be used to support community resilience for each variable.

Table 5.1. ICT and community resilience

Variables in community resilience	How ICT can be used
Economic development/situation Relates to the ability to meet the basic needs of members of the community. Populations at a lower socio-economic level have less instrumental, psychological and social ability to resist disasters than populations with a higher socio-economic standing (Norris *et al.*, 2002a, 2002b). Therefore, wealthier communities with better economic resources have increased resilience and heal more successfully from traumatic experiences than poor communities.	ICT can be used to draw attention to difficult (traumatic) experiences faced by communities, facilitating faster awareness and more effective responses, and ultimately mitigating the resulting trauma.

This is sometimes related to their ability to draw more attention to their problems and, hence, receive more acknowledgement and support.	
Social capital Refers to the networks of community organisations and links between them. It refers to the sense of belonging and, hence, commitment to the community (Perkins & Long, 2002).	ICT can be used to help communities scattered across the globe to remain connected and build community resilience by affirming each other, promoting belonging, and mobilising information and resources.
Reliable information and open communication Refers to accurate and trusted information, which enables members of the community to cope with the outcome of traumatic events and enhances trust in community leaders (Shamai, 2015). Good communication also contributes to the development of meaning (or community narrative).	The provision of reliable information through ICT can create a sense of security among members of the community affected (directly or indirectly) by the traumatic event and among those who are trying to provide help.
Community competence Refers to the ability of community organisations and their leaders to create collective problem-solving and decision-making skills that empower the community to cope with the challenges posed by traumatic events. Where community competence is diminished, or was lacking in the first place, the result is community conflict and helplessness.	Using ICT, communities can develop ways of communicating up-to-date information about protection and problem solving, enabling people to feel safe and have a sense of belonging to a wider network of people who are concerned with issues of mutual importance.

The aim of including some of the findings of this study – which was conducted among Eritrean refugees in Khartoum (Sudan), Addis Ababa (Ethiopia) and refugee camps in northern Ethiopia – was to help explore the potential of providing PTSD support to refugees on the move. The research question was double pronged, seeking to understand both the practicalities regarding prevalence (and connectivity), as well as the regard for the technology in terms of trust.

The original study sought to understand:

- How youth from refugee communities and their counterparts in host communities engage with each other (if at all)
- How youth from the refugee communities and their counterparts in host communities obtain information
- How youth from refugee communities and their counterparts in the host communities engage to build protection and resilience within their community
- What means of communication/sources of information youth from refugee communities and their counterparts in the host communities use most

As mentioned above, the analysis in this chapter mainly relates to elements pertaining to the status and prevalence of mobile phones and social media usage, among Eritrean refugees in refugee camps as well as in urban contexts in Sudan and Ethiopia. The full report details the other elements and combines the perspectives of both the refugees and their counterparts from the respective host communities (see Kidane, 2016).

5.2 Method

5.2.1 Research instrument
This study used structured questionnaires (see Chapter 3) that were translated into Tigrigna and Arabic, as well as being available in English (see Appendix 1). In addition to the questionnaire, the researcher conducted semi-structured interviews to establish the potential of an ICT based project and to understand how it would fit with existing policies and programmes. The semi-structured interviews were in the format of scoping interviews, exploring the possibilities of using radio to disseminate programmes that promoted

community resilience among young people from refugee communities and their peers in the host community. The questions covered:

- Compatibility with other projects with similar objectives, as well as with existing policies, in relation to promoting resilience and community cohesion and societal trends
- Feasibility of the technological aspects of a radio programme to be accessed by refugees, considering the resources and technological advances required
- Feasibility of providing a credible radio service considering the human resources required (presence of adequately trained media professionals)
- Prevalence of similar and potentially competitive initiatives

5.2.2 Procedure

The original study was conducted from April to July 2016 and consisted mainly of a survey of Eritrean, Ethiopian and Sudanese youth in various locations in Ethiopia and Sudan. The part of the study report here is the relevant data gathered using a questionnaire (details of the questionnaire are provided in Chapter 3 and in Appendix 1), to survey Eritrean refugee youth.

5.2.3 Participants

In total, 90 Eritreans took part in the survey, 40 in Ethiopia and 50 in Sudan. Table 5.2 lists the locations and groups surveyed. The participants were all aged between 17 and 35.

Table 5.2. ICT survey locations and groups

Location	Group
Shimelba refugee camp, northern Ethiopia	Refugee youth in camp
Adi Harush refugee camp, northern Ethiopia	Refugee youth in camp
Hitsats refugee camp, northern Ethiopia	Refugee youth in camp
Addis Ababa, Ethiopia	Urban refugee youth
Kassala (refugee camps in the area), Sudan	Refugee youth in and around camps
Khartoum, Sudan	Urban refugee youth

Table 5.3 presents the characteristics of the survey respondents (age, location and nationality).

Table 5.3. Characteristics of survey participants

Location and nationality	Number of Eritrean respondents	Aged 17–19	Aged 20–26	Aged 27–35	Aged 35+
Hitsats	14	3	10	1	0
Adi Harush	4	3	1	0	0
Shimelba	10	1	2	7	0
Addis Ababa	12	3	4	5	0
Kassala	30	4	6	20	0
Khartoum	20	0	6	14	0
Total	90	14	29	47	0

For the semi-structured interview, interviewees were selected for their experience of either the refugee service provision or membership of the community with expertise on media and included:

- One Minister for Communication and Information, Ethiopia
- One refugee protection officer at Shire Ethiopian Agency for Refugees and Returnees Affairs (ARRA)
- Five Ethiopian professionals from the Tigray region
- Four Ethiopian and Eritrean media professionals

5.3 Results

Here I outline the results of the survey that relate to the inquiry of the present research, i.e., the prevalence of mobile phones and the use of social media and Internet access among refugees from Eritrea. Details of other findings can be found in the full report (Kidane, 2016). For the purpose of this research, I have included the results relating to radio listening habits, as background to why we were interested in the devices in use. Social media was then explored to enable us to understand its status as a trusted information source. For the purpose of this research, the latter two (devices in use and social media use) were the crucial considerations.

5.3.1 Radio listening habits

In Ethiopia, with the exception of four participants at Adi Harush refugee camp, all groups reported using FM radios. Very few participants reported listening to international radio stations. However, there was great variation in the proportion of people who accessed radio programmes in the different locations. Generally, fewer refugees reported listening to FM radio in the camps, compared to their refugee counterparts in Addis Ababa. This could be due to technical difficulties with reception in the camps. Similarly, in Sudan (and particularly among Eritrean refugees in Kassala), local FM radio programmes were very popular and many also listen to international radio. Figure 5.1 shows the radio listening habits of participants in each location.

Figure 5.1. Radio listening habits of all participants

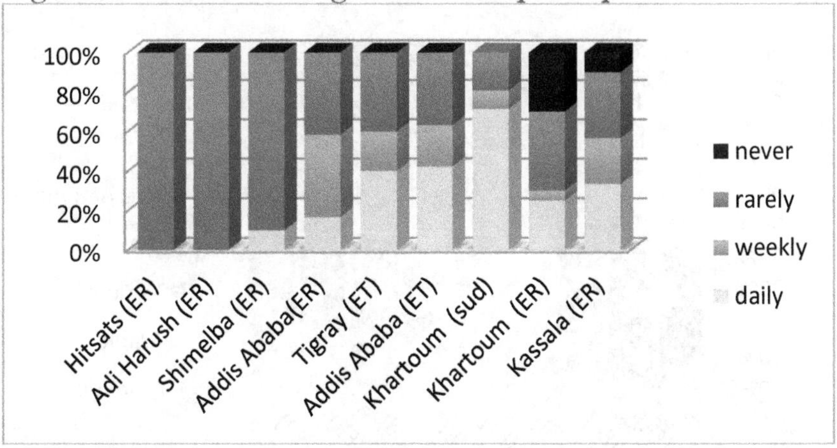

5.3.1.1 Frequency of radio listening

Camp residents reported listening to the radio rarely, with only a few respondents in Shimelba reporting listening daily. The picture is different for refugees in Addis Ababa, where there is wider access, with people listening to the radio daily and weekly. In Sudan, the situation is more diverse with refugees in Kassala almost evenly split among those who listen to the radio daily, weekly and rarely. A greater proportion of refugees in Khartoum than in Kassala reported listening to the radio rarely (see Figure 5.1).

5.3.1.2 Broadcast language

The survey found that Amharic and Tigrigna are the most popular broadcast languages listened to among those surveyed in Ethiopia. In Sudan, Arabic is more popular, but broadcasts in other international languages are also accessed (see Figure 5.2).

Figure 5.2. Broadcast languages listened to by all participants

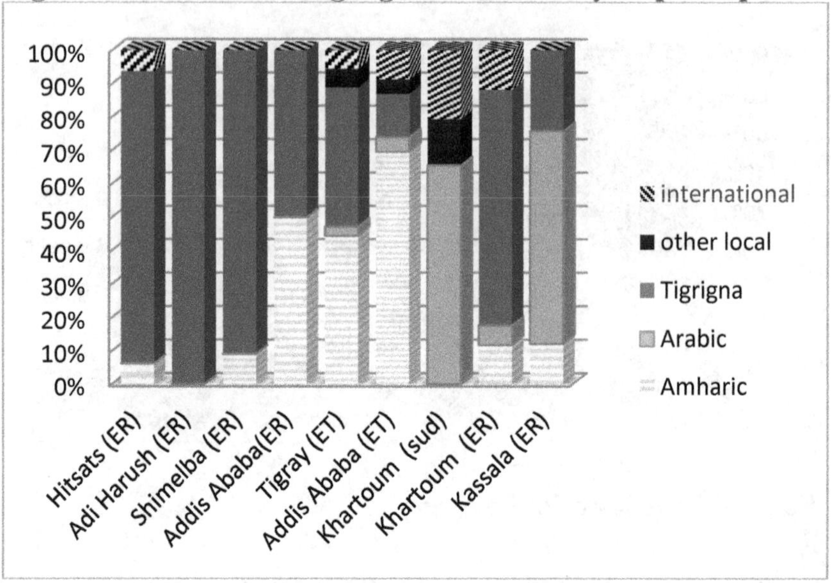

5.3.1.3 Device used

Nearly everyone surveyed listened to the radio on a mobile phone. In Addis Ababa, participants reported listening to the radio on the Internet. Similarly, in Sudan, mobile phones and the Internet were popular, but satellite TV is also widely used for accessing radio programmes. This was particularly so among refugees in Kassala. But a significantly high proportion of refugees in refugee camps use their mobile phones to access radio programmes (see Figure 5.3). This very strongly indicates that mobile phone use is not only prevalent, but already being used to access information, in addition to personal communication.

Figure 5.3. ICT equipment used for accessing radio by all participants

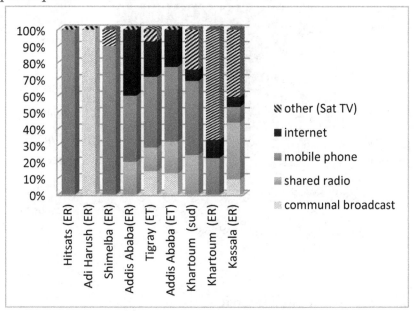

5.3.2 Social media usage

By far the most popular social media platform was Facebook, followed by Viber, which were used to exchange a wide range of communication including family news, current affairs discussions, sport and popular culture, as well as news about safe migration passages and safety in general. This was the case even for the least connected camp in Ethiopia (Hitsats). In Sudan, WhatsApp and MSN Messenger were also in wide use (see Figure 5.4). This was an interesting finding, which indicated that social media was prevalent and already in wide use, as well as being used to exchange a wide range of information, indicating its status as a trusted means. This affirms the possibility of integrating social media as a potential approach for delivering trauma interventions.

Figure 5.4. Social media usage by all participants

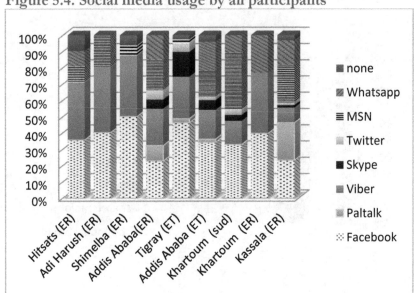

5.3.3 Semi-structured interviews

The semi-structured interviews that were conducted among experts mainly focused on policies, procedures and sustainability of a community radio promoting resilience. Although much of the findings relate to policy and procedural matters (see Kidane, 2016), all of the respondents were clear that while the Internet, mobile phones and satellite television are used to listen to the radio and obtain information, there is also significant widespread usage of social media among refugee youth. This was the case despite the serious connectivity problems, particularly in refugee camps.

As mentioned previously, the objective of the study was wider than the focus in this chapter, hence, the interviews also attempted to understand the policies and procedures regarding information exchange across youth communities. However, as social media and mobile phones are an integral element of youth culture, this became a topic of discussion during the interviews.

5.4 Conclusion

This chapter looked at the prevalence of ICT and its status as a trusted means of communication among refugees to ascertain whether or not it could be used for delivering trauma support. The study identified the prevalence of mobile phones and widespread use of social media, which are both findings pertinent to the current study. The study found that the most prevalent device in use for accessing information on radio is the smartphone, with satellite TV and the Internet as alternatives, where available. This is significant as it indicates that smartphones are already widely available and being used to access information, beyound personal communication, forming a good basis for considering adaptations for delivering TRUST via this technology. Participants also reported widely accessing social media, particularly Facebook and Viber, with nearly all participants in every location reporting having a Facebook account and a significant proportion accessing Viber. MSN Messenger and WhatsApp were also in use, particularly in cities. Only 9 respondents (out of 151) reported not using any form of social media.

The survey clearly identified the centrality of ICT, and particularly the smartphone, for communication, including the communication of information over and above personal and familial use. Social media usage was also almost universal despite the difficulties associated with connectivity. Refugees invest in and rely on technology to obtain information crucial to their lives and access pertinent information. Therefore, the answer to the research question pertaining to the prevalence and status of (trust in) ICT and social media is that its use is significant enough to justify developing a trauma healing programme using ICT as a mode of delivery. The necessary technology is in wide and effective use in Eritrean refugee communities, making ICT, particularly smartphones and social media, an important consideration in discussions regarding refugee trajectories.

We have seen in Chapter 4 how ICT has been used to cause trauma to refugees and their communities at the hands of human traffickers. At the same time, its wide use in the hands of the refugees offers an opportunity to use ICT for their benefit, enabling them to address the trauma that impairs their ability to make rational decisions about their safety and prospects when considering migration trajectories. ICT could circumvent the challenges involved in resourcing trauma support and enable access for those suffering from traumatic stress, no matter where they are located, and at the rate required and to the standard necessary to achieve healing. This understanding was crucial to the development of the trauma support that was later adapted for use via ICT.

Although we had a potentially viable solution to the problem of access to our intervention, this was, again, only the start of the process. I was still no closer to an actual intervention using ICT. In fact, at this point it felt like I might have put the cart before the horse and, if an intervention could not be developed, there was no point in determining the prevalence of ICT use among Eritrean refugees.

Chapter 6

Development of a self-help low-cost post-traumatic stress programme

The development of a trauma intervention required a paradigm shift on a slow burner. I remember exactly where I was when I first heard about EMDR [Eye Movement Desensitisation Reprocessing] – a tapas bar in Rotterdam on a dark winter evening. I was struggling to keep up with the half Dutch, half English conversation my colleagues were having and struggling even harder to envisage a therapy approach that involved eye movement to process traumatic memory. The whole concept irked me on several levels, particularly as a psychotherapist who knew Eritrean culture. Psychotherapy was alien enough and here was a technique that looked absolutely bizarre. That I wasn't convinced is an understatement.

But I was curious enough to read about it, and I did a whole weekend of reading and listening to podcasts, as well as testing out some of the self-help resources later. I was curious and I decided to attend the complete training and find out more. I was also interested to see if it could be adapted. This was the begin of developing a self-help technique for refugees based on EMDR. At that point, I had no idea if it would work.

This chapter outlines the process that led to the development of a six-week self-help programme, called Trauma Recovery Understanding Self-Help Therapy (TRUST), that addresses trauma and, consequently, lowers individual and collective trauma affecting individuals and their communities. The effectiveness of the intervention was first tested among internally displaced women in Northern Uganda and details of this will be discussed in Chapter 7. Following the research in Uganda, the programme was adapted for use with highly-mobile Eritrean refugees in the Tigray region of Northern Ethiopia, the details of the latter are discussed in Chapter 8.

The essence of any intervention to heal trauma in the contexts here needs to be two-pronged: it needs to address individual and collective trauma, simultaneously. As both of these aspects shape the reality of the traumatic experiences, healing should address both to be complete. This is a serious consideration, as it is not necessarily the usual approach used by psychological interventions, often developed in Western contexts, which focus on individual trauma.

Simply focusing on individual trauma de-contextualises the collective suffering in post-conflict communities. The context for such collective suffering is the social and historical fabric of society, which comes under immense stress during the traumatising events and, subsequently, can become the cause of additional and ongoing trauma. Leaving this out of the healing process leads to further atrocities, such as human rights violations, as the mistrust and polarisation prohibit healing through cohesion and support, hampering the recovery of those who are suffering from PTSD and other mental health problems (Lykes, 2001; Van Reisen & Mawere, 2017). Therefore, in addition to contextualising trauma therapy to account for cultural and language differences (widening the focus), locating trauma not just in the individual, but in the community, affords opportunities for practitioners to focus on the community-wide potential to effect healing and is beneficial for those who have not yet been identified as suffering from post-traumatic stress (Bonanno, 2004; Kidane, 2015).

6.1 Trauma and the human brain

In addition to the collective nature of trauma, the development of this trauma intervention also considered the neurological impact of trauma on the individual. In this respect approaches such as EMDR proved a good starting point. As we saw in Chapter 2, trauma affects a person in a way that results in the reconfiguration of the nervous system. Traumatised people become stuck and stop growing and developing, as they are unable to integrate their traumatic experiences into their ongoing life. Instead, they organise their lives as though the trauma is still happening. Energy is focused on suppressing the inner chaos, rather than spontaneous involvement in day-to-day activities (Van der Kolk, 2014).

Without intervention, trauma victims can continue to live their lives as if they are still in danger, weeks, months, years and even decades after the traumatic experience. This is particularly the case for victims of events of 'human design' (American Psychiatric Association, 2000), such as war and political violence, which causes many refugees to flee their homes. It is believed that the element of betrayal entailed in these events makes traumatisation more likely (Van der Kolk *et al.*, 2007) and recovery more complicated (Salter, 1995).

Understanding this impact of trauma on processes in the brain is essential when developing interventions for supporting victims of atrocities perpetrated to torment and terrorise entire communities. In a sense, trauma treatment is essentially helping victims overcome the imprint of the traumatic experiences, which keeps being re-activated, resulting in the fight-flight-freeze response to the slightest trigger, potentially causing ongoing flight in the form of secondary migration. Given that the disintegration of brain functioning and dissociation are problematic in the aftermath of war trauma, treatment based on creating and embedding associations and restoring integration is highly desirable. EMDR therapy is an approach that has been highlighted for the effective integration of traumatic memories in PTSD sufferers (Shapiro, 1989).

6.2 EMDR as a trauma healing intervention

EMDR works by getting victims of traumatic stress to focus intensely on the emotions, sensations and meanings of their traumatic experiences, in a safe setting, while engaging them in a bilateral stimulation. The approach was first developed by Francine Shapiro in 1988 and has since been found to be an effective treatment for PTSD across many fields (Chemtob, Tolin, Van der Kolk & Pitman, 2000), including refugees (Mooren, De Jong, Kleber & Ruvic, 2003). WHO has approved EMDR as top-level evidence-based therapy (World Health Organization, 2013).

The effectiveness of EMDR in healing trauma across many contexts and cultures makes it an ideal choice for addressing trauma among the refugee communities of concern here. Encouraged by the success of EMDR in treating PTSD across many cultures and contexts, the objective of the current initiative was to develop sustainable community-based support using EMDR techniques.

Due to the impossibility of providing trained clinicians (even at basic levels) to provide full-protocol interventions and support in the locations required, it was decided to model the intervention on the self-help guide developed by Francine Shapiro (2012). The main objective of Shapiro's self-help guide is to enable people to understand why they are the way they are and then learn what they can do about pain and negative reactions. Techniques are designed to enable people to attain wellbeing by taking control over the choices they make on a daily basis. The model developed had to include psycho-education, as well as techniques for addressing traumatic memories and dealing with distress. However, because this form of trauma healing is new to the potential recipients, people would need more than mere self-help instructions, and would require coaching, support and demonstrations of techniques to go through the programme. It was, therefore, necessary to include a coaching element demonstrating the various techniques and encouraging victims to persist when difficulties arose. The role of a coach here is not to provide opportunities to talk through the trauma, but to demonstrate the techniques and provide support, for instance, if participants suffered demotivation following the activation of traumatic memories. Hence, the specialisation and training required is minimal and this can also be provided remotely via ICT (videos, text and voice messaging). In addition to being cost effective and sustainable, this approach also leaves the agency with the community, enabling people to train and support each other using the techniques they have mastered for their own use.

Traumatic stress shatters its victims' sense of trust in others, particularly in relation to the events that made them frightened or ashamed. It is, therefore, also important to create a context in which those undergoing the intervention are not stigmatised, but celebrated for their courage in facing their experiences and overcoming them. As mentioned previously, ICT can support interventions. However, it is important to establish that the ICT medium is indeed a trusted platform, before any attempts at utilisation. The opportunity that ICT provided in Northern Uganda was to use community radio personalities, who are trusted by their respective communities, to deliver the education and information element of the intervention and to provide support and encouragement via messages on podcasts and radio broadcasts. These messages reinforced and promoted the need to address and overcome trauma, and the collective and individual benefits thereof, making use of ICT facilitated access as well as trust, by making trusted voices accessible to the wider community. This has the potential to unlock healing, both at the individual and collective levels, enabling whole communities to support the healing of the most vulnerable, while being aware of the community-wide impacts and generating healing conversations on a broader scale. In Ethiopia, there was wide utilisation of ICT on an App that will be detailed in a separate section below.

In addition to the radio broadcasts and podcasts, the programme also included opportunities for community-wide celebration of the steps taken by participants towards healing, as well as their contribution to collective healing. These events were supported by community radio broadcasters and community elders, who were invited to commend and acknowledge the courageous steps taken by victims of atrocities to heal themselves and their communities. These events are intended to address the collective trauma suffered by whole communities, by bringing the community together to bond around addressing issues that are difficult or overwhelming due to traumatic stress. Community-wide benefits include to children who were not yet born during the atrocities, but would have been brought up by the adults who were.

When the intervention was adapted in a more mobile community, i.e., Eritrean refugees in the refugee camps in Ethiopia, the coaching and community support elements were transferred onto an App that was intended to give coaching through videos and support and encouragement through text messages in real-time. The work at the community level was intended to also be via social media postings and testimonials.

6.3 Multilevel healing of trauma in post-war contexts

The approach taken, in the development of the intervention, was based on a conceptualisation of trauma healing as supporting the many individuals with symptoms of traumatic stress, while at the same time addressing collective trauma, addressing both the healing of the traumatised community and traumatised individuals within it. This is intended to affect post-traumatic growth for the individual and their community. If collective trauma represents the disruption of relationships at many levels of the human system, recovery should also involve collective processes of adaptation and the mobilisation of capacities across all these levels (Saul, 2014). Therefore, healing trauma simultaneously at the individual and collective levels is crucial for post-conflict recovery, and neglecting trauma healing has a detrimental impact on the wellbeing of not only the individual, but the whole community. Widespread unaddressed trauma also hampers post-conflict reconstruction and peace building, with the impacts of collective trauma affecting subsequent generations, as traumatic memories and reactions are passed on through collective narratives, norms and societal structures, extending the cycle of violence and vulnerability.

Having justified the need for multilevel healing in post-conflict communities, the challenges of providing such support become evident. These challenges include factors such as the degree of human and material devastation, the resources available to the community, and the prioritisation of other needs over the need for psychological healing, be it individual or collective. Gelbach and Davis (2007) state that, although the treatment of psychological distress in individuals and families is generally believed to expedite community recovery, the provision of effective and affordable psychotherapy is not yet a priority in post-disaster support. Although there are many other reasons for this, including the timing of interventions, as well as the type and effectiveness of some of the available techniques, a recurring concern, particularly in non-Western cultures, is whether psychotherapy itself is culturally biased and stigmatising, pathologising normal responses to danger and labelling trauma survivors as mentally ill (Miller & Rasco, 2004).

The EMDR Humanitarian Assistance Programme (HAP) reports that clinicians trained in EMDR have been able to overcome some of these difficulties to develop a post-disaster treatment method that focuses on supporting the brain's natural capacity to reprocess disturbing information to an adaptive resolution (HAP Volunteers, 2005). In addition, HAP found that training local clinicians helps to circumvent the problems caused by delayed international responses to traumatic events and builds sustainable resources in communities plagued by natural disasters or violent conflict. The positive outcomes of EMDR HAP interventions have been published in several articles (e.g., Jarero, Artigas, Mauer, López Cano & Alcalá, 1999; Adúriz, Knopfler & Bluthgen, 2009; Fernandez, Gallinari & Lorenzetti, 2004; Jarero, Artigas & Hartung, 2006; Jarero & Artigas, 2010; Zaghrout-Hodali, Alissa & Dodgson, 2008).

However, in poor post-disaster contexts, such as in Uganda or refugee camps in Ethiopia, even this successful and relatively cost-effective protocol is not easy to implement due to the unavailability of clinicians, even at the most basic level. This is particularly the case given the extent of the traumatisation and the deprivation of the regions affected. If EMDR-based techniques are to be effectively implemented to address individual and collective trauma in these communities, there is a need to find a realistic and sustainable approach to facilitate their accessibility.

As we have seen in Chapter 4, one of the features of communities in current day Africa is the fast expansion of ICT; this is both a challenge and an opportunity (Van Reisen & Gerrima, 2016). For our purposes, it is important to discuss the opportunities for using ICT to facilitate the cost-effective and sustainable provision of trauma intervention in resource-deprived communities, such as those under consideration here. In Uganda, the approach taken was to use podcasts and community radio, and, for the Eritrean refugees in Tigray region, an App was developed.

6.4 Contextualising and enlarging the impact of trauma support

A defining component of mass trauma, such as the trauma that took place during the civil war in Uganda, is the betrayal of social trust, which leaves victims devalued and humiliated, undermining their sense of communal trust and decency (Saul, 2014). Restoring social trust is, therefore, a foremost task of any intervention, as it enables the community to become the context for healing trauma, rather than causing it or obstructing healing (the community becomes a protective factor). Without restoring trust, an intervention does not have a chance of having any meaningful impact on recovery, as recipients will not access or engage with it. Therefore, trust, and specifically community-wide trust, was the core contextualisation in the development of the intervention for this research.

Media can play an important role in building post-conflict recovery, as it can facilitate collective narration, which can shape the meaning ascribed to traumatic events, as well as providing resources and solutions to difficult challenges (Landau & Saul, 2004). With this in mind, the project liaised extensively with local, trusted media personalities. This was achieved using podcasts with information for participants, as well as providing additional community-wide information on trauma and recovery, to promote trust and build confidence by creating platforms for the establishment of common meaning and understanding. This allowed members of the community to open up to each other and express their needs, views and attitudes. In mobile communities, this role could be adapted to social media through which community-wide discussions could be encouraged and facilitated and trusted personalities could share their experiences and stories of trauma and healing.

6.5 Development and implementation of an App for healing trauma

24COMS is an App offering a communication platform that enables secure and efficient communication through mobile devices, with 100% data ownership and care for privacy. The services offered through the App can be deployed with ease and flexibility for chatting, posts, news feeds, newsletters, brochures, location-based services, and track and trace, among other things. All these solutions and applications are managed by an administrator from a web-based control centre.

A special page on the App was developed with a view to delivering TRUST for use by mobile communities. It provides access to the six support videos developed for the programme. Two of the videos provide education (first of the six sessions) on the impact of trauma and the remaining five give instructions and demonstrations on techniques to enable victims of trauma to take control of distressing emotions in their day-to-day life. During the research, videos were uploaded onto Vimeo, a video-sharing site, and were individually password locked for controlled access. The videos were released to each user by giving them the password after they had completed the previous session. The first two were provided upon completion of the IES-R, SER and ISCS questionnaires, after the administrator had checked suitability. The passwords for subsequent videos were released a few days after the participant had completed the previous video. In addition, users were able to comment on each video, as well as send messages and questions to the administrators of the App. All content, including videos and instructions, were in Tigrigna to enable users to receive information in their first language on a group page called 'Support and Encouragement' (name selected to remove potential stigmatisation regarding trauma and mental illness).

6.6 Outline of TRUST sessions

The discussion above outlines how the trauma intervention was designed to take into account the neurobiology of trauma, as well as the impact of collective trauma on healing and post-traumatic growth. There is increasing recognition that working to engage all areas of the brain is the key to reintegrating the post-traumatic body and brain, including integrating emotions, sensations, awareness and thoughts. These are the connections that are often disrupted by complex trauma (Cozolino, 2006; Ogden, Pain & Fisher, 2006; Siegel, 2001). Clinicians treating either complex PTSD or PTSD endorsed the phased approach (Cloitre *et al.*, 2011) taken in the development of TRUST. In accordance with guidance and good practice examples, TRUST adopted a three-phase approach to address the extensive impact of trauma; these phases are outlined in Table 6.1.

Table 6.1. Outline of sessions for six-week TRUST programme for survivors of traumatic stress

Session	Objective of session and activities	Guidance and support either through ICT or live coaching
1.	Introductory session to outline what trauma is and how it affects the brain and behaviour, as well as the community; outlines the techniques that will be used to address the impacts of trauma	Guidance and support for safe calm place
2.	Identifying the negative feelings, words and reactions that people want to address, remembering the touchstone memories that anchor those feelings and reactions, and making a plan for support with this	Guiding and supporting Subjective Units of Distress (SUDs) and touchstone memories Finishing with a safe calm place
3.	Introducing bilateral stimulation	Guiding and supporting SUDs, touchstone memories and butterfly hugs; checking with SUDs again and repeating butterfly hugs Finishing with a safe calm place
4.	Practicing bilateral stimulation	Guiding and supporting SUDs, touchstone memories and butterfly hugs; checking with SUDs again and repeating butterfly hugs Finishing with a safe calm place

5.	Consolidating the use bilateral stimulation	Guiding and supporting SUDs, touchstone memories and butterfly hugs; checking with SUDs again and repeating butterfly hugs Finishing with a safe calm place
6.	Preparing for closure and thinking about sustainability of the approach for the community event, at which participants are able to raise awareness of trauma and trauma healing in their community and teach the techniques learnt	Guiding and instructing people how to do the four elements and encouraging them to use these regularly, in combination with other techniques or on their own
7.	Holding a community celebration where the whole community comes together to celebrate the participants and their achievements	Preparing something that the participants can take with them as a memento or a certificate of the work that was undertaken, to be given at a community-wide event

In light of the risk of participants losing motivation, which is endemic to the context of working with traumatic memory, this intervention, which works without a therapist's involvement, was much shorter than the average recommended under such circumstances. Much of the work was, thus, directed towards education and coaching on specific coping and processing skills, followed by a session dedicated to psychosocial rehabilitation. This is based on the understanding that participants are able to practice outside sessions and revisit the information as required. Community-wide awareness was also provided, giving participants both the tools and the opportunity to talk about trauma and demonstrating how trauma processing allows the whole community to heal.

The TRUST programme was offered over weeks with sessions covering the following:

- Sessions 1–2: Psychosocial education, understanding trauma and the brain
- Sessions 3–5: Learning skills for managing trauma symptoms
- Sessions 6–7: Preparing a reorientation towards a supportive community

Session 7 is intended to be a community-wide event that could either take place in the same week, as the culmination of the 6 sessions, or later if the community prefers (the bulk of the therapeutic work is completed over 6 sessions). The sessions are detailed in Table 6.1. As mentioned above, the programme uses concepts from EMDR, making adaptations to fit the cultural and linguistic context where it is being implemented. The exercises used in the videos and podcasts/coaches are explained in Shapiro (2012). The concepts taken from Shapiro's self-help book are generally divided into five main categories integrated in the sessions of the TRUST programme:

- **Psycho-education:** This gives people the opportunity to learn about the effects of trauma on the human brain, and the analogy of a 'busy desk' (Shapiro, 2012) (or adaptations, such as 'busy kitchen') used to show how the trauma-activated brain becomes too chaotic for appropriate information transmission and how the essence of trauma support is to create order and enable effective information retrieving and processing.

- **Measuring distress:** Here Subjective Units of Distress (SUDs) are used to help people assess their own level of distress, ranking them on a scale of 1 to 10 (using beads or matches to make it accessible), as a way of measuring progress, but also of understanding and managing their symptoms and taking precautionary action to relax or avoid further distress if SUD levels are high.

- **Resourcing:** These are techniques to equip people to manage their distress; in TRUST there are breathing exercises and what is known as a 'safe calm place', both fully described in Shapiro (2012). A 'safe calm place' is a technique whereby participants are guided to picture an internal emotional sanctuary that generates feelings of calm and safety that they can retreat to during the stress of everyday life, as well as during the processing of traumatic memory.

- **Processing distressing memories:** These are self-administered bilateral stimulation techniques that facilitate the processing of traumatic memories. Bilateral stimulation is the use of alternating right, left stimulation such as tapping or eye movements to activate and integrate information from the brain. While knee tapping could be used, the main technique used is known as 'butterfly hugs' (wrapping arms around themselves, so that each hand touches the opposite upper arm or shoulder and then move their hands like the wings of a butterfly to tap shoulders in an alternating rhythm. The technique has been effective in emergency contexts. Prior to processing the distressing memory, people are trained on identifying the original memory, through what is referred to as 'touchstone memories' (earliest memory related to the presenting feeling); this enables participants to trace the origins of the traumatic memory and identify it for processing.

- **Reintegration and maintenance:** Reintegration took the form of community-wide acknowledgement of the steps taken to heal trauma and recognition of the valuable skills in understanding and addressing traumatic distress, while maintenance relates to helping participants maintain a healthy balance. The 'Four Elements' exercise (Shapiro, 2012), which is designed to follow the body from the feet to the stomach, to the throat and mouth, and, finally, to the head, was used for this purpose.

6.7 Conclusion

The TRUST programme was designed to deliver therapy, combining a robust understanding of trauma and its healing with consideration of the context of high levels of trauma, deprivation and mobility. Basing it on self-help activities made the programme sustainable within the low resource settings of the communities involved. The approach fostered improved understanding of trauma without re-narration, to limit the possibility of re-traumatisation in a context in which trauma support is limited.

In addition to accessibility, the intervention had to be highly contextualised to take into account the specific difficulties of the refugees and their cultural background to create a level of trust and relevance for communities. This contextualisation included the creation of a strong collective community base for the support programme, including support from community leaders and families. The community support was in addition to the practical instruments provided for reducing PTS, based on a scientific understanding of the effect of trauma in post-war and conflict settings. This gave communities an opportunity to examine and address their previous negative attitudes towards traumatised members of the community and also ensured community-wide ownership of the programme (and, hence, the healing of trauma). All of the developments and adaptations were carried out with close attention to integrating contemporary knowledge of psychiatric treatment of PTSD. The adaptations made for delivery using ICT were aimed at setting the approach within the realistic boundaries of a low-cost context with an extreme shortage of health-care provision, as well as taking the high level of mobility of the community into consideration. As much as ICT was an asset, there were challenges regarding its use including the lack of connectivity, which meant that real-time coaching and encouragement were not possibly as participants entered the challenging phase of trauma processing. In addition, virtual community-wide awareness raising and support and encouragement for those undergoing the therapy required extra work, as virtual communities do not always translate to the physical community that participants engage with on a day-to-day basis.

I am always humbled when people come to me for therapy; it represents the ultimate form of trust in another human being, often a stranger, to share some of your most difficult experiences in the anticipation that the therapist will help you process them. Developing TRUST took this a step further, as I was in the situation of not only asking people to trust me, but to trust an approach that I myself was still fairly new to. It was one giant voyage of discovery for all involved.

Chapter 7

Testing the effectiveness of the TRUST programme in Uganda

Practising bilateral stimulations and breathing techniques with Ugandan women under a tree in Kitgum or Lira was a perk of this research that I never anticipated. If being a psychotherapist in a clinic in London was an experience that still humbled me many years after qualifying as a therapist, here was an experience that taught me about the value of meeting people at the point of their need and giving them something, even a little something, to help them unlock their own ability to do the rest of the work. I am a student of life and this was my classroom, these women were the professors who taught me what was neither in the courses I attended nor the reading I had done in preparing TRUST – the power of the human brain to heal itself.

7.1 Introduction

In previous chapters we addressed the research questions regarding the levels of traumatic stress among Eritrean refugees, as measured on the IES-R (Chapter 4), we also looked at the prevalence of ICT and its status as a trusted means for offering trauma support (Chapter 5). In Chapter 6 we explored the development of the TRUST programme. Here we examine the effectiveness of TRUST in reducing trauma among survivors of war trauma. The programme's effectiveness was first tested as part of *A Cost-Benefit Analysis of Cash-Transfer Programs and Post-Trauma Services For Economic Empowerment of Women in North Uganda*; the full outcome of that research is detailed in Van Reisen *et al.* (2018b). This chapter addresses the fourth research question: Q.4. Is it possible to lower levels of PTS and enhance socio-economic resilience by delivering a short self-help trauma intervention in a high trauma/low resource context? We do so by looking at a study that involved the implementation of TRUST in Northern Uganda.

In relation to the current research, the Uganda project was an opportunity to test the effectiveness of the intervention in an area of similarly high traumatic stress, but with a relatively settled community. This was a crucial study, ahead of the additional developments required for the delivery of TRUST via ICT among highly-mobile Eritrean refugees in northern Ethiopia. This chapter concerns the findings of the broader Uganda research that are relevant to the effectiveness of TRUST.

The objective of the Uganda study was to understand the impact of trauma support on the effectiveness of social protection in building social economic resilience. The programme was developed after an initial research had shown that trauma counselling was having some impact on social economic resilience (Van Reisen *et al.*, 2018b). The implementation of TRUST was, therefore, intended to maximise the impact of trauma support by responding more effectively to the contextual realities in low resource contexts, where trained counsellors and mental health workers are not available.

As mentioned previously, the Ugandan context has similarities with the Eritrean context in terms of the presence of high level and sustained political violence that led to the traumatic displacement of vulnerable members of the society. The participants of this project were women who had been victims of war atrocities and were found to have similar levels of trauma as those seen among Eritrean refugees, discussed in Chapter 4 (Van Reisen *et al.*, 2018b).

Over two decades, since the late 1980s, the Lord's Resistance Army (LRA) waged a war against the Ugandan People's Democratic Army and the people of Northern Uganda. The extreme brutality of the conflict resulted in the total destruction of the region, and the displacement of over 1.5 million people, turning Northern Uganda into a humanitarian disaster. Tens of thousands of adults and children were abducted to serve as soldiers, porters, and sex slaves for commanders (Baines, Stover & Wierda, 2006; Allen & Schomerus, 2006).

In response to all this, the International Criminal Court (ICC) issued warrants of arrest on 13 October 2005 against LRA leader Joseph Kony and four of his top commanders for crimes against humanity and war crimes, including the forced conscription of children (ICC, 2005). However, the pressure only resulted in pushing the LRA out of Uganda into neighbouring countries. The LRA continues to cause widespread displacement and terror in the Northern Democratic Republic of Congo, South Sudan and Central African Republic. Although indicted by the ICC for war crimes and crimes against humanity, Kony and his high-level commanders remain at large.

Ending conflict and achieving durable peace in Northern Uganda presents a challenge. The Government of Uganda continues to successively, and sometimes simultaneously, pursue military action, peace negotiations, and amnesty for the rebels. The abduction of children and youth into the LRA was a brutal feature of the conflict in Uganda. The United Nations estimates that during the prolonged civil war, in total, over 25,000 children were forced to enrol as soldiers, with the girls being forced into sexual slavery (Pham, Vinck & Stover, 2007). An estimated 10,000 girls became forced child mothers due to abduction by the LRA between 1988 and 2004. Another 88,000 girls, who were not abducted, also became child mothers due to conditions in the internally displaced persons camps contributing to the risk of rape (Akelo, 2013).

Until early 2007, community and international humanitarian organisations in Northern Uganda were operating 12 reception centres for LRA abductees, who were either captured in battle or who had managed to flee their captors (Human Rights Watch, 2005; Derluy, Broekaert, Schuyten & De Temmermann, 2004). On arrival, former abductees were provided with medical examination and treatment, as appropriate. Those suffering from war wounds were sent to hospitals in Gulu and Kampala. Most returnees stayed at the centres for two to six weeks and participated in a range of activities, including counselling. However, the violence in LRA-affected territories traumatised all members of the communities from which the victims had been abducted, not only the abductees.

It is in this context of extremely high trauma and resource limitations that the TRUST programme was implemented with the aim of reducing levels of trauma to enhance the impact of the social protection offered to these women, as they reintegrate back into their communities. Participating women were already in receipt of social protection assistance to address poverty, in the form of material help and/or counselling (this counselling was provided by churches and non-governmental organisation [NGOs] independently of TRUST). The overall research question in this study was: Does support to trauma relief positively affect the relationship between social protection and socio-economic resilience? The expectation was that trauma had a mediating effect on reducing socio-economic resilience, explained by the depressing effect of trauma on the processing of information.

7.2 Method

7.2.1 Research design

Using a natural research design, the TRUST programme was implemented in four groups based on the combination of other social support they received. There was also a control group consisting of women who did not receive any social protection/support package. The groups were:

- Cash/in-kind only and TRUST
- Counselling and TRUST
- Cash/in-kind, counselling and TRUST
- Only TRUST
- Cash/in-kind only and no TRUST
- Counselling only and no TRUST
- Both cash/in-kind and counselling, no TRUST
- No programme (control group)

This design allowed us to study the direct (main) effect of the TRUST programme, as well as investigate the interactions between the different types of programmes (cash/in-kind, counselling) and the TRUST programme.

7.2.2 Participants

A total of 475 women took part in the project, of which 356 took part in the part of the research under report here. The participants were selected by local leaders who identified them based on their observed needs, indicating that they could benefit from trauma support to enable them to make best use of the social protection on offer. To this end participants were purposively assigned to the trauma support programme developed by the researchers in collaboration with local authorities, who identified communities where there were high levels of trauma and low socio-economic resilience. Arrangements were made for mental health support to participants, referred – when needed, by the researchers.

Participants in this part of the research came from the following districts in Northern Uganda: Amuria (18.0%), Lira (29.8%), Katakwi (20.5%) and Kitgum (31.7%). Table 7.1 outlines the participants and their respective region.

Table 7.1. Participants and their region of residence

District	Number of participants
Amuria	64
Lira	107
Katakwi	73
Kitgum	113

7.2.3 Research instruments

The study used a number of tools specifically designed for the research (SER) as well as a standardised psychometric test (IES-R). These are fully described in Chapter 3. Here I give a brief recap of the tools for ease of reference. In addition to questionnaires, structured interviews and observations were also used (see Appendix 5 for details) to elaborate on the experiences of participants.

7.2.3.1 Impact of Events Scale-Revised

The IES-R consists of three subscales: intrusion (8 items), avoidance (8 items) and hyperarousal (6 items). The scale values of the items range from 0 to 4 (0 = not at all; 1 = a little bit; 2 = moderately; 3 = quite a bit; 4 = extremely). For each subscale, a mean is calculated to obtain an index of the scale. The total score of the scale is calculated by summing the three subscales (minimum 0, maximum 12).

7.2.3.2 Social and Economic Resilience tool

The SER tool was developed specifically for this research and consists of Likert scales on six areas: social embeddedness (5 items), capability (6 items), income (13 items), empowerment (12 items), trust in the system (2 items), and worriedness (10 items). The scale values of the items ranges from 1 to 5 (1 = strongly disagree; 2 = disagree; 3 = neutral; 4 = agree; 5 = strongly agree). Most statements are stated positively (high score indicates a positive mindset), however, for the subscale worry a high score indicates more worry (a negative mindset).

7.2.3.3 Interviews and observations

Interviews were conducted as part of a field study for this research and observations were made about social interactions and physical appearance during the field study (see Appendix 5 for topic list and observation format). The interviews comprised both in-depth individual interviews with 29 women and focus group discussions in the following sites: Barlonyo (two sites), Ogur, Amida and Usuk (one site in each). The transcripts of each individual interview and group discussion were analysed under three headings that related to the original traumatic experience, their impression and experiences of the intervention, and any changes in day-to-day life since the intervention.

7.3 Results: Effects of TRUST on the reduction of trauma

A full description of the results with an analysis of the impact of TRUST on social protection is available in the extensive report on the project (Van Reisen *et al.*, 2018b). Here we focus on the effect of the TRUST programme on trauma as an indication of the effectiveness of the programme for the purpose it was designed for. In addition to the statistical analysis, the results of semi-structured interviews and focus groups are also considered.

In reading the statistical analyses it should be noted that the time between finishing the TRUST programme and the measurement was not very long (under six weeks). This may be a too short a time for the effects to be fully observable, based on the length of time that trauma counselling usually takes to be effective (several months depending on the approach used and responsiveness). TRUST is a self-help therapy and the focus during implementation of the programme was on training the participants on the techniques and their sequencing; hence, the effect of the programme may not follow the time line of the research.

7.3.1 Quantitative results

In order to explore the effects of TRUST, we first analysed the total mean score of the IES-R. Table 7.2 gives the key statistics of the total mean IES-R score for each group of participants, showing that for all groups the post-test average score for post-traumatic stress is about 7 (IES-R-total: sum of the three subscales; minimum 0, maximum 12; higher score means more trauma). This is quite similar to the stress level reported in the pre-test setting, where the 357 participants' results were tested using the IES-R pre-intervention and post-intervention. This indicates that the change in level of trauma as a result of the provision of TRUST to groups in the social protection programme was not statistically significant, based on the IES-R data collected. However, as shown in Van Reisen *et al.* (2018b), there was significant effect on some SER scales; specifically, there was significant effect on 'social embeddedness'.

Table 7.2. IES-R: Total mean IER-S score for each group of respondents

	N	Average	Standard deviation	Skewness	Kurtosis
Cash/in-kind only and TRUST	25	7.03	2.20	-0.53	-0.27
Counselling and TRUST	56	7.81	1.66	-0.78	0.32
Cash/in-kind, counselling and TRUST	85	7.67	1.74	-0.87	0.93
Only TRUST	21	7.95	1.41	-1.43	1.61
Cash/in-kind only and no TRUST	37	6.76	2.37	-0.53	-0.61
Counselling only and no TRUST	37	7.90	1.79	-1.35	2.15
Both cash/in-kind and counselling, no TRUST	37	7.00	2.09	-1.31	0.84
No programme (control group)	58	7.68	1.98	-1.24	1.49
Total	356				

173

In addition to the question raised regarding timing, there might be issues about the way the IES-R was administered by research assistants or interpreted by participants. The IES-R is reliant on precise instruction being given to the participants completing the test. Although no special training is required to administer the questionnaire, the wording of the questions has to be precise. The respondent is asked to report the degree of distresses experienced for each item in the past 7 to 10 days; this may have not been strictly adhered to when local researchers were administering such a sensitive instrument to such a large cohort, which could have resulted in people reporting distress levels for periods that included pre-test, spanning many years. As mentioned above, selection was done by local authorities who prioritised women based on their need for support, this could have resulted in more needy women being offered the highest package of services, which included TRUST, and, hence, scoring high for traumatic stress and still reporting it in the post-test period. To avoid the difficulties arising from the sensitivity of IES-R in the Ethiopian research, the main researcher completed all the questionnaires and work was also undertaken to develop a shorter version (as detailed in Chapter 3).

In addition to the quantitative data, a series of interviews and focus group discussions were carried out by the researcher to give a fuller insight into the impact of the TRUST programme. Interestingly, the narratives here fully covered the women's experiences of living with trauma, their impressions of the TRUST programme and reductions in symptoms of PTS. These were conducted through the interpretation of local research assistants. The result of these interviews and focus group discussions (qualitative results) are outlined in section 7.3.2.

7.3.2 Qualitative results

This section presents the results of the qualitative data, regarding traumatic stress and day-to-day life experiences, based on interviews and focus group discussions illustrating the experiences of women who received TRUST in recognition of their rather high trauma levels and low socio-economic resilience (see Appendix 5 for topic list and observation format). The local leaders who selected the women for participation expressed the belief that behaviours associated with trauma were a common occurrence in their communities. Many people in their communities were known to behave in ways that required counselling. However, most of these communities lacked facilities where traumatised people could seek assistance. The local leaders identified the war as the main cause of trauma among members of their community, although they acknowledged that there were also other events that could have a similar impact, such as domestic violence.

Below is a report of the in-depth individual interviews and focus group discussions conducted in January 2017. The transcripts of each interview and focus group discussion were analysed under three main headings, which were used as a general guide when interviewing the women (the descriptions were used to guide the interviews, but the titles came from the interview data collected during the interview):

- *When the rebels came: experiences of traumatic events*
  - Traumatic experiences faced by the women, their families and communities as a result of the many years of conflict in the region
  - Types of loss and suffering experienced by the women
- *The rebels will come back: experiences of living with severe symptoms of trauma*
  - Impacts of the traumatic stress suffered by the women, their families and communities after the rebels left or they escaped from them, including the many years of uncertainty in the IDP camps
  - Symptoms of traumatic stress described during the interviews
- *The rebels are not coming back: experiences of healing*
  - Impact of the trauma support (training) on individual stress levels
  - Examples of healing within the family
  - Examples of wider community healing

7.3.2.1 When the rebels came: Prevalence of traumatic experiences

The quotes and comments below detail the experiences of trauma symptoms experienced by participants before they received TRUST.

> *I remember the first time the rebels came, there were no camps then, so we had to hide in the bushes, it was very scary. The second time they came we had camps, so we ran there. I was 18 years old and was married. I lost my mother-in-law who is one of the people buried in these grounds here.* (07/24/01/B[3] age 29)

The women described a wide range of extremely traumatic events and a lot of loss and devastation, associated with not just the immediate impact of the conflict, but the extremely stressful life they are leading as a result of the devastation and its aftermath.

About half of the women described the war years and particular incidents, while the remainder either just mentioned it in passing or not at all; this was perhaps PTSD induced avoidance of traumatic memories. The most dominant theme of these descriptions is loss. Loss of loved ones, loss of health and wellbeing, loss of a home and loss of livelihood. There was not a single participant who did not report loss and who was not suffering from the devastating consequences of that loss.

Some lost their parents at an early age and, as a result, have lived with no one taking care of them and continue to feel the loss and abandonment. A respondent from Barlonyo said:

> *I have four children aged ten, eight, four and one; after so much trouble with my husband I left him and came back to this village. I lost my parents and have no one to take care of me or the children.* (03/24/01/B, age 28)

---

[3] These codes were used to identify the timing of the interview as well as the site

A participant from Usuk described her multiple loss as follows:

In 1986 the rebels attacked our home they beat and killed people, they tied my father up and raped my mother, and took me and my siblings with them, they also took three sacks of grain and destroyed everything we had. (22/27/01/U, age not stated)

During the focus group discussion in Amida, a woman said:

I lost my mother when I was very young. She was abducted, raped and then killed and ever since everything has been difficult for me. Every time I remember her I get a terrible headache and I feel like killing myself too. I wished I was dead. (16/26/01/A, age 35)

There were many who spoke about the loss of children, siblings, and husbands. Each of these losses represents not only the loss of a loved one, but also the loss of status in the community, as well as protection, compounding the damage. A respondent reported becoming feverish and collapsing every time she remembered the dead.

…my husband told me not to think about the dead and about dying all the time, as he believed that if you think about the dead a lot, they draw you to them and that was why I was having the fever and collapsing, I just couldn't help but think about all that, all the time. (16/26/01/A, age not stated)

A woman, described the loss of her children and the implications of that as follows:

I had three boys, I lost two during the war and their father too. My one remaining son sustained some injuries and so I am responsible for looking after the grandchildren now. (08/24/01/B, age 50)

177

An elderly mother from Barlonyo described the enormity of the death of her husband, who had been ill and bedridden since the end of the war:

My husband died and left me 20 children, biological and adopted. All are male except one. My husband was ill and bedridden for a long time and then he died, and I used to worry about the fact that I had no one to help me after his death. I used to also think a lot about the war years and all the pain. (04/24/01/B, age 61)

Others continued to mourn entire generations of their family. The following quote is from an 18-year-old mother:

I used to constantly think about the death of the elders and it was such an evil thought that disturbed me. It caused me pain in the chest. I used to fight people a lot when I have those thoughts and I used to cry remembering my mum, my father and my grandparents. (02/24/01/B, age 18)

The other major and devastative loss was the loss of a place, a home and the status associated with a home, and a piece of land that one can cultivate. This was described both in terms of having to run away from the chaos and then having to go into the IDP camps, which were described as harsh due to the constant problem of security, as well as lack of basic provisions.

In Ogur, a woman described her life between 2001 and 2006 as follows:

From 2001 to 2006 we lived a very hard life. In 2001 our home was attacked, we ran away and hid in the bushes. We were very scared, we came back later but we were still scared and had to sleep in the bush. On the 18th of November 2002 we went to camp after my mother-in-law was shot and killed we were in that crowded and dirty camp until 2006. And there the children saw many things they shouldn't have seen. (09/25/01/O, age 46)

Another woman in Ogur said:

Even at the camp many people died. My brothers were caught and were taken with them [the rebels]. I was with my parents, but then my father was killed by the rebels. A lot of were killed and it is difficult not to think about that. (12/25/01/O, age 21)

In Amida, a respondent puts her experiences in the camp in the context of a long history of loss and devastation going back to 1979:

Actually, our troubles go back to 1979 at least, during Idi Amin's time; we have been experiencing problems ever since. We have had no experience of peace… not much. During [President] Museveni's years it was insurgence and LRA. All we know is cattle raids, abductions of children. Our ears were cut off, our people were killed and then we had to go to the camp. We lost everything.

The camp in many ways was worse than the insurgency. Our movements were restricted and so we were confined. We had meagre food supply, there was a lot of illnesses, children didn't go to school. The HIV epidemic also took hold then, spreading very fast with more devastation. In 2008 we moved from the main camp to a satellite camp which was a bit better, we had a bit of freedom there; three years later we moved back home. (14/26/01/A, age 50)

Loss of livelihood was another type of loss that was a constant theme across the sites. This was particularly devastative for the women, who were forced to return home to their families empty handed, when the cattle that were their dowry was raided and looted. In Usuk many families suffered double devastation, as they were not just affected by the rebels, but also by the *Karamoja* warrior nomads who raided their cattle and looted during the chaos of the conflict.

A respondent in Usuk talked about what happened to her at a very young age:

In 1980 the Karamoja came and raided our house and they killed my father, I was still a little girl, but was taken by them and raped, many people were raped. On the way we ran away from them and some good people helped us and took us to the mission and we got a lot of help there. Things were a bit better for a while, I grew up and got married ,but then the rebels came there too... (21/27/01/U, age not stated)

Similarly, another woman from Usuk narrated the double devastation as follows:

Karamojas and rebels both affected my life. Karamojas took all our cattle including those that were my dowry and so my husband sent me back home and my parents sent me back to him. Me and my five children were in limbo, but then my husband died, and I went back to my family with three children, but they didn't accept me and refused to give me any land. (23/27/01/U, age not stated)

The looting and material loss affects the women's prospects for the future too. One respondent described it as follows:

When the Karamojas attacked and took all our cows there was nothing left for my schooling (and that of my siblings). They took cows and nuts and chickens and left us nothing at all and they also used us, as servants and we had to do all they asked. School and studying became an impossibility and I was depressed. (25/27/01/U, age not stated)

In addition to all the losses suffered alongside the rest of the community, there were specific gender-based atrocities that many of the women suffered, including rape and abduction for domestic and sex slavery. During the abductions many suffered mutilation and physical injuries, as well as contracting HIV and other sexually transmitted diseases and unwanted pregnancy.

A woman from Barlonyo described her predicament as follows:

In 2003 we were attacked, they were actually inside my house and ordered me out. I tried to run away but they caught me and took me to Ocholi land and they made me carry their loot. On the way I spilled something because I was very tired, and they beat me up so badly and cut my ear. Later I got the opportunity to escape them and came back here.

In 2004 the rebels came back again, and the soldiers also made this their barracks. The soldiers told us to stay indoors and so the rebels burnt our houses. Many people died, I only escaped because I fell on dead bodies and hid there. It is after all this that I discovered that I had contracted HIV. Over the years since then I didn't sleep much, I had dreams and very vivid memories (flashbacks) if I slept; I never could sleep indoors. (09/24/01/B, age 45)

A respondent also from Barlonyo had her stomach cut open as a punishment for dropping things she was carrying for the looting rebels:

The rebels came and attacked people in this side and burnt our houses and only those who were able to run away survived, but even then, we were caught, and I sustained injuries as a result. I was raped too. To date my body is weak all over as a result. When I dropped the luggage they had me carry, they slit my stomach open, I have a great cut across my stomach as a result. (08/24/01/B, age 50)

7.3.2.2 The rebels will come back: Prevalence of traumatic stress

The following quotes detail the experiences of participants living with PTSD.

In December 2006 we came back, and I honoured my pledge to give my life to God upon my return. I prayed a lot and that helps me, but I still had bad dreams and up to now I worry that the rebels will come back; for example, last month they were talking [about] massacres and that made me think about all that bad time we had. (09b/25/01/O, age not stated)

181

These symptoms affected the whole family including children who were not born or were too young to actually remember the events themselves.

The children were worried too, they used to say that the rebels are still out there, and they can come any time. One day my girl dreamt that they had actually come back and came into the house and she started screaming in terror. (10/25/01/O, age 44)

Even many years after the events described above nearly all the women interviewed were suffering from a range of symptoms that indicate PTSD. Table 7.3 lists the range of symptoms described by the women. Descriptions of symptoms were categorised into the known PTSD symptoms as listed in the table.

7.3.2.3 The rebels are not coming back: Impact of trauma intervention

This section details the participants' descriptions, of how their lives have been impacted on following their engagement in TRUST. The main objective of the TRUST intervention was to enable participants to learn strategies to help them overcome the symptoms of traumatic stress affecting their day-to-day functioning. Achieving this, has had positive effects on the participants' physical and psychological wellbeing, their relationships with their families, their role within the wider community, and their ability to function in the community. It has enabled them to look forward, rather than back in fear of the rebels coming back. A participant from Balornyo described it as follows:

Everyone sees the difference it has made to all of us. We work together and are happier working together. Before I used to think back and feel that rebels would come back, but now we look forward to life. We even have a dance group and have had the opportunity to go to different villages to perform. (09/24/01/B, age 45)

182

As mentioned above, improvements to both physical and psychological wellbeing were reported as a result of the intervention. A woman from Barlonyo shared:

The breathing exercises help a lot, I have been breathing in and out and it helps. Although I have not taken any medication for it, the pain in my chest is now gone. (01/24/01/B, age not stated)

Several women reported healthy weight gain. This is a crucial indicator, particularly for those who are HIV positive, as it indicates that their physical health is in better shape following the mental health support they received.

I showed my children and they like it, they can see I am less stressed and have put on weight too, because I am not too worried about things like before. I used to tell them about the training even during the training but now they can see it both in the way I am and how I look too. (09/25/01/O, age 46)

I am more positive about things now, I have a safe place under a tree and if things get really bad I take myself there and calm myself down. I am healthier, and my weight is also healthy. I have gained a lot of weight. (15/26/01/A, age 26)

The relief from stress related chest pain and the attainment of a healthy weight actually led one woman from Usuk to conclude that the intervention probably saved her life:

I was so thin at the time, I would say malnourished. I was in a lot of pain too. All that has changed; I have since put on weight and also my chest pain is gone. The training probably saved my life. (24/27/01/, age not stated)

Interestingly, several participants used the Subjective Unit of Distress (SUD), a 0 to 10 scale of emotional disturbance, to report back on levels of anxiety and stress – a technique that was taught during the training.

During the training my SUD was 10, maybe even more; now I feel it is 1 and maybe 2 sometimes, but not more. I am very grateful for the training, it saved me from a lot of difficulties and pain. (07/24/01/B, age 29)

When we were training at the start my SUD was 10 and more if I could do more, and then gradually it became 8 and then 5 and now there are days when I can say it is 1 or even 0. (14/26/01/A, age 50)

During the training my SUD became 6 first and then 3. (20/26/01/A, age 26)

Another recurring theme was the reduction in quarrelling and violent outbursts:

The training helped; now when I am at home and these frightening things happen I know how to handle them. Even with other things happen, like when someone quarrels, I breath in and out properly before responding. When I am agitated I go to my safe calm place and I feel free there. (10/25/01/O, age 44)

One day someone was quarrelling, and I got really annoyed I just walk back indoors and got myself into my quiet calm place and did my breathing there and I felt relieved. (10/25/01/O, age 44)

I live with my mother in-law and she sees the difference, I don't quarrel with her much anymore. We have a better relationship now. My husband as well, we have started sharing everything with each other. (01/24/01/B, age not stated)

My husband saw how different I am, I can sit calmly and talk about things and we don't quarrel a lot like before, he says this training has been good for me. (12/25/01/O, age 21)
I don't get into many quarrels around the village anymore as I am able to handle things better. (15/26/01/A, age not stated)

In many cases, this has led to a calmer family atmosphere and improved relationships with children, husbands and in-laws, as described in the following:

As a result of this training my family is calmer and is a role model for the whole community. Before, we used to have a lot of trouble and quarrels and even violence at home, now we get invited to community gatherings to share our experiences and even at church. Even my appearance has changed, I have put on weight and wash more and look after myself better. The children are proud of this and I am happy. (14/26/01/A, age 50)

My husband even came and told the group leaders how things are a lot better now and how the house is at peace now. The children are a lot happier too, even if it meant that when I was at the training I was away from them. (16/26/01/A, age 35)

I have been living with my current husband for many years, but we never married, but after the training he saw how I had changed and how happy we all were and wanted to make that permanent and so he suggested we get married in a church. I agreed and we got married. Everyone from my training group came to support me and we were happy to have them around. (09/24/01/B, age 45)

I don't get frustrated a lot like before and my daughters see this too; they have learnt the breathing and safe calm place. (15/26/01/A, age not stated)

The improvements in wellbeing and family relationships have also had a positive impact on members of the wider community, who have noticed the changes and ask to be trained too, giving the women opportunities to train others.

It [the training] makes my brain think about other things, other than the war and death of my family. The rest of the family see that I don't cry all the time and so do our neighbours and everyone else too. We all feel like we can now think about ourselves and not just about the war. (08/24/01/B, age 50)

185

Participants understand that the problems are shared across the community and want to have an input into the healing of the whole community and use every opportunity to share their new skills with their neighbours.

I tell my neighbours all about it and teach them the exercises; they see how it helps us with many bad memories. My grandfather was killed in the war and also we had to run away a lot. It is not easy, being shot at is all I can remember clearly. These were the things that made living very difficult. (13/25/01/O, age 28)

People ask me why I smile a lot and also how I managed to change myself like this. They notice that I wash and look after myself better these days. (15/26/01/A, age not stated)

I have taught the breathing and knee tapping to my family and they say it works too. (01/24/01/B, age not stated)

The women are so pleased with the impact of the training for themselves, their families and communities, that they are now looking for ways to expand its impact and are also developing ways of sustaining it.

We have developed like a cooperative and we put money together and buy things and then we sell that. We discuss and agree on what we invest in and then sell. (09/24/01/B, age 45)

We have only got about 20 women trained and we do our best to support each other and others too, but many people ask us for help and we try, but it would have been good if there were more of us trained, as the community is big and has many people that need this training. (14/26/01/A, age 50)

Mama Anna [group leader] is working on making the group permanent, as the women seem to be getting a lot of support from each other and have also been supporting others. (20/26/01/A, age 26)

The interviews and focus group discussions were clear on the presence of a range of PTSD symptoms that affected participants in their daily lives, including their physical health and relationships. As Table 7.3 indicates, the symptoms reported are consistent with the Diagnostic and Statistical Manual of Mental Disorders (DSM) criteria for PTSD. The participants were also consistent in their descriptions of the implications of the symptoms. Finally, their description of their current experiences reflects what would be expected after successfully processing trauma, including reduced symptoms associated with low mood, re-experiencing and numbing, as well as a change in physical symptoms such as weight loss and weakness. Weight gain and improvements in physical appearance (self-care) were also visible among participants whom the researcher was familiar with, when observed during the pre-test and post-test visits.

Table 7.3. Symptoms described by the women interviewed about their pre-intervention experiences of trauma

PTSD symptoms	Description
Hyperarousal	
Physical reactions	When anxious, my heart beats fast. (12/25/01/O, 21, from Ogur)
Reduced tolerance to noise	When I hear a loud noise that sounds like gun shots I go into a panic. (11/25/01/O, 48, from Ogur)
Panic attacks and depression	I also had a lot of anxiety and used to be easily frightened, had nightmares. Oftentimes I felt like I was back in the war and used to get really frightened. (14/26/01/A, 50, from Amida)
Difficulty falling or staying asleep	I didn't sleep much, I had dreams and very vivid memories (flashbacks), if I slept, I could never sleep indoors. (09/24/01/B, 45 from Barlonyo)
Difficulty concentrating	I was forgetful, since the problems we had here my memory wasn't so good. (01/24/01/B from Barlonyo) But even here we were worried, I used to imagine that one day the rebels would come back again

	maybe from Barlonyo. The children were worried sick too, they wanted to study and do good at school, but they were too unsettled. (11/25/01/O, 48, from Ogur)
Being easily moved to tears	I cried a lot, I cried all the time. (17/26/01/A, 45, from Amida)
Anger/aggressive behaviour	I was very short tempered and quarrelled a lot with people. (17/26/01/A, 45, from Amida)
Tensing of muscles	I was so angry and I would feel my muscles tense. (21/27/01/U, from Usuk)
Avoidance	
Frequent periods of withdrawal	I have a lot of worries and many problems that make me sad. (03/24/01/B, 28, from Barlonyo) Since long ago, I used to always get preoccupied with thoughts of the war and sometimes dream about being back there and dream about all the people who died there. (12/25/01/O, 21, from Ogur)
Inability to remember important aspects of the experience	My memory isn't good, as I tend to forget things since the war and because of all my injuries. (08/24/01/B, 50, from Barlonyo)
Intrusion	
Flashbacks	I could see blood everywhere, the wells, and when it got too much I used to run through the village sometimes screaming. (09/24/01/B, 45, from Barlonyo) When I dropped the luggage they had me carry they slit my stomach open. I have a great cut across my stomach as a result. (08/24/01/B, 50, from Barlonyo) Sometimes I hear trucks running inside my head. I can hear things. I think about my husband and sons all the time. (08/24/01/B, 50, from Barlonyo) I felt like someone was calling my name even when there was no one. (17/26/01/A, 45, from Amida)

	Every time I am stressed I see the mutilated body of my father. (23/27/01/U, 22, from Usuk)
Nightmares	I used to also think a lot about the war years and all the pain. Running from place to place, losing a lot of people and also losing your place and home. I used to have bad dreams and sometimes flashbacks, it was frightening. (04/24/01/B, 61, from Barlonyo) After we came back, I used to have nightmares about burning homes and being chased. I used to be worried that the rebels are coming back and fear a lot (10/25/01/O, 44, from Ogur)
Feelings of intense distress when reminded of trauma	I used to constantly think about the death of the elders and it was such an evil thought that disturbed me. (04/24/01/B,18, from Barlonyo) I used to also always think about how I have lost everyone and was only left with my husband and our children. That used to put me into this deep mood that would stay with me all day. (04/24/01/B, 35, from Barlonyo)
Other symptoms	
Feeling suicidal	I was almost becoming a mad woman. I lost my mother when I was very young she was abducted, raped and then killed and ever since everything has been difficult for me. Every time I remember her I get a terrible headache and I feel like killing myself too. I wished I was dead. (16/26/01/A. 35, from Amida) My life had a lot of stress and stress took over my life. I often thought about killing myself, but worried about how much worse it would be for the children if I did that. (24/27/01/U, from Usuk)
Exhaustion	We were caught, and I sustained injuries as a result. I was raped too. To date my body is weak all over as a result. (08/24/01/B 50, from Barlonyo)

Physical aches and pain	I used to have vivid dreams about those times and used to also get a very sharp pain in my chest. (07/24/01/B, 29 from Barlonyo) I had a constant headache. (17/26/01/A, 45, from Amida)

Through their experiences of trauma and living with the devastating implications, as well as their experiences of finding healing, the women of Northern Uganda demonstrated that TRUST has been effective in enabling women to process traumatic stress from the atrocities experienced by women in Uganda.

7.4 Conclusion

The main findings regarding the effectiveness of the programme in lowering trauma, according to the data collected using the IES-R, is that while TRUST had no effect on the reported trauma, as measured by the IES-R six weeks after implementation, the qualitative data gathered from in-depth interviews and focus group discussions indicate that post-traumatic stress symptoms had reduced with positive implications for the day-to-day functioning and relationships of participants. This is encouraging, given the level of trauma that was identified in participants for them to be selected for the programme in the first place.

Ideally the statistical indication (IES-R scores) would have been strong enough to fully conclude that the intervention was effective in addressing trauma, as measured by the tools selected for the process. However, contrary to our expectations, the impact of the intervention was not reflected in the IES-R results (Van Reisen *et al.*, 2018b). As mentioned previously, the length of time between the completion of the programme and potential discrepancies in the data collection, given the sensitivity of the instrument used, may have impacted on the reporting of symptoms. In hindsight, given the very specific way IES-R is supposed to be administered, although no specialist training is required to use the scale, it would have been better to extensively brief and fully train research assistants on the effective gathering of data using the IES-R.

Discussions among the members of the project team also hypothesised that this might be a consequence of raised awareness of the impact of trauma and the associated symptoms. For example, people who had never previously considered their lack of sleep or lack of concentration as trauma related became more aware of this and were, therefore, reporting it more. This holds some veracity, as all other indicators, including the social and economic measures on the SER (taken for the wider project, but not included in this particular research), indicate improvements in post-intervention resilience (Van Reisen et al., 2018b; Van Reisen et al., 2019).

Although the statistical analysis was not conclusive about the effectiveness of TRUST on levels of traumatic stress (as measured by IES-R), we took the results of the qualitative data, as well as indications of improvement in resilience (as measured by the SER tool) as being enough of an indication of the effectiveness of TRUST to continue with further development of the programme, adapting it for use via ICT and making the IES-R shorter (hence, the development of IES-S), as well as the careful gathering of data by a researcher familiar with the IES-R ad IES-S. The results of that study will be discussed in Chapter 8.

"Selam do you remember me?", a woman asked me excitedly following one of the focus group meetings under yet another tree somewhere in Northern Uganda. I tried to think back to my previous visit when I had first met some of the women. I couldn't remember her (which was not unusual, as I have a terrible memory for faces). I could not be sure, but I thought her voice was familiar, and then she smiled, and I recognised her smile. She was one of the women who had contracted HIV as a result of the rape she suffered during her abduction by the LRA. She was so thin the last time I saw her, and now, here she was, and she had visibly gained weight. I asked what happened and she enthusiastically told me how she had been doing her butterfly hugs and how she especially liked the breathing techniques. She told me about her 'safe calm place' too. My mind went back to when I was doing touch-stone memories with her, how she cried relating her original trauma, not only of the rape as an abductee, but being hungry all the time as a shepherd girl long before she was abducted. It was tough, but something worked. I was encouraged, I was grateful and I looked forward to the next step in the journey.

Chapter 8

The effectiveness of delivering TRUST using ICT among Eritrean refugees in Ethiopia

I was back in the refugee camps in Ethiopia and I was actually going to stay in the camps and live among the refugees for longer than I have ever done. Needless to say, I was apprehensive. I was putting the programme on autopilot, uploading it onto all sorts of mobile phones and it felt surreal. What if it doesn't work? It would be three years of work down the drain, but, more crucially, the therapist in me was worried that I would have failed to deliver therapy to the neediest people I had ever come across. At this point I felt I needed a therapist myself, and then I remembered that that was the whole point! There were no therapists, and so my participants and I were in the same boat in that respect. Of course, my confidence crisis was no comparison to the extremely high levels of post-traumatic stress they were suffering from.

This chapter answers the fifth research question: Q.5. Will a short self-help trauma intervention delivered using ICT have an impact on reducing PTS and enhancing resilience in the high trauma and low resource contexts of young Eritrean refugees? And, what are the key elements of such a short self-help trauma intervention in a high trauma/low resource context for it to impact on social economic resilience? As mentioned in previous chapters, the programme was developed with the understanding of the individual and collective impacts of trauma, as well as the challenges of delivering trauma support in contexts where resources are severely limited.

8.1 Introduction: Eritrean refugees in Tigray

This chapter focuses on a study carried out in the summer of 2017 among Eritrean refugees in two refugee camps in the Tigray region of northern Ethiopia. Before delving into the research and its findings, a brief overview is given of the mobility of Eritrean refugees. The country's recent history, as it relates to the situation of refugees, was provided in Chapter 1 and the presence and severity of

PTSD among members of the Eritrean refugee communities was discussed in Chapter 4.

Following the official independence of Eritrea from Ethiopia in 1993, Eritrean refugees have been coming to Ethiopia, fleeing persecution and, increasingly, the open-ended national service in their country. In Ethiopia, they mainly live in four refugee camps in the Tigray region (although there is an increasing number of people who use the off-camp policy and live elsewhere in the country, provided they have the means to do so). Shimelba, the oldest camp, which opened in 2004, and Hitsats, the newest camp, which opened in 2013, are the camps included in this study.

UNHCR's Country Refugee Response Plan for 2018 states that, since 2014, Ethiopia has received an average of 2,300 refugees per month. In 2017, the country hosted 164,668 Eritrean refugees (UNHCR, 2018). According to the plan, the main challenge in providing assistance to these refugees is the high number of people who leave the camps to pursue onward movement. In 2016, up to 80% of newly arrived refugees, including up to 300 unaccompanied children per month, left the camps within the first 12 months of arrival. This extraordinary rate of mobility was also mentioned in earlier reports: in 2014 it was found that out of 382 Eritreans surveyed, 84% identified 'moving to another country' as their plan for the future (Samuel Hall Consulting, 2014). Similarly, an Amnesty International survey conducted in 2015 found that two thirds of Eritrean refugees in Ethiopia were pursuing secondary movement (Amnesty International, 2015). Many of these people would be travelling via irregular means, with the substantive majority crossing the Sahara and the Mediterranean Sea to reach Europe (UNHCR, 2017).

This high rate of mobility is the main difference between the Northern Ugandan population that participated in previous trials of TRUST (see Chapter 7) and the participants of the study under discussion here. This mobility necessitates the use of ICT to address the challenges of delivering effective trauma support. As we saw in Chapter 5, social media and smartphones are technological developments that the refugees have invested in financially, as well as in terms of trust and use, for much more than personal

193

communication. Developing an App to deliver TRUST was, therefore, considered a practical next step in this study. The App 24COMS, which is a commercial App geared towards delivering the kind of services we were aiming at, was used.

However, there are other challenges that come with high mobility and lack of community stability. Unlike in Uganda, in the refugee camps in Tigray community-wide ownership of the intervention and, consequently, community-wide healing was not straightforward. This was most apparent in relation to community-based support to maintain motivation to complete the programme, even when trauma processing becomes hard. A lot of thinking went into replicating the functions virtually, by encouraging participants to use social media to make their friends and family aware of their involvement in the intervention; however, this could not always be guaranteed due to difficulties with Internet connectivity, limiting the support that participants could access.

In addition to general effectiveness, we also wanted to understand if the various components of TRUST could be provided separately to the same effect. For instance, we were keen to see if the psycho-education (understanding trauma) component could be delivered as a stand-alone intervention with the same effect of lowering trauma. This was done by splitting our participants into two groups and giving half of them access to two videos containing only the psycho-education element of the programme and the other half full access to all videos (as will be described below).

8.2 The development and implementation of the 24COMS App

The 24COMS App, also described in Chapter 6, is a communication platform that enables secure and efficient communication through mobile devices, with 100% data ownership and care for privacy. Services offered through the App can be deployed with ease and flexibility including chatting, posts, news feeds, newsletters, brochures, location based services, and track and trace, among other things. An administrator from a web-based control centre manages all these solutions and applications.

A special page on the App was developed with a view to delivering the TRUST programme for use by mobile communities. The page has the facility to provide access to the seven videos that were developed to give six sessions of support. Two of the videos provide education on the impact of trauma and five give instructions and demonstrations on techniques to enable victims of trauma to take control of distressing emotions in their day-to-day life and their relationship and communication with members of their family and community.

Videos were uploaded onto Vimeo, a video-sharing site, and were individually password locked for controlled access. The release of video links and passwords was coordinated by the researcher, in liaison with research assistants. The first two were released after participants were briefed and had signed a consent form to take part in the research. Subsequent videos were released a few days after completion of each previous video (when participants sent a message indicating completion). A few days gap was given to enable participants to process the information, practise the skills and complete the associated tasks. In addition, users were able to comment on each video and send messages to the administrators of the App.

All content, including videos and instructions, were in Tigrigna, enabling users to receive information in a language accessible to the participants. The whole programme was put in a section of the App called 'Support and Encouragement', a name selected to remove the taboo surrounding mental health, as well as indicate the availability of support and encouragement.

8.3 Method

8.3.1 Overview

The initial plan for the research was as follows: following their selection for participation in the research, participants were given a whole group briefing and then allocated to their respective group (those assigned to receive a shorter intervention of two videos versus those assigned to receive a full intervention of seven videos). This enabled us to test if a shorter version could be as effective as the full version in lowering the level of post-traumatic stress. Having a group that received psych-education was also seen as more ethical than having a control group that received no support.

All participants were then interviewed to complete the short versions of the IES and SER, as well as the ISCS adapted for the research. As detailed in Chapter 3, the IES-S was used to measure the traumatic stress levels, while the SER scale measured social and economic resilience, and the ISCS measured social capital (as an indicator of levels of collective trauma). After completing the scales, everyone uploaded 24COMS and was admitted to the 'Support and Encouragement' page, where they confirmed that they had completed the scales and were prompted and given the relevant access codes for the first two videos.

After accessing the first two videos, participants in the 2-videos group were notified that they would be invited to a community-wide event at which they would be commended for the steps taken in addressing the impacts of their difficult experiences. They were also given information about follow-up data collection and encouraged to share their knowledge and experience on their social media platforms and with the people they live with in the camp. The group assigned to the full version of the intervention (the 7-videos group) were prompted to send a message to ask for the passwords for subsequent videos a minimum of a two days after viewing the videos. After the last video, they too were invited to the community celebration event and given information relating to follow-up data collection, as described above. As with the 2-videos group, this group was asked to share the information about trauma on the first two videos with their community in the camp, as well as virtually, if connectivity allowed; however, we asked them to refrain from sharing the other techniques until the end of the research project, when we promised to make the remaining videos available to everyone who took part. Finally, all participants were invited back for the follow-up data collection, to complete the post-test IES-S, SER-S and ISCS. The collection of the second set of data took place six weeks after completion of the intervention with those who had completed the full version.

As mentioned by Schoenmaeckers (2018), unfortunately, due to connectivity problems, it was impossible to use the App in the way it was envisaged, despite all participants having uploaded the App and being registered on the Support and Encouragement page. As a consequence, videos had to be uploaded to one phone and research assistants then shared it with participants via Bluetooth using an App called SHAREit. As a result, the exchange of support and guidance messages was not live and discussions on the App were not as free flowing as initially envisaged.

SHAREit is a free application used for transferring files between phones by creating hotspot connections between two mobile phones that have the application. Once the connection was created, research assistants were able to select the relevant video and complete transmission. This technology was already in widespread use in the camps, through which photos, videos, contacts and anything else on SD cards was transferred. This was a good enough alternative to complement 24COMS in delivering TRUST through ICT. It was, however, necessary to give the role of ensuring the videos were disseminated appropriately to research assistants on the ground, as opposed to the 24COMS administrator remotely.

The objective of the aforementioned community event, at which participants and their families were commended for the steps taken in addressing trauma, was to address collective trauma by encouraging the acknowledgement of collective pain and collective healing. The event was organised by the camp community and participants invited their friends, family and community leaders. In keeping with the concept of using social media, participants were also encouraged to create posts about their experience and encourage other members of their community to take steps to address trauma too.

8.3.2 Research design

The research was carried out using a natural experimental design. We assigned participants at random to one of the two groups (the 2-videos group and 7-videos group). In this particular case, it would have been both unethical and impractical to have a control group without any treatment (Bonell *et al.*, 2010). It would have been unethical because it would have denied trauma support to groups of highly vulnerable refugees assigned to a control group, even after they had come into contact with, and opened up to (in the process of completing IES, SER and ISCS) people who could have given them support. In addition, it would have been impractical. Given that the intervention relied on videos available on a mobile phone, and we were asking people to share the psycho-education material with others, it would be impossible to stop people from sharing their newfound knowledge with those who were supposed to receive no intervention at all. So, it was felt that it would be easier to convince participants in the 2-videos group that they would be given the remaining videos at the conclusion of the intervention, together with reimbursement of any expenses incurred in accessing the remaining videos.

All participants were given phone cards, which were initially supposed to be in reimbursement of the cost of accessing the videos and downloading the App. However, even though it was not always needed, as videos were mostly accessed via a Bluetooth application, we decided to not remove the promised reimbursement. Instead the phone cards became our way of encouraging participants to persevere with the programme and remain in contact with the research assistants.

In addition to the two intervention groups, we also had groups based on the level of livelihood support received, collaborating with NGO ZOA. In recognition of the fact that some participants received additional livelihood support from NGOs in the camps, we separated their scores from the rest of the group and they were randomly assigned to take part in one of the two interventions to see if this made any difference to their scores. With MSF, operating for mental health support in the camps, it was agreed that refugees who needed mental health support could be referred. In the period three participants were referred. Table 8.1 outlines the distribution of participants across the groups.

Table 8.1. Research participants and conditions (N=103)

Intervention	2-videos group	7-videos group	Total
With livelihood support	14	18	32
Without livelihood support	36	35	71
Total	50	53	103

The experiment is based on a pre-test, post-test (within subjects) design using formal interviews and psychometric tests. Before gaining access to the videos, participants were interviewed by the researcher on a one-on-one basis, which gave participants an opportunity to ask any questions they had and also gave the researchers an opportunity to get to know the participants to enable observations to be made throughout the various stages of the research. Six weeks after completion of the intervention participants were invited for a second interview using the same scales as in the first interview. In addition to one-on-one interviews, participants were also invited to focus group discussions, at which they gave their impressions of their experiences and were able to ask questions. At the focus group discussions, participants also commented on the impressions of the rest of the community about TRUST and their participation in it.

8.3.3 Participants

Participants were selected using purposive sampling approaches, relying on the research team's intimate understanding of the camps and their populations. The research assistants selected from the refugee community were briefed to use their judgement in selecting a sample of participants to comprehensively answer the research questions (Cresswell & Plano Clark, 2011). In addition, as this research sought to explore difficult experiences, there needed to be an assessment of their willingness to participate, as well as their ability to reflect and communicate that reflection, while remaining as near to the theoretical norm of their respective community as possible

(Allen, 1971). The local research assistants were briefed on the selection criteria, as listed in Table 8.2, and then asked to draw up a list of potential participants. The list was then finalised during team-wide discussions. All interactions were in Tigrigna, which is the mother tongue of most participants; there were a few participants for whom Tigrigna was not their most preferred language, but they indicated their proficiency to use it and confirmed that they were comfortable to do so.

Table 8.2. Sampling criteria

Criteria
Having experiences that are typical of fellow members of the community
Living in the geographical locations included in the research
Having a phone with the capacity to view the videos
Being available for the duration of the research
Being able to delve into and reflect on their traumatic experiences and cope with the demands of the research

8.3.4 Research instruments

In this research three constructs were measured by means of a scale during a series of formal interviews:

- Level of trauma, measured by a short version of the IES-R, i.e., the IES-S
- Social and economic resilience, measured by a short and slightly adjusted version of the SER tool used in the Uganda research
- Social capital, used as an indicator of the level of collective trauma, measured by the Internet Social Capital Scale (ISCS)

As described in Chapter 3, the construction and validity of these scales was found to be satisfactory for the purpose of this research.

8.3.5 Ethical considerations

As mentioned above, there was a serious ethical consideration that affected the design of the study, as it was felt to be unethical (on top impractical) to leave respondents who had come into contact with the research team, and would have been interviewed across all instruments, answering questions on traumatic experiences, without any support. As a result, the research design was altered and there was no control group of people with no intervention.

In addition to this, there was concern over the potential re-traumatisation of participants who were asked to reflect on traumatic experiences, without immediate access to a mental health professional. Below is an overview of the steps taken to avoid re-traumatisation:

- The design of the intervention focused on equipping participants, with self-help techniques to deal with reactions to post-traumatic stress, rather than on identifying and addressing specific traumatic experiences. This was done to avoid harm to participants and, in particular, to avoid re-traumatisation as much as possible under the circumstances.
- Videos were sequenced in a way that ensured participants were fully briefed and coached on building their resources for stabilising themselves in the event of distress when dealing with post-traumatic stress. Two exercises in the first video following the information/education session (videos) were designated for this purpose (the safe calm place and breathing exercises). No participant was given access to subsequent videos that dealt with processing traumatic stress without first accessing this session, which equipped participants with the necessary techniques.
- In addition, there were meetings with a health sector NGO in the camps to explain the potential need for the referral of participants who were identified during the initial data-collection (pre-test data collection) as needing more support than was available in the videos. The NGO agreed to receive referrals from the researcher at that point and from research

assistants once the videos were distributed. Subsequently, four people were referred (three in Hitsats and one in Shimelba) and were supported by members of the NGO team during and after the conclusion of the research. The researchers had a meeting with the NGO staff prior to collection of the follow up data to obtain updates and ensure that it was safe to collect data from the people referred to them.

- Research assistants were briefed to ask people their views on the preceding video before giving them access to the next session and, as mentioned above, they were aware of the possibility of referral to the NGO.
- Participants also had the option of sending a message on the App (when connectivity allowed), or as a comment on the video, to ask for assistance (most of the requests received were for technical assistance on downloading and accessing videos).

The final ethical consideration concerned data management. All data was gathered, processed and stored in accordance with Tilburg University's data management protocol. Data was analysed and filed in a password locked system to protect the identity of participants, in accordance with the requirements of the Tilburg University Ethics Committee.

8.4 Results

8.4.1 Hypotheses

In the following sections on the quantitative part of the results we focus on the effectiveness of the TRUST programme as a mobile App in terms of decreasing trauma, increasing social and economic resilience, and increasing social capital (decreasing collective trauma). We also compare the effectiveness of the psycho-education component of TRUST with the full programme. The hypotheses to be tested can be summarised as follows:

Hypothesis 1: In the pre-test we expect a negative correlation between post-traumatic stress (IES-Short) and the components of:

- Social and economic resilience (except worriedness, as high values on that scale indicate more worry)
- Social capital (ISCS, both online and offline social capital)

Hypothesis 2: Applying the full TRUST programme (psycho-education and demonstration of exercises) will produce better results than psycho-education alone:

- Decrease post-traumatic stress
- Increase the scores of social and economic resilience (except worriedness, as high values on that scale indicate more worry)
- Increase the score for Internet social capital (both online and offline)

Hypothesis 3: Livelihood support will:

- Decrease post-traumatic stress
- Increase social and economic resilience (except worriedness, as high values on that scale indicate more worry)
- Increase the components of Internet social capital (both online and offline)

8.4.2 Correlation between PTSD, SER and ISCS in the pre-test

To enable us to see the relationship between PTSD (as measured by IES-S), social and economic resilience (as measured by SER-S) and collective trauma levels (as measured by ISCS), we analysed the correlation between them across the data gathered for each of the scales prior to administering TRUST. Table 8.3 outlines the findings of the analysis and indicates that post-traumatic stress correlates negatively with all components of social and economic resilience, except worriedness (as expected) in the pre-test. The analysis also indicates that PTSD correlates negatively with social capital offline too, but the same was not true for social capital online. However, it should be noted that due to lack of connectivity the kind of online interaction envisaged in the development of the research was missing.

Table 8.3. Correlation between PTSD, SER and ISCS

		Correlation	Significance
SER	Income	-0.280**	< 0.01
	Empowerment	-0.343**	< 0.01
	Worriedness	0.487**	< 0.01
	Trust in the system	-0.192	0.052
	Capability	-0.269**	< 0.01
	Social embeddedness	-0.252*	0.010
ISCS	Offline	-0.187	0.058
	Online	-0.068	0.495

8.4.3 Effectiveness of TRUST

In order to explore the effectiveness of TRUST and compare the two versions, as well as the impact of livelihood support, a repeated measurement MANOVA (multivariate analysis of variance) was carried out. We analysed the difference between the first and second measurements of IES-S, SER-S and social capital (within factor) as related to TRUST and livelihood support (between factors) in a 2x2x2 repeated-measures MANOVA. The results of each of these analyses are outlined below, enabling us to identify the effectiveness of TRUST in reducing (individual and collective) trauma and enhancing perceptions of socio-economic prospects. In addition, the analysis enabled us to identify which version was more effective and the impact of additional livelihood support.

8.4.3.1 Is TRUST effective in reducing traumatic stress?

The results of the IES-S indicate that post-traumatic stress changed between the first and second measurement ($F(1.90) = 64.594$, $p<0.01$). Furthermore, the interaction time*TRUST is significant ($F(1.90) = 91.80$, $p<0.01$). This indicates that TRUST did bring down the levels of trauma, as measured by the IES-S.

Furthermore, inspection of the estimated means indicate that those who received seven videos of TRUST (i.e., the full programme) reported less post-traumatic stress during the second measurement, than their counterparts who received the shorter version with two videos (see Figure 8.1).

Figure 8.1. TRUST programme and post-traumatic stress levels

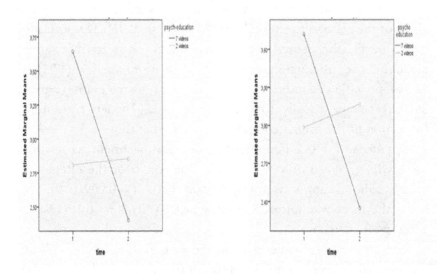

8.4.3.2 Can TRUST increase social and economic resilience as measured on the SER-S?

Similarly to above, 2x2x2 repeated-measure MANOVAs were carried out to see if TRUST had a specific impact on the various elements of the SER-S (subscales).

On the subscale for 'income', the results indicate that the perception of income did not change between the first and second measurement ($F(1.91) = 0.358$, $p<0.551$). So, in general, it can be said that the perception of income did not change during the research. However, the interaction time*TRUST is significant ($F(1.91) = 15.084$, $p<0.01$), which indicates that during the research the perception of income did change for the 2-video and the 7-video conditions. Inspection of the estimated means indicates that those who received seven videos of TRUST reported higher income scores and those who received two videos reported lower income scores during the second measurement. However, the interaction between time*livelihood was not significant (F(1.91) = 1.112, p=0.294), which indicates that livelihood support did not alter the participants' perception of income. Finally, the (three-way) interaction time*TRUST*livelihood is not significant (F(1.91) = 0.842, p=0.361). So, receiving both the livelihood programme as well as the TRUST programme does not result in a multiplier effect.

For the subscale 'empowerment', the results indicate that the main effect of time is significant (F(1.91) = 17.662, p<0.01). This indicates that, overall, the scores for empowerment changed during the research. The interaction time*TRUST is significant (F(1.91) = 42.344, p<0.01) and indicates that during the research empowerment did not change equally for the 2-video and 7-video conditions. Inspection of the estimated means indicates that those who received seven videos of TRUST reported higher empowerment scores than those who received only two videos. The result for the interaction time*livelihood support is not significant (F(1.91) = 0.069, p=0.793), nor is the three-way interaction time*TRUST*livelihood (F(1.91) = 1.921, p=0.169).

Regarding the subscale 'trust in the system', the results indicate that the main effect of time is significant (F (1.91) = 23.480, p<0.01). This indicates that, overall, the scores for trust in the system changed during the research. The interaction time*TRUST is significant (F(1.91) = 38.632, p<0.01), which indicates that during the research the scores for system did not change equally for the 2-video and 7-video conditions. Inspection of the estimated means indicates that those who received seven videos of TRUST reported higher scores for trust in the system. The two-way interaction time*livelihood support and the three-way interaction time*TRUST*livelihood are not significant (F(1.91) = 1.983, p=0.162; F(1.91) = 0.311, p=0.579, respectively).

For the subscale 'worriedness', similar results were found. The results indicate that the main effect of time is significant (F(1.91) = 5.090, p=0.026), indicating that, overall, the scores for worriedness changed during the research. The interaction time*TRUST is significant (F(1.91) = 13.438, p<0.01), which indicates that during the research the scores for worriedness did not change equally for the 2-video and 7-video conditions. Inspection of the estimated means indicates that those who received seven videos of TRUST reported less worry. The two-way interaction time*livelihood support and the three-way interaction time*TRUST*livelihood are not significant $(F(1.91) = 0.368, p=0.545; F(1.91) = 0.644, p=0.424,$ respectively).

Regarding the subscale 'capability', the results indicate that the main effect of time is significant $(F(1.91) = 21.708, p<0.01)$. This indicates that, overall, the scores for capability changed during the research. The interaction time*TRUST is significant $(F(1.91) = 69.565, p<0.01)$, which indicates that during the research the scores for capability did not change equally for the 2-video and 7-video conditions. Inspection of the estimated means indicates that those who received seven videos of TRUST reported higher capability scores. Again, the two-way interaction time*livelihood support and the three-way interaction time*TRUST*livelihood are not significant $(F(1.91) = 0.644, p=0.424; F(1.91) = 0.644, p=0.424,$ respectively).

Regarding the subscale 'social embeddedness', the results indicate that the main effect of time is significant $(F(1.91) = 9.105, p<0.01)$. This indicates that, overall, the scores for social embeddedness changed during the research. The interaction time*TRUST is significant $(F(1.91) = 22.474, p<0.01)$, which indicates that during the research the scores for social embeddedness did not change equally for the 2-video and 7-video conditions. Inspection of the estimated means indicates that those who received seven videos of TRUST reported higher social scores. The two-way interaction time*livelihood support and the three-way interaction time*TRUST*livelihood are not significant $(F(1.91) = 0.808, p=0.371; F(1.91) = 0.091, p=0.763,$ respectively).

It seems that livelihood support was not significant in any of the SER-S subscales, indicating that the presence of livelihood support did not change perceptions of social and economic resilience. Inspection of the estimated means indicates that those who received seven videos of TRUST reported better scores on all components of the social and economic resilience scale after completion of the programme.

Regarding 'income', those who received two videos reported lower income scores during the first and the second measurement (see also Figure 8.2). This finding is surprising as it indicates that even prior to the intervention those who were allocated to the full intervention (7-video group) perceived their income levels to be higher than those who were allocated to the shorter version. In discussions with research assistants, this was thought to be due to the fact that those who were allocated to the full version had more phone cards (as this was initially envisaged to be a reimbursement of the expenses they would incur in accessing five more videos than their counterparts in the shorter intervention group). While the amount was not large, this difference is significant in the context of the refugee camp where access to cash is a big challenge.

On the rest of the SER subscales ('empowerment', 'worriedness', 'trust in the system', 'capability', 'social embeddedness') the full version of TRUST seemed to result in better outcomes for social and economic wellbeing. Figures 8.2 to 8.7 are graphic representations of the impact of TRUST on SER.

Figure 8.2. TRUST programme and 'income' on SER

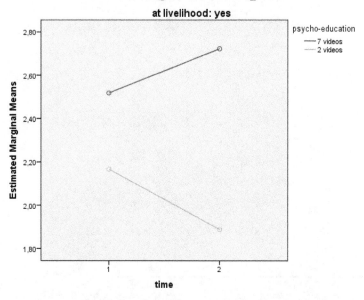

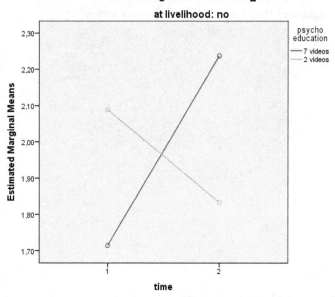

Figure 8.3. TRUST programme and 'empowerment' on SER

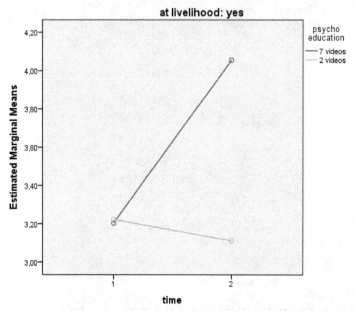

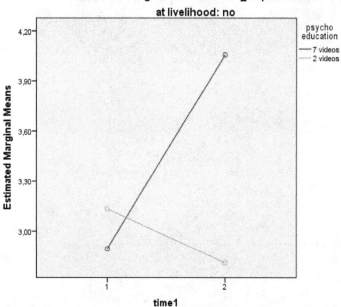

Figure 8.4. TRUST programme and 'worriedness' on SER

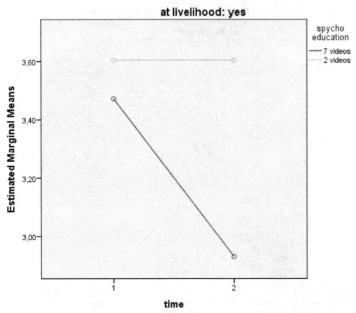

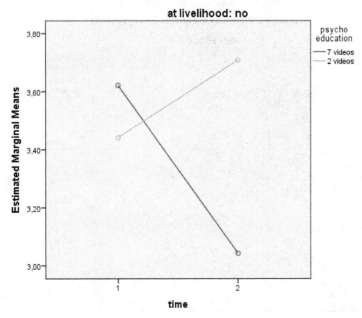

Figure 8.5. TRUST programme and 'trust in the system' on SER

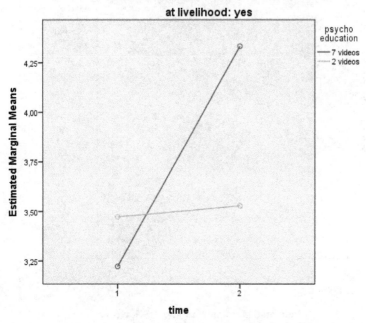

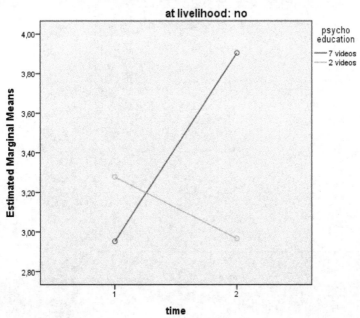

Figure 8.6. TRUST programme and 'capability' on SER

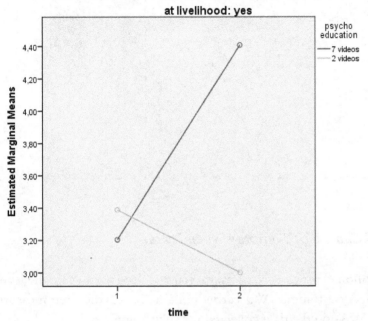

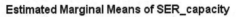

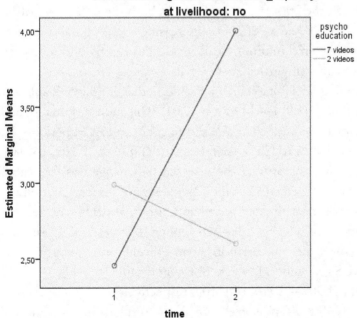

Figure 8.7. TRUST programme and 'social embeddedness' on SER

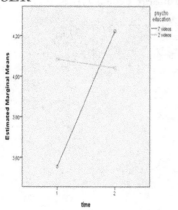
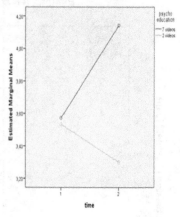

8.4.3.3 Can TRUST improve social capital?

As mentioned previously, social capital was used to indicate the level of collective trauma. We carried out a 2x2x2 repeated-measure MANOVAs on the data collected for social capital offline and social capital online, as the dependent variables. The analysis indicates that the main effect of time was significant in both the online and offline context. TRUST had an effect on increasing social capital (therefore, reducing collective trauma), both inside the camps and across the online networks of participants (see also Figures 8.8 and 8.9).

For online social capital, the results indicate a significant main effect of time ($F(1.90) = 14.859$, $p<0.01$). This indicates that, overall, social capital online changed during the research period. The interaction time*TRUST is significant ($F(1.90) = 32.203$, $p<0.01$), which indicates that during the research the change in social capital online was not equal for the 2-video and 7-video conditions. Inspection of the estimated means indicates that those who received seven videos of TRUST reported higher social capital scores. The results for the interactions time*livelihood support and time*TRUST*livelihood were not significant ($F(1.90) = 0.675$, $p=0.413$; $F(1.90) = 2.719$, $p=0.103$, respectively).

Similarly, for offline social capital, the results show a significant main effect of time ($F(1.90) = 55.409$, $p<0.01$). This indicates that, overall, social capital offline changed during the research period. The interaction time*TRUST is significant (F(1.90) = 82.733, p<0.01), which indicates that during the research the change in social capital offline was not equal for the 2-video and 7-video conditions. Inspection of the estimated means indicates that those who received seven videos reported higher social capital offline. The results for the interactions time*livelihood support and time*TRUST*livelihood are not significant (F(1.90) = 0.359, p=0.551; F(1.91) = 1.109, p=0.295, respectively). Inspection of the estimated means indicates that those who received seven videos of TRUST reported higher on social capital offline and online.

Figure 8.8. TRUST programme and 'social capital offline'

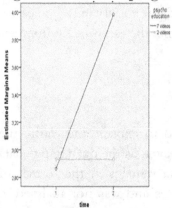 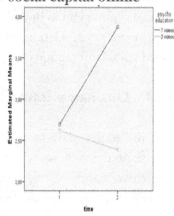

Figure 8.9. TRUST programme and 'social capital online'

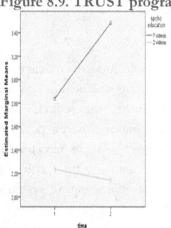 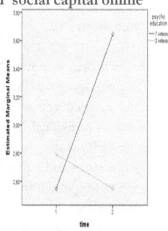

As mentioned above, the ISCS was specifically used as an indicator of collective trauma and so an improvement in social capital following the intervention is an indication of the positive impact of the intervention on reducing the level of collective trauma. This could be the combined effect of improvements in perceptions of economic resilience, leading to a reduction in the need to over rely on others for assistance and support, leading to improved, mutually-beneficial, and rewarding relationships. In addition, the reduction in the level of PTSD could also mean that people are more sociable and less preoccupied with their symptoms, such as mistrust. Moreover, community activities are positive social experiences that counter the mistrust and isolation that are features of collective trauma. This change is prevalent in both online and offline social capital, indicating improvements in relationships, both within the camp and in Internet-based social interactions.

8.4.4 Qualitative results

The qualitative data gathered was used to explain and clarify the quantitative data where necessary. However, as the quantitative data was clear, much of the qualitative data remains in the format of interview transcripts and fieldwork notes and was not analysed in detail. Some of the findings are incorporated in the discussions in Chapter 9, where they were used to expand on the quantitative data.

8.5 Conclusion

The research demonstrated that TRUST could indeed be delivered via ICT with positive impacts on alleviating the symptoms of individual and collective trauma. Furthermore, the reduction in symptoms of individual and collective trauma also had a positive impact on SER scores, with significant improvements in perceptions of empowerment and capacity, as well as enhancing the quality of social networks and improving reliance on the support systems available to refugees.

It was also found that the full programme (with seven videos) delivered superior results than the short version (with two videos), although the short version resulted in improvements too. Interestingly, the livelihood support available in the camps to beneficiaries who met the criteria set by NGOs operating in the field did not seem to have an impact on either trauma (collective or individual) or perceptions of social and economic resilience (prospects) across all the SER subscales. The support we are referring to here is varied and refers to any additional support over and above the basic UNHCR ration. Many received solar lights and access to fuel for cooking, a few received access to training on income generating activities, and fewer still received financial assistance to set up a business. None of these initiatives seem to have contributed to reducing trauma or improving perceptions of social and economic resilience among refugees.

Figure 8.10 summarises the effect of the trauma intervention on IES-Short, the various elements of social and economic resilience (using the SER), and social capital (using the ISCS). The partial eta-square can be interpreted as the percentage of variance in change between the first and second measurement, plus the associated error variance (Pierce, Block & Aguinis, 2004). From this perspective it can be said that TRUST has had a strong effect on post-traumatic stress, capability (on the SER) and social capital offline (ISCS).

Table 8.4. Summary of results of the effect of TRUST

		F value	Partial eta-square
IES-Short		$F(1.90) = 91.80, p < 0.01$	0.505
SER	Income	$F(1.91) = 15.084, p < 0.01$	0.142
	Empowerment	$F(1.91) = 42.344, p < 0.01$	0.318
	Worriedness	$F(1.91) = 13.438, p < 0.01$	0.129
	System	$F(1.91) = 38.632, p < 0.01$	0.298
	Capability	$F(1.91) = 69.565, p < 0.01$	0.433
	Social embeddedness	$F(1.91) = 22.474, p < 0.01$	0.198
Social capital (ISCS)	Offline	$F(1.90) = 82.733, p < 0.01$	0.479
	Online	$F(1.90) = 32.203, p < 0.01$	0.264

Some of the challenges posed by lack of connectivity were overcome by incorporating the adaptations already in use in the camps to overcome the problem, however, this continues to be a challenge and has inhibited the full implementation of the support that would have been available through the App. For instance, if there was better connectivity, participants could have accessed more interactive support, encouragement and motivation when watching the videos and processing traumatic stress. They would also have had more opportunities to engage with fellow refugees through their own posts on social media.

These findings will be discussed in more detail in Chapter 9, together with findings from the studies presented in previous chapters, to fully address the main research question and all sub questions together. Here, suffice it to say that, despite the technological challenges and the challenges associated with introducing an approach to providing support that hitherto had not been tried, we have indeed demonstrated the effectiveness of TRUST. This short programme can significantly reduce trauma and improve the quality of relationships, as well as enhance refugees' perceptions of social and economic resilience in a community with limited resources and high levels of post-traumatic stress. Moreover, while the psycho-education elements of the programme can play a role in reducing individual and collective trauma to enhance resilience, the full version of the programme works better than the short version, yielding better results across the board.

These findings are crucial to our understanding of the decision-making processes of traumatised refugees who are considering secondary (and often dangerous) migration. The decision to embark on these dangerous journeys could indeed be the result of the inability to process all available information due to the fact that the cognitive processes of refugees are hampered by the post-traumatic stress, as well as their tendency to assess their social and economic resilience poorly due to high levels of trauma. The other significance of the findings is in relation to the development and delivery of services in the camps and other refugee hosting contexts. High levels of traumatic stress are prevalent in refugee communities, and this research has demonstrated that delivering effective trauma support does not necessarily have to be complicated or expensive. Lastly, when it comes to refugees' own assessment of social and economic, resilience, trauma support, rather than livelihood support, seems to have a better outcome.

My 'eureka' moment came in a dusty café in the middle of the refugee camp that I was using as a makeshift office. I worked through the day fuelled by endless cups of sweet tea and with no time to reflect on the data I was collecting to see if any pattern was emerging, despite the fact that people were telling me encouraging things about how much the intervention had helped. And, then, in came Merhawit. I remembered her instantly as she was one of the most severely traumatised people I had met in the camp. I remember thinking (during the baseline data collection); if it works for her, it will work for real. Nearly two months later, she was telling me how tough it was going through the programme. She particularly found processing all the old memories difficult. She told me how many times she stopped, as well as how she somehow managed to force herself to restart, because she was desperate for something that would help. And, finally, she told me how it all came together for her at last (but painfully slowly). She told me exactly what made TRUST work for her. She emphasised that it does indeed work, but needs a significant level of support, even remotely via ICT. Apologetically, Merhawit told me that there were times when she resented hearing my voice on the video, as it meant having to face things that she had been avoiding for so long. She explained how it would have been good to be able to ask me if this was normal. With a properly connected system Merhawit would have been able to ask me such questions in a text message. As it transpired, she only had access to my voice on the video and limited access to text support; she made do, however, and was able to go through the programme – and it worked for her. I realised that if TRUST had worked for the most complicated trauma case, then it did indeed work. And it would work even better if we could improve the level of support and encouragement available and overcome connectivity issues.

Chapter 9

Discussion and conclusion

This research has been a long process, resulting in a small contribution to our understanding of refugees. Along the way, I have met people who have taught me a lot from their personal journeys of pain and suffering, recovery and resilience. Most importantly, I have developed a trauma support intervention that can help alleviate some of that pain and I have been able to contribute my thoughts to explain how refugee migration needs to be understood comprehensively for policies and practices to actually work. In addition, it has been a personal journey for me, of living through my own despair and using it to navigate questions and arrive somewhere good, where there is hope.

In this chapter the results of the research are discussed in four sections addressing the five sub questions. This leads us to the **main research question**, which is twofold: Firstly, o what extent does trauma affect the appraisal of social economic resilience and explain decisions regarding the ongoing migration of refugees? Secondly, are low resource trauma treatment programmes delivered using ICT effective in enhancing refugees' perceptions of safety and socio-economic resilience?

This main question was elaborated through five sub questions, each of which dealt with an element of the overarching question. The **first sub question** sought to understand the level of PTS among refugees from Eritrea, as measured on a recognised trauma scale (IES-R). This was followed by the **second sub question**, which looked at the effect of PTS levels among refugees on the processing of information regarding safety and socio-economic resilience during decision making about ongoing migration. These two questions were looked at through a single study conducted among Eritrean refugees in Tel Aviv (Israel), Kampala (Uganda), refugee camps in the Tigray region (Ethiopia) and Asmara (Eritrea).

As the objective of this research was to find an approach to address trauma in highly-mobile communities, the **third sub question** sought to determine if the use of ICT is indeed prevalent among refugees and if it is a trusted method of receiving information, beyond personal communication among friends and family. This was answered through the second study, which was conducted using a questionnaire administered in Khartoum (Sudan), Addis Ababa (Ethiopia) and refugee camps in the Tigray region (Ethiopia). This was done to investigate the feasibility of delivering therapy via ICT and, as a result, a six-week programme of self-help trauma support for individuals and communities – Trauma Recovery Understanding Self-Help Therapy (TRUST) – suited to low resource communities was developed in a third study.

Before delivering TRUST, the intervention was tested in a less mobile community in Uganda, in the fourth study, using a combination of community coaches and technology, based on the IES and SER scales. Hence, the **fourth sub question** looked at whether or not it was possible to lower levels of PTS and enhance socio-economic resilience by delivering a short self-help trauma intervention in a high trauma/low resource context. Finally, a shorter version of the therapy, delivered via ICT, was tested among Eritrean refugees in Tigray (Ethiopia) to see if it would have an impact on reducing PTS and enhancing resilience in the high trauma and low resource contexts of young Eritrean refugees. This **fifth sub question** also sought to determine the key elements of such a short self-help trauma intervention in a high trauma/low resource context for it to impact on social economic resilience.

These sub questions are answered in the sections below, towards answering the main research question.

9.1 Trauma levels among Eritrean refugees

This section answers **sub questions one and two** about the level of trauma among Eritrean refugees and the implications of this for their appraisal of their socio-economic resilience as they consider ongoing migration (Chapter 4).

9.1.1 A high level of trauma

The research looked into the level and prevalence of traumatic stress among Eritreans in various refugee communities, as well as inside Eritrea, in the specific context of migration and human trafficking. The study, which was conducted in Tel-Aviv (Israel), Kampala (Uganda), refugee camps in the Tigray region (Ethiopia), and Asmara (Eritrea), identified a high prevalence of PTSD, measured using the IES-R. All participants, who had been victims of human trafficking in the Sinai scored above the threshold for likely PTSD and many scored high enough to impact on functioning even 10 years after the traumatic event, potentially altering the victim's functioning permanently.

This high level of PTSD is not confined to those who had direct experiences of traumatic events. Although the participants in the groups not directly involved in human trafficking (as an abductee) showed lower levels of PTSD than abductees, only one participant (an Eritrean refugee in Kampala) scored below the 'cut-off' point for PTSD. Nearly all scores constituted levels of trauma consistent with PTSD, some indicating severe impact with long-term impairment of functioning. Hence, the study found that the traumatic impact of Sinai trafficking has resulted in extremely high levels of PTSD, including among those who did not experience the trauma first-hand, indicating the existence of collective trauma.

9.1.2 Collective trauma and social capital

As mentioned in Chapter 3, the need to examine social capital emanates from our understanding of collective trauma and its implications for societal wellbeing. In light of the role of ICT in the lives of refugees on the move (see Chapter 5), we measured social capital across both online and offline networks. The findings of this study indicate that there is a negative relationship between PTSD and social capital offline. This is an important indication that levels of trauma may be eroding community resilience (Murphy *et al.*, 1987), while the diminished social capital might be simultaneously depriving individual refugees of a crucial protective factor against PTSD and social support for dealing with PTSD.

The findings also indicated that the impact of the intervention was slightly lower for social capital online than social capital inside the camp (offline). This could mean that, due to the cost of connectivity as well as the generally limited access to the Internet, people are not making the best use of their online social networks, thus reducing the impact on (online) social capital and leaving refugees to deal with the impact of their traumatic experiences without support from friends and families.

Often times, contact with those who could be accessed only online was considered essential on many levels, both for obtaining practical information and maintaining social links. Many participants told of their worry that 'those abroad' might be weary of the constant needs of those in the camps and on route for support, information and financial resources.

9.1.3 Implications for ongoing migration

It is well established that PTSD affects cognitive processes and functioning, including the strategies adopted in response to danger, potentially effecting decision-making abilities (Lerner & Kennedy, 2000). The need to keep moving, whatever the risk, can be seen as being induced by a strategy developed in response to PTSD. This makes trauma a crucial consideration in refugee trajectories, as it has implications for rational decision making. This finding is important, as it provided a basis for developing and implementing an intervention to reduce the levels of post-traumatic stress and enhance socio-economic resilience in the high trauma/low resources settings of Eritrean refugees.

9.2 The prevalence of ICT among Eritrean refugees

This section answers **sub question three** about the prevalence of the use of ICT among Eritrean refugees and the status of technology as a trusted means for exchanging information, as well the role it might play in the provision of trauma interventions (see Chapter 5).

9.2.1 Prevalence of ICT among Eritrean refugees

The prevalence of the use of ICT among Eritrean refugees was determined using a survey of Eritrean refugees in Khartoum (Sudan), Addis Ababa (Ethiopia) and refugee camps in Tigray region (northern Ethiopia). The findings of the study were clear on the relevance of ICT in the lives of the refugees we interviewed in the refugee camps, as well as off camp, namely, that ICT provides crucial and trusted information and resources, as well as a way of maintaining networks and relationships. The study found that nearly everyone participating in the survey owned a smartphone and accessed social media platforms, despite difficulties with connectivity. Participants reported widely accessing social media, particularly Facebook and Viber, with nearly all participants in every location reporting having a Facebook account and a significant proportion reporting accessing Viber. MSN Messenger and WhatsApp were also in use, particularly in cities. Only 9 respondents (out of 151) reported not using any form of social media. For this research, it was important to understand the role of ICT, as it led to the consideration of ICT as an instrument for delivering trauma support to refugees on the move.

9.2.2 ICT as a trusted means of communication

In addition to establishing the fact that nearly everyone owned and used a smartphone, we also found that these smartphones were used to access information beyond personal and social contexts. Refugees were using their phones to listen to the radio. This indicated that smartphones are a trusted means of communication, both for personal use as well as for accessing information. While nearly everyone surveyed listened to the radio on a mobile phone, it was found that a significantly high proportion of refugees in refugee camps use their mobile phones to access radio programmes, indicating that the technology is already trusted to access information, in addition to being used for personal communication.

9.2.3 ICT as a means of delivering trauma therapy

For refugees on the move, owning and being able to use a smartphone can save one's life; it helps refugees to stay connected with friends and family members, as well as providing a link to crucial information and resources. Therefore, smartphones are treasured possessions that refugees invest in, as an absolute necessity. This study found that the vast majority of Eritrean refugees owned and used a smartphone as a trust form of communication and to obtain information. This was key to the consideration of ICT as an instrument for delivering TRUST, the self-help trauma therapy intervention, potentially overcoming issues to do with high mobility and low resources in the refugee camps in northern Ethiopia. The fact that refugees were already investing in and using mobile technology to exchange information showed a level of trust in the technology and opened up the possibility of delivering a trauma intervention using the same technology, which was already in the hands of Eritrean refugees. However, the use of technology, and particularly mobile phones, is not without its challenges These challenges include issues with connectivity in the camps and the difficulties that arise with making adaptations to overcome lack of connectivity, including the crucial loss of real-time interactive coaching.

9.3 A self-help trauma intervention for high trauma/low resource contexts

Having established a high level of PTS among refugees from Eritrea (sub question one) and the negative effect of this on the processing of information regarding safety and socio-economic resilience during decision making about ongoing migration (sub question two), as well as the prevalence of the use of ICT among refugees as a trusted method of delivering information (sub question three), the possibility of delivering therapy via ICT was considered. This section answers **sub question four**, which asks if a short self-help trauma intervention could lower levels of PTS and enhance socio-economic resilience in a high trauma/low resource context (see Chapter 7).

9.3.1 Development of TRUST

One of the main objectives of this research was to see if trauma levels could be lowered through an intervention in a setting with low resources and extremely high levels of trauma. This led to the development of TRUST, a trauma support intervention designed to respond to the needs of refugees suffering from post-traumatic stress (see Chapter 6).

9.3.2 Testing TRUST in Northern Uganda

Once TRUST was developed, it was important to see if it was effective in lowering trauma levels enough to improve refugees' appraisal of their social and economic resilience. This was done in Northern Uganda, among women who had been victims of atrocities during the war with the LRA, which was a less mobile community, but with similar levels of PTS as we had found among Eritrean refugees (see Chapter 7). The work was carried out with some reliance on podcasts and radio broadcasts to complement the work of community coaches, who provided support and encouragement to women, removing the taboo surrounding mental health and traumatisation. Although, as mentioned earlier, the statistical analysis of trauma levels, as measured by the IES-R, did not yield the expected lower scores following the implementation of TRUST as an intervention for trauma, participants clearly indicated fewer symptoms during group and individual interviews. This was confirmed by observations during the collection of post-intervention data. The discrepancy between the quantitative and qualitative data could be due to the design of the research, which measured the effect between groups (as opposed to a repeat measure). This means that the design was less sensitive to change. It could also be due to the lack of training given to research assistants on using the IES-R, which, although it does not require specialist training, is still a sensitive psychometric test. The qualitative results obtained through individual interviews and focus group discussions were thought to be enough of an indication of the effectiveness of the intervention for use in the next step of the research. Adaptations were made to the

IES-R, leading to the development of the IES-Short, to enable more effective data gathering.

9.4 Delivering TRUST through ICT

This section answers **sub question five**, which asks if a shorter version of this self-help trauma intervention delivered using ICT could have an impact on reducing PTS and enhancing socio-economic resilience in a high trauma/low resource context with Eritrean refugees, and, if so, what are the key elements of such an intervention (see Chapter 8).

9.4.1 Delivering TRUST among Eritrean refugees in Tigray

Having noted the effectiveness of TRUST in Uganda, we moved to testing the potential of making even more use of ICT, given our understanding of the highly-mobile nature of Eritrean refugees and the prevalence of social media and smartphones as both a reliable source of information and a means of social contact across the scattered communities. In addition, we wanted to see if the different components of TRUST could be delivered to the same effect of lowering trauma levels. More specifically, here we wanted to consider the effect of delivering psycho-education in two videos, as compared to seven videos (the full intervention).

The high PTSD levels were found to negatively affect the self-assessment of socio-economic resilience (prospects) as measured by the SER scales. The scale measured resilience across several spheres and those with high PTSD scores were found to have lower SER scores. This finding reflects clinical experience and research findings, indicating that low socio-economic positions are overrepresented in trauma populations (Brattström, Eriksson, Larsson & Oldner, 2015).

Resource loss is an integral part of becoming a refugee. The conservation of resource (COR) theory (Hobfoll, 1989) states that individuals strive to obtain, retain, protect and foster their resources. COR theory predicts that stress will occur following the actual loss of resources, threat of loss of resources, or failure to gain resources following significant resource investment. Studies carried out after disasters have found that resource loss is a key predictor of psychological distress (Benight, Swift, Sanger, Smith & Zeppelin, 1999). Similarly, studies in the context of conflict and disaster also support the assertion in COR theory that the initial resource loss is likely to contribute to long-term loss cycles, hampering recovery (King, King, Foy, Keane & Fairbank, 1999; Kaniasty & Norris, 1995). In this manner, those who have the fewest resources are most affected in the crisis stage and, as they have fewer resources for recovery, they continue to be vulnerable in the aftermath of traumatic events (Hobfoll, Stevens & Zalta, 2015). Here, it can be concluded that the resource loss entailed in becoming a refugee in a camp, where there is little prospect of recovering lost resources, can diminish resilience and contribute to high levels of PTSD. In the same vein, there is little prospect of recovering from PTSD when you have few resources to assist that recovery. This is an important consideration when assessing the type, level and manner of delivery of support. In the study, the livelihood support provided did not seem to result in enhanced resilience. This could be due to the type of support provided (e.g., not relevant in the context of mobility, such as small businesses in refugee camps) or the limited nature of the opportunities available (too few to meet the actual need for rebuilding). It seems that, in order to have an impact on levels of trauma (or assist trauma recovery), the livelihood support needs to be proportionate to the loss and also be given with recognition of the impacts of trauma and collective trauma.

A particularly detrimental aspect of trauma is helplessness and its implications for self-efficacy. Self-efficacy (an individual's belief in their ability to manage their symptoms resulting from unexpected events and to produce desired effects in a given activity) is considered to be a protective factor for PTSD (Bandura, 1997), as it enables people to consider anxiety and stress symptoms as controllable and temporary (Leganger, Kraft & Røysamb, 2000). Without trauma support, the situation can result in motivational deficit. Livelihood support ought to be complemented by trauma support to enable the rebuilding of self-efficacy, individuals with low self-efficacy report more traumatic symptoms (Benight & Harper, 2002; Johansen *et al.*, 2007). Differences in levels of self-efficacy have been found to persist over time, determining long-term adjustment and recovery (Benight & Harper, 2002; Heinrichs *et al.*, 2005; Johansen *et al.*, 2007). One of the advantages of TRUST has been the fact that, as a self-help tool that also relies on community support and community-wide engagement, it inculcates a sense of self-efficacy and agency, both in the individual and the community. Indeed, in talking to participants, the one thing that they found surprising was the fact that there was no doctor, or even a priest, present when they were practicing the techniques and finding relief. In addition, the educational element (psycho-education) was an opportunity to learn about something new and was helpful to the refugees on two levels: Firstly, they felt that they learnt something important about what had happened to them and how their brain can be helped to process the difficult experiences and, hence, help them cope better. Secondly, people felt included in their own healing and this built self-efficacy. Indeed, research has identified that self-efficacy also determines the acuteness (or otherwise) of the symptoms experienced (Benight & Harper, 2002).

In this sense, it seems that the assessment of social and economic resilience was also an assessment of self-efficacy or the perceived ability to cope with the level of economic resources available (as actual incomes did not increase pre- and post-intervention to account for the rise in SER). Hence, the responses indicate that those with high PTSD and low SER scores had low self-efficacy.

Self-efficacy relates to an individuals' perception of their capability to effect a change in their situation. People with self-efficacy are more likely to proactively engage with opportunities around them as they believe in their ability to succeed in the tasks involved. This is also confirmed by other research that had similar findings with regards to trauma and self-efficacy in similarly devastated communities. For example, Saigh, Mroueh, Zimmerman and Fairbank (1995) assessed diverse spheres of self-efficacy in three groups of Lebanese adolescents. The research found that traumatised adolescents with PTSD exhibited a lower level of perceived efficacy in diverse aspects of their lives than traumatised adolescents without PTSD and non-traumatised adolescents.

In accordance, the study in Ethiopia conducted for this research, despite the short length of the intervention (given the levels of traumatic stress and its complex nature), as well as the difficulties associated with delivering therapy through ICT, clearly shows that the intervention did lower levels of traumatic stress. This has been shown to have a positive impact on social capital and social and economic resilience, which means that treating PTSD has positive impacts on mental health, perceptions of social and economic status, and community-wide relationships (social capital). Self-efficacy in coping is the "core belief that one has the power to produce desired effects by one's actions" and "plays a key role in stress reactions and quality of coping in threatening situations" (Benight & Bandura, 2004, p. 1131). Individuals with low self-efficacy see challenges as dangerous and areas for potential personal failure, focus on these, and have low confidence in themselves. Self-efficacy is thus a key component of resilience to trauma (Bandura, 1997), which seems to have been addressed by TRUST. Here, an approach that focused on helping survivors of war atrocities and traumatic experiences to understand and be able to process their own difficult experiences and learn to reconnect to their communities as resourceful members (who have a new set of knowledge and skills) achieved positive results.

Moreover, the full 7-video intervention was shown to be more effective than the 2-video psycho-education sessions. The first two videos, which everyone received, incorporated only one phase of the intervention, concerned with educating participants to enhance their understanding about trauma and its impacts. The remaining five videos included the other phases, which resourced participants to process trauma, followed by the reintegration phase of teaching them everyday skills in the community. The full intervention was consistently better at reducing PTSD and bringing about associated improvements in SER and social capital (ISCS).

Much of the PTSD found in the camps can be described as complex PTSD, as it occurred due to prolonged exposure to traumatic events in the context of political violence. Trauma treatment literature is relatively consistent that the phase-oriented approach that was taken in developing TRUST is most effective in treating complex trauma (Briere & Scott, 2006; Brown, Scheflin & Hammond, 1998; Courtois, Ford & Cloitre, 2009; Ford, Courtois,

Steele, Van der Hart & Nijenhuis, 2005; Van der Hart, Nijenhuis & Steele, 2006). The intervention focuses on both understanding symptoms as well as developing skills to improve the management of symptoms and enhance functioning and relationships. And, it seems these improvements resulted in lower individual trauma and collective trauma (as measured on the ISCS), as well as positive perceptions of social and economic resilience.

Perhaps surprisingly, neither trauma levels, social and economic wellbeing, or social capital were affected by the availability of livelihood support of the kind that was available in the camps. This is surprising given the link between resources and trauma. It seems that the level of livelihood support available in the camps is not perceived by the recipients as contributing to their social and economic resilience/prospects, nor does it seem that livelihood support is currently contributing to protection against trauma or loss of social capital. However, it could well be that the process in which the livelihood support is provided does not take the situation of refugees into account. NGOs often select the most destitute and focus on individual support, rather than empowering communities to manage resources and support the most vulnerable. The current system fails to recognise the amount of support required by the most vulnerable (including trauma support) and works against the collective by selecting and targeting very limited numbers for support. This leaves the individual without support to build their self-efficacy and the community without the agency to support its most vulnerable.

Given that the objective of most of the projects being implemented by NGOs in the camps is to support and protect refugees, with a particular emphasis on providing them with the skills and resources to regain economic viability through the provision of livelihood support, it is important to address this concern and ensure that livelihood support is objectively related to reducing levels of PTSD and, thereby, enhancing self-efficacy to result in the desired improvement in social and economic resilience. This means that in contexts where trauma and collective trauma is an issue of concern, the provision of livelihood support needs to be well integrated with meeting the mental health needs of refugees and their communities.

9.4.2 Challenges of delivering TRUST via ICT

The results in terms of the psychosocial improvements seem to speak clearly of the potential of the ICT-delivery approach. Indeed, focus group discussions, as well as individual feedback, highlighted the main advantages of delivering trauma support using ICT. The ability to choose your own time and space was a great advantage, reinforcing the idea of regaining control over one's own healing. The ability to obtain information and treatment in an accessible language was another advantage mentioned by many participants. Finally, the ability to go over things again and gain additional information on things that were not clear at the start was a unique advantage of the approach (Van Reisen *et al.*, 2019).

However, the approach was not without its challenges. Delivering an intervention via an App and through social media proved difficult and, even impossible, in some cases due to the lack of connectivity and the unreliability of the connection for downloading videos. Alternatives suggested by the refugees themselves addressed some of these concerns. Adaptations were made to the intervention following consultations with refugees and in recognition of the challenges posed by connectivity, this enabled delivery of the intervention via ICT, but without reliable connectivity. One approach was to download all videos to one phone (from a memory card) and then have the research assistants share them via Bluetooth. This worked well in resolving the technical hurdles, but it also meant that the level of interaction envisaged, via the Support and Encouragement page on the App, was lost. Participants were unable to leave messages and feedback, or access additional text-based support and encouragement, as was original envisaged. The situation resulted in the loss of crucial social support for those involved in the process of addressing traumatic memories. This reduced the community-wide input as well. In Uganda, when TRUST was first tested, entire communities were aware of the intervention (through the radio programmes and podcasts) and, hence, able to provide support to the women in the programme. The community coaches and women had t-shirts they wore at the community event that highlighted their status as people with information on addressing trauma – this was validating as well as encouraging. This function would ideally have been replicated virtually on social media for Eritrean refugees, through Facebook posts, profiles and tags to create a sense of online community-wide support and encouragement, as well as interaction, but this was curtailed due to lack of connectivity, leaving extremely limited communication, which could not take place in real-time, as the little connectivity that was available in the camps was at night.

This led to an additional and more serious problem: participants felt alone as they were confronted with the potentially difficult material they were trying to cope with. This could result in participants losing motivation to fully engage with traumatic memories or dropping out altogether, as trauma healing is a process that takes whole communities to be truly effective. Many people found the resourcing techniques (breathing exercises and 'safe calm place') more attractive than the bilateral stimulation, which required greater commitment and a deeper engagement to focus on and process traumatic memories. Feedback from one of the most severely traumatised participants captured this well during an interview. She said:

> ... [the intervention] is really helpful, it made sense to me, it touched everything I felt and everything that was happening to me and eventually the butterfly hugs were helpful too, but I felt physically tired every time I did them. I really hated how it initially made me feel, I hated your voice on the video. There were times when I felt physically ill, but then I started to notice I was calmer later and less anxious. I started sleeping better and now I see how it helped. But it really is tough and there should be a contact person to tell you it will be okay in the end. (A0011, Hitsats Camp, 14/08/2017, age not stated)

Without major improvements to the technology, delivering the whole intervention via ICT risks either a high dropout rate or unnecessarily high levels of distress for those committed to carrying on with the intervention. In retrospect, an opportunity was missed by not developing text-messaging support by collecting the telephone numbers of participants and sending regular messages of support and encouragement. Texting does not require Internet connectivity and, as the participants were provided with phone cards, these could have been used to respond to text messages, in addition participants could have been prompted and encouraged to send messages to each other to simulate the community aspect of the programme. In addition, even with connectivity, it is not prudent to assume that the online community, as it exists, can be geared towards providing a community hub for trauma work. It is important to do additional work to raise general awareness of mental health and the importance of the community and to create a focus on supporting each other, as well as to protect participants from random unsupportive or even hostile comments, which often abound with the anonymity that the Internet affords. I envisage closed groups, like the Hitsats Refugee Community Facebook page or Youth on the Move page, which were in use at the time, being used for such purposes. Groups like these could be carefully utilised to develop a sense of community and a supportive forum.

9.4.3 Trauma and the ongoing refugee trajectory

TRUST enabled survivors of trauma to gain an understanding of their symptoms and regain some control over them, through the use of simple self-help exercises that enabled them to experience better relationships in their day-to-day life within their community. Without trauma intervention, symptoms of PTSD (i.e., flashbacks, nightmares, intrusive thoughts, increased arousal) are experienced as uncontrollable and unavoidable, often diminishing the victim's cognitive and emotional control. Perceived life control is the cognitive appraisal that has been shown to be significantly associated with PTSD symptoms (Bolstad & Zinbarg, 1997; Regehr, Cadell & Jansen, 1999); in fact, the development of PTSD is strongly associated with loss of control. Rothbaum *et al.* (1992) concluded that PTSD is most likely to develop when the stressful event is perceived as both dangerous and uncontrollable. Perceptions of control felt during the trauma, or controllability in the future, are important determinants of ongoing functioning among trauma survivors (Kushner, Riggs, Foa & Miller, 1993). Regaining control over aspects of their symptoms and their reactions to the symptoms gives people options that are not open to them otherwise. TRUST reduced trauma levels enhancing social capital (reduced collective trauma), as well as social and economic resilience. As this cannot be attributed to increases in income levels in the context of a refugee camp, where there was no difference in the amount of material resources available to participants, the change can be attributed to the agency and efficacy that was afforded as a result of the ability to gain control over hitherto uncontrollable symptoms.

Arnkoff and Mahoney (1979) suggested the following four beliefs as protecting individuals against ongoing pathology resulting from an extremely stressful event: having the skills to control one's response, having the skills to control the occurrence of reinforcement, being able to regulate one's mental activities, and the ability to inhibit distressing mental activities. PTSD undermines these control-related beliefs and the resulting reduction in locus of control renders the sufferer a victim to ongoing trauma. Inability to take control of one's life reduces the sufferer's belief in their ability to exert any control over their environment (Mikulincer, Glaubman, Wasserman, Porat & Birger, 1989). Consequently, being able to take some of that control back and, hence, overcome the trauma-induced helplessness resulted in a significant change to the participants' perception of their environment and the community of people who share that environment. The skills learnt through the intervention gave people a significant level of control over their response to day-to-day challenges in their extremely difficult environment. These small victories in alleviating symptoms and controlling reactions resulted in an enhanced sense of capability to improve perceptions of social and economic reality, resulting in a sense of personal self-efficacy.

As mentioned above, a sense of personal efficacy is the foundation of human agency (Bandura, 1997, 2001). People who believe that potential threats are unmanageable view their entire environment as fraught with danger; thus, they magnify the severity of possible threats and worry about potential perils that are unlikely to happen. This triggers a negative cycle of thoughts that ends up hampering functioning (Bandura, 1997; Jerusalem & Mittag, 1995; Lazarus & Folkman, 1984). With little perceived control over their sense of agitation and anxiety, participants felt that there was little going well for them and that more hardship and danger was inevitable. However, once they regained control over their symptoms, they were able to more realistically appraise their environment and their own capacity to influence it, as well as their prospects.

Studies where researchers managed to vary perceived control in the experimental design found that those who exercised some level of control over unfavourable events had lower levels physiological arousal in addition to lower rates of performance impairment of efficient performance. This was in contrast to those who experienced lack of personal control, despite the fact that both groups were faced with similar circumstances (Geer, Davison & Gatchel, 1970; Glass, Singer, Leonard, Krantz & Cummings, 1973; Litt, Nye & Shafer, 1993; Sanderson, Rapee & Barlow, 1989). This research has demonstrated that giving people information about traumatic stress and enabling them to learn techniques that allow them to take control of these symptoms results in reducing PTSD levels. Reduced trauma levels then enabled people to perceive their social and economic standing positively, enhancing their SER as well as improving their relationships with those around them. It is thought that a better appraisal of their current environment will have implications for refugees when assessing the need to move again.

Trauma, particularly the kind of trauma caused by prolonged and devastative events, such as political conflict and war, is not an isolated transient phenomenon, rather it entails a whole catalogue of losses: loss of life, physical injuries, and property destruction. Often, victims suffer stress not only from the catastrophic event itself, but also from the strain of continuing adaptations in the wake of the devastation. In addition to personal physical and psychological injury, as well as death and injury of family members, there is often a widespread loss of social connection, extensive damage to or loss of property and, in many, instances the loss of one's livelihood (Van Reisen *et al.*, 2019). Moreover, the trauma is collective, not just personal, which means that everyone is undergoing similar levels of loss and devastation and, hence, do not have the ability to support others. Survivors find themselves in a community in severe shock, which can accentuate the traumatic experience (Benight & Bandura, 2004). In the face of such daunting devastation and enduring hardship it requires a solid sense of self-efficacy to persevere with recovery efforts, and even dealing with relief agencies that assist can be a source of further strain (Bolin, 1982).

Trauma support, such as that provided by TRUST, can be a good starting point for regaining control and self-efficacy and breaking the vicious cycle, both by unlocking personal and community resilience and by preparing the ground for the better utilisation of social support initiatives, such as the livelihood support provided in refugee camps. The experimental conditions in this research had certain advantages that would not necessarily be available in all circumstances (e.g., availability of mental health provision in the camps that prioritised the cases we identified as needing urgent support). Nonetheless, the validity of the intervention was established by the fact that that the full programme resulted in a similar effect of reducing collective and individual trauma and enhancing SER across two contexts (Uganda and Ethiopia). The fidelity of the full intervention was also established during the final study, which compared a shorter version of the intervention, which was not as effective as the full version.

The central point of this study related to the extent to which trauma affected Eritrean refugees' perceptions of their protection and prospects, and whether or not this explains ongoing refugee trajectories. However, rather than explore the motivations and decision making directly, we took the approach of creating enhanced cognitive capacity, enabling people to regard their social and economic resilience more positively by lowering levels of individual and collective trauma. The idea was that the kind of rational thinking assumed in the push and pull theory of migration is made impossible by trauma, and most certainly by the levels of trauma we found among the refugees who took part in this research. With their sense of self-efficacy diminished, and in a trauma induced state of hypervigilance that elevates the threat perceived in their current environment, refugees are almost programmed to see their environment as fraught with insurmountable danger – livelihood support and refugee protection notwithstanding. It is, therefore, important to rethink the push and pull theory to incorporate the unreliability of the information available to a traumatised brain and their (lack of) capacity for a rational assessment of push and pull factors.

This research did not specifically ask about imminent decisions pertaining to secondary migration, as such questions are seldom answered truthfully in formal circumstances; however, there was evidence during discussions that suggests a gradual ability to take in and process contextual information regarding situations outside the camp. One such example came at the end of a focus group discussion in Hitsats refugee camp. The participant, a young man, who was part of the group who took up the full six-week sessions, asked hesitantly (because he was not sure whether it was an appropriate question):

> ... *this may not be relevant, but ever since listening to you on the videos I have been wondering if... in Europe, where you live, there are traumatic events and if people there also suffer from PTSD?* (D0014, Hitsats Camp, 12/08/2017, age not stated)

Nearly everyone in the group resonated with this question and they all wanted to hear the response. The question and the enthusiasm to hear the answer reflected the increased capacity of the refugees to begin taking in contextual information that had not previously been taken on board, as, in their hypervigilant, low self-efficacy state, they only looked for danger in their current environment and prepared for flight.

9.5 Conclusion and recommendations

Going through TRUST was a journey of healing for the participants in this research, both in Uganda and in Ethiopia. For me, as a researcher, it was a journey of understanding trauma a whole lot better than I have ever done. The search for an intervention that works has taken me in a direction that made me discover the brain's capacity to unlock its own healing through processes that are naturally available even in the most deprived contexts (understanding, breathing, and bilateral movement). I also discovered that trauma healing does not require an unrealistic amount of resources. In this research, we showed that what was required to heal trauma was to put the refugees at the heart of the conceptualisation of their travels and troubles, and then build services out of that understanding.

This section answers the main research question, before providing recommendations based on the findings of this research.

9.5.1 Main research question

The results of the last two studies (see Chapters 7 and 8) point in the same direction: that the full TRUST programme (psycho-education, exercises to gain control over distressing PTSD symptoms, and encouragement to share experiences with members of the community) is capable of reducing PTSD, increasing social and economic resilience, and increasing social capital.

Measuring PTSD using the IES-R and IES-Short was found to be an effective instrument for monitoring levels of trauma and also assessing the effectiveness of the intervention. The IES-R was effective in reliably measuring levels of trauma in the various contexts and the IES-Short was effective in addressing concerns raised about the length of the instrument for use in mobile communities.

The research found that the self-help exercises, together with the information/education element of the intervention, were more effective than the education/information sessions on their own. The lower trauma levels, as a result of the intervention, were associated with improved appraisal by refugees of their resources, as well as improved capacity within their community. In addition to this, in the Ethiopian study, it was found that, despite the need to improve connectivity and adapt Apps to work in low-connectivity contexts, delivering trauma support via ICT is a viable option. This presents a crucial opportunity for delivering trauma support that can have an impact on raising social capital, as well as increasing social and economic resilience, in a highly-mobile community with high levels of trauma. The fact that TRUST can be delivered through a medium that is already known, trusted and used by the refugees themselves, and the fact that language barriers can be surmounted, makes this particular approach attractive. This is particularly true if one is able to overcome the challenges of connectivity, either by adapting functions already available without connectivity (e.g., text messaging, Bluetooth) or making as much information and support as possible available through questions and answers in the videos to inform participants about the need for perseverance. However, it should be noted that the latter is less interactive and may fail to cover issues specific to individuals.

The main finding of this research is that reducing traumatic stress among refugees in a refugee camp can enhance their social capital and improve their perception of their protection and prospects in their current location. This is important for those trying to improve the situation of refugees in their current location by providing them with opportunities to improve their livelihoods and prevent them from embarking on dangerous secondary migration journeys in search of better prospects. Hence, the findings of this research answer the main research question in the positive: *Trauma can greatly affect the appraisal of social economic resilience by refugees and explain decisions regarding their ongoing migration. Furthermore, low resource trauma treatment programmes delivered using ICT can be effective in enhancing refugees' perceptions of safety and socio-economic resilience, thereby positively affecting their appraisal of their prospects in their current location and, hence, better informing decision making about onward migration.*

9.5.2 Recommendations

Based on this research, recommendations can be made regarding the development of refugee support, with a view to providing stability and preventing secondary migration.

The **first recommendation** concerns the delivery of livelihood support to refugees in camps. The main objective of such projects is to prevent vulnerable refugees from embarking on secondary migration due to the harsh living conditions and lack of opportunities for refugees to earn an income and support themselves and their families. However, as we have seen above, agencies providing support need to ensure that refugees are enabled to enhance their self-efficacy to enable them to take advantage of opportunities, maximise the benefits, and enhance their social and economic resilience.

The **second recommendation** pertains to the anti-human trafficking information projects that abound in the camps and across refugee communities elsewhere. These projects seem to focus on giving a lot facts and figures regarding the risk of secondary migration. While we have not evaluated the efficacy of such projects, the fact that many refugees continue to take perilous onward journeys seems to suggest that a rethink of this strategy is warranted. Given our understanding of the impacts of trauma on processing factual information, the nature of these campaigns need to be reviewed so as to present the information only once trauma has been addressed. In addition to facts and figures, the information billboards and other materials feature details of the traumatic experiences of others. Given that one of the symptoms of traumatic stress is avoidance, this approach needs to be revised. We recommend messages that inculcate self-efficacy and agency to enable sound assessments and decision making. TRUST can be used in conjunction with such programmes to achieve the desired goal of enabling refugees to enhance their social and economic resilience and feel more in control of their future.

9.5.3 Final words

Since the research for this thesis was completed, a new study was conducted on the lagged effect of TRUST, compared to the effect of material or financial support on social economic resilience. This study found that the trauma treatment can enhance the psychological aspects of social and economic resilience (empowerment, capability and worriedness) significantly over time. In addition, it was found that trauma treatment effectively enhanced perceptions of income security, despite the fact that there was no material increase in actual levels of income. The study also concluded that the success of the programme is based on two important pillars: self-help to gain control over the symptoms of PTSD and ownership of the programme by the community. These results show that TRUST is effective in enhancing social economic resilience (Van Reisen, Stokmans, Malole & Kidane, 2021, forthcoming).

In explaining the validity of this research, the following two points should be made about the starting point of the research and the sampling approach used. Firstly, the research started with a theoretical framework defining the constructs and their operationalisation, as well as the interaction between the various constructs. This framework is used as a guide throughout the studies undertaken as part of this research and is supported by the (qualitative and quantitative) results. Secondly, in relation to the sampling approach used, the samples were not (nor were they intended to be) representative of populations. This may have had an impact on the level of trauma identified (the research may have attracted people with high levels of trauma, as sampling was not random); however, this is not thought to have impacted on the findings regarding the effectiveness of the TRUST programme, as the reduction in trauma levels was across the board and was not compared to the rest of the population. In addition, the full version of TRUST has been demonstrated to lower trauma and enhance social and economic resilience.

Going back to the opening story – of the monkey who fell out of his tree and his futile attempt to get out of the situation by himself, before being helped by someone who plucked the crucial thorn from his backside, enabling him to sit down and do the rest by himself – this is an apt description of how a strategic approach to addressing trauma using ICT can enhance self-efficacy enabling victims to help themselves. Without such strategic support, the only option left would be to continue to futilely toss and roll in the bush of thorns, acquiring more pain and injury.

I no longer feel the desperation I felt on the morning of the Lampedusa disaster, not because we have been able to avert such disasters (we are still far from that), but because I have something, albeit limited, to offer by way of averting a similar disaster. I am no longer helplessly staring at my screen in bewildered grief. I have made that screen – and technology – deliver some relief, and I am certainly no longer stunned, asking 'why?' I have arrived at an explanation that offers an answer.

For many Eritreans, an element of these tragedies, which take place thousands of miles away from home, is the inability to find the closure that comes from burying your dead. I feel that this research has given me closure in some way, and for that I am grateful to all the people who gave me closure by supporting and participating in this research.

In October 2013, I reached for some closure by expressing my grief through the following poem, which actually resonates better now than it did then.

The Return Flight

Eritrea
Hide little brother hide
They have come to get you again
Please hold your breath… don't make any noise

Kassala
Run little brother run
They want to sell you and sell you kidneys
Please don't stop to breathe… run, don't halt your pace

Lampedusa
Swim little brother swim
They refuse to come rescue you
Take a deep breath and swim…there is no time to think

Eritrea
Fly little brother fly
To the clouds above the sea
To the mountains beyond the borders
To the streets you knew like the back of your hand
Then finally to the home whose very life and light you were
To the side of your forlorn mother who lived for you and will die with you

Rest
Dear brother
Now rest in peace
There is no need to run
And there is nowhere to hide
It really is the end… it is all over now
Rest dear little brother, rest in eternal peace

References

Aarts, P. G., & Op den Velde, W. (1996). Prior traumatization and the process of aging: Theory and clinical implications. In Van der Kolk, B. A., McFarlane, A. C. & Weisaeth, L. (eds), *Traumatic Stress: The Effect of Overwhelming Experience on Mind, Body and Society* (pp. 359–377). New York: Guilford Press.

Adger, W. (2000). Social and ecological resilience: Are they related? *Progress in Human Geography* 24 (3), 347–364.

Adger, W. N., Kelly, P. M., Winkels, A., Huy, L. Q., & Locke, C. (2002). Migration, remittances, livelihood trajectories, and social resilience. *Ambio* 31, 358–366.

Adúriz, M. E., Knopfler, C., & Bluthgen, C. (2009). Helping child flood victims using group EMDR intervention in Argentina: Treatment outcome and gender differences. *International Journal of Stress Management* 16 (2), 138–153.

Akelo, G. (2013). Experiences of forced mothers in Northern Uganda: The legacy of war. *Intervention* 11 (2), 149–156.

Alexander, J. C. (2004). Toward a theory of cultural trauma. In Alexander, J. C., Eyerman, R., Giesen, B., Smelser, N. J., & Sztompka. P. (eds), *Cultural Trauma and Collective Identity* (pp. 1–30). Berkeley: University of California Press.

Allen, H. B. (1971). Principles of informant selection. *American Speech* 46, 47–51.

Allen, T., & Schomerus, M. (2006). *A hard homecoming: Lessons learnt from the Reception Center processes in Northern Uganda. An independent study commissioned by USAID and UNICEF.* Washington, DC: Management System International.

American Psychiatric Association. (2000). *Diagnostic and statistical manual of mental disorders: DSM-IV-TR.* Washington, DC: American Psychiatric Association.

American Psychiatric Association. (2013). *Diagnostic and statistical manual of mental disorders* (5th ed.). Washington, DC: American Psychiatric Association.

Amnesty International. (2004). *Eritrea: 'You have no right to ask' – Government resists scrutiny on human rights.* AFR 64/003/2004, 19 May 2004. London: Amnesty International.

Amnesty International. (2015). *Just deserters: Why indefinite national service in Eritrea has created a generation of refugees.* London: Amnesty International.

Arnkoff, D. B., & Mahoney, M. J. (1979). The role of perceived control in psychopathology. In Perlmutter, L. C. & Monty, R. A. (eds), *Choice and Perceived Control* (pp. 245–272). Hillsdale NJ: Erlbaum.

Astur, R. S., St Germain, S. A., Baker E. K., Calhoun V., Pearlson G. D., Constable, R. T. (2005). FMRI hippocampal activity during a virtual radial arm maze. *Journal of Applied Psychophysiology and Biofeedback* 30, 307–317.

Asukai, N., Kato, H., Kawamura, N., Kim, Y., Yamamoto, K., Kishimoto, J., Miyake, Y., & Nishizono-Maher, A. (2002). Reliability and validity of the Japanese-language version of the Impact of Event Scale-Revised (IES-R-J): Four studies of different traumatic. *Journal of Nervous and Mental Disorders* 190 (3), 175–182.

Augsburger, M., & Elbert, T. (2017). When do traumatic experiences alter risk-taking behavior? A machine learning analysis of reports from refugees. *PLOS ONE* 12(5).

Avnet, T., Tuan, M., Pham, M. T., & Stephen, A. T. (2012). Consumers' trust in feelings as information. *Journal of Consumer Research* 39 (4), 720–735.

Babu, A. R. M., Babu, S., & Wilson, A. (2002). *The future that works: Selected writings of A.M. Babu*. Trenton, NJ: Africa World Press.

Baguena, M., Villarroya, E., & Belena, A. (2001). Propiedades psicometricas de la version Espanola de la Escala Revisada de Impacto del Estressor (EIE-R) [Psychometric properties of the Spanish version of the Impact of Event Scale-Revised (IES-R)]. *Analisis Modificacion de Conducta* 27 (114), 581–604.

Baines, E., Stover, E., & Wierda, M. (2006). *War-affected children and youth in Northern Uganda: Toward a brighter future: An assessment report* (pp. 13-17). Chicago, IL: John D. and Catherine T. MacArthur Foundation.

Baingana, F. (2003). *Conflict prevention and reconstruction*. Social Development Notes, No.13. Washington, DC: World Bank.

Baingana, F. K., Alem, A., & Jenkins, R. (2006). Mental health and the abuse of alcohol and controlled substances. In Jamison, D. T., Feachem, R. G., Makgoba, M. W., Bos, E. R., Baingaa, F. K., Hofman, K. J., O Rogo, K. (eds), *Disease and Mortality in Sub-Saharan Africa* (pp. 329–350). Washington, DC: The International Bank for Reconstruction and Development / The World Bank.

Bandura, A. (1997). *Self-efficacy: The exercise of control*. New York, NY: Freeman/Times Books/ Henry Holt & Co.

Bandura, A. (2001). Social cognitive theory: An agentic perspective. *Annual Review of Psychology* 52, 1–26.

Bandura, A. (2006). Going global with social cognitive theory: From prospect to paydirt. In Donaldson, S. I., Berger, D. E. & Pezdek, K.

(eds), *The Rise of Applied Psychology: New Frontiers and Rewarding Careers* (pp.53–79). Mahwah, NJ: Erlbaum.

Banerjee, N., & Ray, L. (1991). *Seasonal migration: A case study from West Bengal*. New Delhi: Centre for Women's Development Studies (Mimeo).

Baron, R. A. (2008). The role of affect in the entrepreneurial process. *Academy of Management Review* 33 (2), 328–340.

Barudy, J. (1989). A program of mental health for political refugees: Dealing with the invisible pain of political exile. *Social Science and Medicine* 28 (7), 715–727.

Başoğlu, M., Yetimalar, Y., Gürgör, N., Büyükçatalbaş, S., Kurt, T., Seçil, Y., & Yeniocak, A. (2006). Neurological complications of prolonged hunger strike. *European Journal of Neurology* 13 (10), 1089–1097.

Bass, Judith K., Jeannie Annan, Sarah McIvor Murray, Debra Kaysen, Shelly Griffiths, Talita Cetinoglu, Karin Wachter, Laura K. Murray, and Paul A. Bolton. "Controlled trial of psychotherapy for Congolese survivors of sexual violence." New England Journal of Medicine 368, no. 23 (2013): 2182-2191.

BBC. (2015). Why do so many people want to leave Eritrea for Europe? 10 November 2015, BBC News, Africa. Available at: https://www.bbc.com/news/av/world-africa-34774133 (accessed 3 February 2021).

Bell, C., & Newby, H. (1971). *Community studies: An introduction to the sociology of local community*. London: Allen and Unwin.

Benight, C. C., & Bandura, A. (2004). Social cognitive theory of posttraumatic recovery: The role of perceived self-efficacy. *Behaviour Research and Therapy* 42 (10), 129–148.

Benight, C. C., & Harper M. L. (2002). Coping self-efficacy perceptions as a mediator between acute stress response and long-term distress following natural disasters. *Journal of Traumatic Stress* 15 (3), 177–186.

Benight, C., Swift, E., Sanger, J., Smith, A., & Zeppelin, D. (1999). Coping self-efficacy as a mediator of distress following a natural disaster. *Journal of Applied Social Psychology* 29 (12), 2443–2464.

Ben-Zur, H. & Zeidner, M. (2009). Threat to life and risk-taking behaviours: A review of empirical findings and explanatory models. *Personality and Social Psychology Review* 13 (2), 109–128.

Bergstrand, J. H., Larch, M., & Yotov, Y. V. (2015). Economic integration agreements, border effects, and distance elasticities in the gravity equation. *European Economic Review*, 78, 307–327.

Bernard, H. R. (2002). *Research methods in anthropology. Qualitative and quantitative approaches* (3rd Edition). Walnut Creek, CA: Altamira Press.

Biernacki, P, & Waldorf, W. (1981). Snowball sampling: Problem and techniques of chain referral sampling. *Sociological Methods and Research* 10 (2), 141–63.

Boehnlein, J. K., Kinzie, J. D., & Sekiya, U. *et al.* (2004). A ten-year treatment outcome study of traumatized Cambodian refugees. *Journal of Nervous and Mental Disorder* 192 (10), 658–663.

Bolin, R. C. (1982). *Long-term family recovery from disaster.* Boulder, CO: Institute of Behavioural Science, University of Colorado.

Bolstad, B. R., & Zinbarg, R. E. (1997). Sexual victimization, generalized perception of control, and posttraumatic stress disorder symptom severity. *Journal of Anxiety Disorders* 11 (5), 523–540.

Bonanno, G. A. (2004). Loss, trauma, and human resilience: Have we underestimated the human capacity to thrive after extremely aversive events? *American Psychologist* 59 (1), 20–28.

Bonell, C. P., Hargreaves, J., Cousens, S., Ross, D., Hayes, R., Petticrew, M., & Kirkwood, B. R. (2010). Alternatives to randomisation in the evaluation of public health interventions. *Journal of Epidemiology and Community Health* 65 (7), 582–587.

Borjas, G. J., Bronars, S. G., & Trejo, S. J. (1992). Self-selection and internal migration in the United States. *Journal of Urban Economics* 32(2), 159–185.

Boss, P. (2007). Ambiguous loss theory: Challenges for scholars and practitioners. *Family Relations* 56 (2), 105–111.

Boyer, T. W. (2006). The development of risk-taking: A multi-perspective review. *Developmental Review* 26 (3), 291–345.

Bramsen, I., & Van der Ploeg, H. M. (1999). Fifty years later: The long-term psychological adjustment of ageing World War II survivors. *Acta Psychiatrica Scandinavica* 100 (5), 350–358.

Brattström, O., Eriksson, M., Larsson, E., & Oldner, A. (2015). Socio-economic status and co-morbidity as risk factors for trauma. *European Journal of Epidemiology* 30 (2), 151–157.

Brave Heart, M. Y. H. (2004). The historical trauma response among natives and its relationship to substance abuse: A Lakota illustration. In Philips, M. & Nebelkopf, E. (eds), *Healing and Mental Health for Native American: Speaking in Red* (pp. 7–18). Walnut Creek, CA: Alta Mira Press.

Bremner, J. D. (1999). Does stress damage the brain? *Biological Psychiatry* 45 (7), 797–805.

Bremner, J. D., Vermetten, E., Schmahl, C., Vaccarino, V., Vythilingam, M., Afzal, N., Grillon, C., & Charney, D. S. (2005). Positron emission tomographic imaging of neural correlates of a fear acquisition and extinction paradigm in women with childhood sexual-abuse-related post-traumatic stress disorder. *Psychological Medicine* 35 (6), 791–806.

Brhane, M. O. (2016). Understanding why Eritreans go to Europe. *Forced Migration Review* (51), 34.

Briere, J., & Scott, C. (2006). *Principles of trauma therapy: A guide to symptoms, evaluation, and treatment.* London: Sage Publications.

Brown, D., Scheflin, A., & Hammond, C. (1998). *Memory, trauma treatment, and the law.* New York, NY: Norton.

Brunet, A., St Hilaire, A., Jehel, L., & King, S. (2003). Validation of a French version of the Impact of Event Scale-Revised. *Canadian Journal of Psychiatry* 48 (1), 56–61.

Burawoy, M. (1998). The extended case method. *Sociological Theory* 16 (1), 4–33.

Cairns, E. (1996). *Children and political violence.* Cambridge: Blackwell Publishers.

Cater, J., & Jones, T. (1989). *Social geography: An introduction to contemporary issues.* London: Edward Arnold.

Chapman, C. R., & Gavrin, J. (1999). Suffering: The contributions of persistent pain. *The Lancet* 353 (9272), 2233–2237.

Chemtob, C., Roitblat, H. L., Hamada, R. S., Carlson, J. G., & Twentyman, C. T. (1988). A cognitive action theory of post-traumatic stress disorder. *Journal of Anxiety Disorders* 2(3), 253–275.

Chemtob, C. M., Tolin, D. F., Van der Kolk, B. A., & Pitman, R. K. (2000). Eye movement desensitization and reprocessing. In Foa, E. B., Keane, T. M. & Friedman, M. J. (eds), *Effective Treatments for PTSD: Practice Guidelines from the International Society for Traumatic Stress Studies* (pp. 139–154). New York, NY: Guilford Press.

Christensson, P. (2010). *ICT definition*. TechTerms. Sharpened Productions.

Chrousos, G. P., & Gold, P. W. (1992). The concept of stress and stress system disorders: Overview of physical and behavioural homeostasis. *Journal of the American Medical Association* 267 (9), 1244–1252.

Cloitre, M., Courtois, C., Charuvastra, A., Carapezza, R., Stolbach, B., & Green, B. (2011). Treatment of complex PTSD: Results of the ISTSS expert clinician survey on best practices. *Journal of Traumatic Stress* 24 (6), 615–627.

Cohen, D. K., Green, A. H., & Wood, E. J. (2013). *Wartime sexual violence*. Special Report, 617. United States Institute of Peace (USIP).

Cohen, J. B., Pham, M. T., & Andrade, E. B. (2008). The nature and role of affect in consumer behaviour. In Haugtved, C., Kardes, F. & Herr, P. (eds), *Handbook of Consumer Psychology* (pp. 297–348). Mahwah, NJ: Erlbaum.

Coleman, J. S. (1988). Social capital in the creation of human capital. *American Journal of Sociology* 94, S95–S120.

Collier, P., Elliott, V., Hegre, H., Hoeffler, A., Reynal-Querol, M., & Sambanis, N. (2003). *Breaking the conflict trap*. Civil War and Development Policy. A World Bank Policy Research Report. Washington, DC: World Bank and Oxford University Press.

Connell, D. (2012). Escaping Eritrea: Why they flee and what they face. *Middle East Report* 264 (Fall), 2–9.

Courtois, C. A., Ford, J. D., & Cloitre, M. (2009). Best practices in psychotherapy for adults. In Courtois, C. A. & Ford, J. D. (eds), *Treating Complex Traumatic Stress Disorders: An Evidence-Based Guide* (pp. 82–103). New York, NY: Guilford Press.

Cozolino, L. J. (2002). *The neuroscience of psychotherapy: Building and rebuilding the human brain.* New York, NY: W.W. Norton & Company.

Cozolino, L. (2006). The social brain. *Psychotherapy in Australia* 12 (2), 12–7.

Creamer M., Bell, R., & Failla S. (2003). Psychometric properties of the Impact of Event Scale-Revised. *Behaviour Research and Therapy* 41 (12), 1489–1496.

Cresswell, J. W., & Plano Clark, V. L. (2011). *Designing and conducting mixed method research* (2nd Edition). Los Angeles, CA: Sage Publications.

Crow, G., & Allen, A. (1994). *Community life: An introduction to local social relations.* Harlow: Pearson Education.

Cukor, J., Spitalnick, J., Difede, J., Rizzo, A., & Rothbaum, B. O. (2009). Emerging treatments for PTSD. *Clinical Psychology Review* 29 (8), 715–726.

Cullen, M., & Whiteford, H. (2001). *The Inter-relations of social capital with health and mental health.* National Mental Health Strategy, Discussion Paper, Commonwealth of Australia.

Danish Immigration Services Report. (2014). *Eritrea – Drivers and root causes of emigration, national service and the possibility of return country of origin information for use in the asylum determination process.* Report from the Danish Immigration Service's fact finding missions to Ethiopia and Eritrea August and October 2014, 5/2014 ENG. Copenhagen: Danish Immigration Service.

Derluy, I., Broekaert, E., Schuyten, G., & De Temmermann, E. (2004). Post-traumatic stress in former Ugandan child soldiers. *The Lancet* 363 (9412), 861–863.

Derogatis, L. R., & Lazarus, L. (1994). SCL-90—R, Brief Symptom Inventory, and matching clinical rating scales. In M. E. Maruish (Ed.), The use of psychological testing for treatment planning and outcome assessment (p. 217–248). Lawrence Erlbaum Associates, Inc.

Dixon, L. E., Ahles, E., & Marques, L. (2016). Treating posttraumatic stress disorder in diverse settings: recent advances and challenges for the future. Current psychiatry reports, 18(12), 1-10.

Dorigo, G., & Tobler, W. (1983). Push-pull migration laws. *Annals of the Association of American Geographers* 73(1), 1–17.

Doyle, M., & Sambanis, N. (2006). *Making war and building peace: The United Nations since the 1990's*. Princeton, NJ: Princeton University Press.

Dubow, E. F., Rowell Huesmann, L., Boxer, P., Landau, S., Dvir, S., Shikaki, K., & Ginges, J. (2012). Exposure to political conflict and violence and posttraumatic stress in Middle East youth: Protective factors. *Journal of Clinical Child & Adolescent Psychology* 41 (4), 402–416.

Dunmore, E., Clark, D. M., & Ehlers, A. (1999). Cognitive factors involved in the onset and maintenance of PTSD. *Behaviour Research and Therapy* 37 (9), 809–829.

Eades, D. (2013). Resilience and refugees: From individualised trauma to post traumatic growth. *Media and Culture Journal* 16 (5).

Ebert, D. D., Zarski, A. C., Christensen, H., Stikkelbroek, Y., Cuijpers, P., Berking, M., & Riper, H. (2015). Internet and computer-based cognitive behavioural therapy for anxiety and depression in youth: A meta-analysis of randomized controlled outcome trials. *PLOS ONE* 10 (3), e0119895.

Economist. (2013). Eritrea and its emigrants: Why they leave. Eritreans are taking to the seas because of worsening conditions at home. *Economist*, Middle East and Africa, 12 October 2013, Nairobi.

Ehlers, A. D., & Clark, A. (2000). Cognitive model of posttraumatic stress disorder. *Behaviour Research and Therapy* 38 (4), 319–345.

Ehlers, A., Hackmann, A., Steil, R., Clohessy, S., Wenninger, K., & Winter, H. (2002). The nature of intrusive memories after trauma: The warning signal hypothesis. *Behaviour Research and Therapy* 40 (9), 995–1002.

El-Bialy, N., Nicklisch, A., & Voigt, S. (2017). Risk-taking, trust, and traumatization among Syrian refugees in Jordan – A Lab-in-the-Field Experiment. *SSRN Electronic Journal* (2017).

Epping-Jordan, J. E., Harris, R., Brown, F. L. Carswell, K., Foley, C., Garcia-Moreno, C., Kogan, C., ... Van, O. M. (2016). Self-help plus (SH+): A new WHO stress management package. *World Psychiatry* 15 (3), 295–296.

Ergun, D., Cakici, M., & Cakici, E. (2008). Comparing psychological responses of internally displaced and non-displaced Turkish Cypriots. *Torture* 18 (1), 20–28.

Erikson, K. (1976). *Everything in its path: Destruction of community in the Buffalo Creek Flood.* New York, NY: Simon and Schuster.

Erikson, K. (1995). Notes on trauma and community. In Caruth, C. (ed.), *Trauma: Explorations in Memory* (pp. 183–199). Baltimore: Johns Hopkins University Press.

Estrada, C. A., Isen, A. M., & Young, M.J. (1997). Positive affect facilitates integration of information and decreases anchoring in reasoning among physicians. *Organizational and Human Decision Processes* 72 (1), 117–135.

Faist, T. (2000). *The volume and dynamics of international migration and transnational social spaces.* Oxford and New York, NY: Oxford University Press.

Farhood, L., Dimassi, H., & Lehtinen, T. (2006). Exposure to war-related traumatic events, prevalence of PTSD, and general psychiatric morbidity in a civilian population from Southern Lebanon. *Journal of Transcultural Nursing* 17 (4), 333–340.

Fernandez, I., Gallinari, E., & Lorenzetti, A. (2004). A school-based EMDR intervention for children who witnessed the Pirelli Building airplane crash in Milan, Italy. *Journal of Brief Therapy* 2 (2), 129–136.

Ferreira-Lay, P., & Miller, S. (2008). The quality of Internet information on depression for lay people. *Psychiatric Bulletin* 32 (5), 170–173.

Figley, C. R. (ed.) (1995a). *Compassion fatigue: Coping with secondary traumatic stress disorder in those who treat the traumatized.* New York, NY: Brunner/Mazal.

Figley, C. R. (1995b). Compassion fatigue: Toward a new understanding of the costs of caring. Secondary traumatic stress: Self-care issues for clinicians, researchers, and educators. In Stamm, B.H. (ed.), *Secondary Traumatic Stress: Self-care Issues for Clinicians, Researchers, and Educators* (pp 3–28). Baltimore, MD: The Sidran Press.

Figley, C. R. (1998). *The traumatology of grieving: Conceptual, theoretical, and treatment foundations.* Philadelphia, PA: Brunner/Mazel.

Fleming, M. (2015). The death boats: A survivor's tale. UNHCR. Available at: https://www.unhcr.org/uk/news/stories/2015/6/56ec1e9f8/the-death-boats-a-survivors-tale.html (accessed 27 February 2021).

Fletcher, D., & Sarkar, M. (2012). A grounded theory of psychological resilience in Olympic champions. *Psychology of Sport and Exercise* 13 (5), 669–678.

Ford, J. D., Courtois, C. A., Steele, K., Hart, O. V. D., & Nijenhuis, E. R. (2005). Treatment of complex posttraumatic self-dysregulation. *Journal of Traumatic Stress: Official Publication of the International Society for Traumatic Stress Studies* 18 (5), 437–447.

Foresight, U. K. (2011). *Migration and global environmental change: Final project report.* London: The Government Office for Science.

Gaillard, J. C. (2007). Resilience of traditional societies in facing natural hazards. *Disaster Prevention and Management: An International Journal* 16 (4), 522–544.

Gampel, Y. (1988). Facing war, murder, torture and death in latency. *Psychoanalytic Review* 75 (4), 499–509.

Gates, S., Nygård, H. M., Strand, H., & Urdal, H. (2016). Trends in armed conflict, 1946–2014. *Conflict Trends* 1, 1–4.

Geer, J. H., Davison, G. C., & Gatchel, R. I. (1970). Reduction of stress in humans through nonveridical perceived control of aversive stimulation. *Journal of Personality and Social Psychology* 16 (4), 731–738.

Gelbach, R. A., & Davis, K. E. (2007). Disaster response: EMDR and family systems therapy under communitywide stress. In Shapiro, F., Kaslow, F. W. & Maxfield, L. (eds), *Handbook of EMDR and Family Therapy Processes* (pp. 385–404). Hoboken, NJ: John Wiley & Sons Inc.

Gerritsen, A. A., Bramsen, I., Deville, W., Van Willigen, L. H., Hovens, J.E., & Van der Ploeg, H. M. (2006). Physical and mental health of Afghan, Iranian and Somali asylum seekers and refugees living in the Netherlands. *Social Psychiatry and Psychiatric Epidemiology* 41 (1), 18–26.

Giacaman, R., Abu-Rmeileh, N. M. E., Husseini, A., Saab, H., & Boyce, W. (2007). Humiliation: The invisible trauma of Palestinian youth. *Public Health* 121 (8), 563–571.

Glass, D. C., Singer, J. E., Leonard, H. S., Krantz, D., Cohen, S. & Cummings, H. (1973). Perceived control of aversive stimulation and the reduction of stress responses. *Journal of Personality* 41 (4), 577–595.

Gunderson, L. H. (2000). Ecological resilience-in theory and application. *Annual review of Ecology and Systematics* 31 (1), 425–439.

Hallegatte, S., Bangalore, M., & Vogt-Schilb, A. (2016). *Socioeconomic resilience: Multi-hazard estimates in 117 countries.* The World Bank.

Hamilton, N., & Chinchilla, N. S. (1991). Central American migration: A framework for analysis. *Latin American Research Review* 26 (1), 75–110.

Hampton, J. (2014). *Internally displaced people: A global survey.* New York, NY: Routledge.

HAP Volunteers. (2005). Informal reports of EMDR Humanitarian Assistance Program volunteers in India, Sri Lanka, Thailand and US Gulf Cost. *Journal of EMDR Practice and Research* 2 (2), 1933–3196.

Hashemian, F., Khoshnood, K., Desai, M. M., Falahati, F., Kasl, S., & Southwick, S. (2006). Anxiety, depression, and posttraumatic stress in Iranian survivors of chemical warfare. *Journal of the American Medical Association* 296 (5), 560–566.

Hayes, S. C, Luoma, J. B., Bond, F. W., Masuda, A., & Lillis, J. (2006). Acceptance and commitment therapy: Model, processes and outcomes. *Behaviour Research and Therapy* 44 (1), 1–25.

Heinrichs, M., Wagner, D., Schoch, W., Soravia, L. M., Hellhammer, D. H., & Ehlert U. (2005). Predicting posttraumatic stress symptoms from pretraumatic risk factors: A 2-year prospective follow-up study in fire fighters. *American Journal of Psychiatry* 162 (12), 2276–2286.

Hensel, J. M., Ruiz, C., Finne, C., & Dewa, C. S. (2015). Meta-analysis of risk factors for secondary traumatic stress in therapeutic work with trauma victims. *Journal of Traumatic Stress* 28 (2), 83–91.

Hepner, T. R. (2009). *Soldiers, martyrs, traitors, and exiles: Political conflict in Eritrea and the diaspora*. Philadelphia, PA: University of Pennsylvania Press.

Herman, J. (1992). *Trauma and recovery: The aftermath of violence – from domestic abuse to political terror*. New York, NY: Basic Books.

Hilty, D. M., Chan, S., Hwang, T., Wong, A., & Bauer, A. M. (2017). Advances in mobile mental health: Opportunities and implications for the spectrum of e-mental health services. *mHealth* 3 (8), 34.

Hirschberger, G. (2018). Collective trauma and the social construction of meaning. *Frontiers in Psychology* 9, 1441.

Hobfoll, S. E. (1988). *The ecology of stress*. Washington, DC: Hemisphere Publishing.

Hobfoll, S. E. (1989). Conservation of resources: A new attempt at conceptualizing stress. *American Psychologist* 44 (3), 513–524.

Hobfoll, S. E., Stevens, N. R., & Zalta, A. K. (2015). Expanding the science of resilience: Conserving resources in the aid of adaptation. *Psychological Inquiry* 26 (2), 174–80.

Horbaty, G., Gollp, A., Daita, S., & Carballo, M. (2006). *Migration in Central Asia and its possible implications for women and children.* Geneva: International Centre for Migration and Health.

Horowitz, M., Wilner, N., & Alvarez, W. (1979). Impact of Event Scale: A measure of subjective stress. *Psychosomatic Medicine* 41 (3), 209–218.

Hotline for Migrant Workers. (2011). *"The dead of the wilderness": Testimonies from Sinai desert, 2010.* Hotline for Migrant Workers.

Hou, C., Liu, J., Wang, K., Li, L., Liang, M., He, Z., ... & Jiang, T. (2007). Brain responses to symptom provocation and trauma-related short-term memory recall in coal mining accident survivors with acute severe PTSD. *Brain Research* 1144, 165–174.

Hu, C., Kung, S., Rummans, T. A., Clark, M. M., & Lapid, M. I. (2015). Reducing caregiver stress with Internet-based interventions: A systematic review of open-label and randomized controlled trials. *Journal of the American Medical Informatics Association* 22 (e1), e194–e209.

Human Rights Watch. (2005). *Uprooted and forgotten: Impunity and human rights abuses in Northern Uganda.* Human Rights Watch Report, 20 September 2005. Available at: https://www.hrw.org/reports/2005/uganda0905/ (accessed 3 February 2021).

Human Rights Watch. (2009). *Service for life: State repression and indefinite conscription in Eritrea.* New York, NY: Human Rights Watch.

Human Rights Watch. (2018). *World Report 2018 – Eritrea*. Annual Report, 18 January 2018. Available at: https://www.hrw.org/world-report/2019/country-chapters/eritrea (accessed 3 February 2021).

Hunt, N., & Gakenyi, M. (2005). Comparing refugees and non-refugees: The Bosnian experience. *Journal of Anxiety Disorders* 19 (6), 717–723.

ICC. (2005). *International Criminal Court. Warrant of arrest unsealed against five LRA commanders.* Press release, 14 October 2005. The Hague: International Criminal Court (ICC).

ICMC Europe. (2013). *Eritrean refugees in eastern Sudan.* International Catholic Migration Commission Europe (ICMC), European Res Resettlement Network. Belgium: Édition & Imprimerie.

IresearchNet. (2021). Psychology: Risk appraisal. Available at: https://psychology.iresearchnet.com/social-psychology/social-cognition/risk-appraisal/ (accessed 10 September 2021).

Isen, A. M. (2001). An influence of positive affect on decision making in complex situations: Theoretical issues with practical implications. *Journal of Consumer Psychology* 11 (2), 75–85.

Janoff-Bulman, R. (1985). *The aftermath of victimization: Rebuilding shattered assumptions. Trauma and its wake: The study and treatment of post-traumatic stress disorder.* New York, NY: Brunner/Mazel.

Janoff-Bulman, R. (1989). Assumptive worlds and the stress of traumatic events: Applications of the schema construct. *Social Cognition, Special Issue: Social Cognition and Stress* 7 (2), 113–136.

Janoff-Bulman, R. (1992). *Shattered assumption: Towards a new psychology of trauma.* New York, NY: Free Press.

Jarero, I., & Artigas, L. (2010). The EMDR integrative group treatment protocol: Application with adults during ongoing geopolitical crisis. *Journal of EMDR Practice and Research* 4 (4), 148–155.

Jarero, I. N., Artigas, L., & Hartung, J. (2006). EMDR integrative group treatment protocol: A post-disaster trauma intervention for children and adults. *Traumatology* 12 (2), 121–129.

Jarero, I., Artigas, L., Mauer, M., López Cano, T., & Alcalá, N. (1999). *Children's post-traumatic stress after natural disasters: Integrative treatment protocol.* Poster presented at the annual meeting of the International Society for Traumatic Stress Studies, Miami, FL.

Jerusalem, M., & Mittag, W. (1995). Self-efficacy in stressful life transitions. In Bandura, A. (ed.), *Self-Efficacy in Changing Societies* (pp. 177–201). New York, NY: Cambridge University Press.

Johansen, V. A., Wahl A. K., Eilertsen, D. E., & Weisaeth, L. (2007). Prevalence and predictors of posttraumatic stress disorder (PTSD) in physically injured victims of non-domestic violence. A longitudinal study. *Social Psychiatry and Psychiatric Epidemiology* 42 (7), 583–593.

Johnson, K. (2006). *After the storm: Healing after trauma, tragedy and terror.* Berkeley, CA: Publishers Group West.

Johnston, R. (2000). Community. In Johnston, R., Gregory, D., Pratt, G., & Watts, M. (eds), *The Dictionary of Human Geography* (4th Edition). Oxford: Blackwell.

Kaldor, M. (2014). In defense of new wars. *Stability* 2 (1), 1–16.

Kaniasty, K., & Norris, F. H. (1995). Mobilization and deterioration of social support following natural disasters. *Current Directions in Psychological Science* 4 (3), 94–98.

Kaplan, A. (2005). Virtually possible: Treating and preventing psychiatric wounds of war. *Psychiatric Times* 22 (4), 7–10.

Kawachi, I., & Subramanian, S. V. (2006). Measuring and modelling the social and geographic context of trauma: A multilevel modelling approach. *Journal of Traumatic Stress* 19 (2), 195–203.

Kawamura, N., Yoshiharu, K., & Nozomu, A. (2001). Suppression of cellular immunity in men with a past-history of post-traumatic stress disorder. *American Journal of Psychiatry* 158 (3), 484–486.

Kibreab, G. (2009). Forced labour in Eritrea. *Journal of Modern African Studies* 47 (1), 41–72.

Kibreab, G. (2015). Why thousands of asylum-seekers are fleeing Eritrea and risking their lives in the Mediterranean. *The Conversation*, 5 May 2015.

Kidane, S. (2015). Deserts high seas and hope. In Van Reisen, M. (ed.), *Women's Leadership in Peace Building Conflict, Community and Care* (pp. 289–300). Trenton, NJ: Africa World Press.

Kidane, S. (2016). *Refugee community radio: Baseline study, Sudan and Ethiopia.* Tilburg: Tilburg University.

Kidane, S., & Van Reisen, M. (2017). Collective trauma from Sinai trafficking: A blow to the fabric of the Eritrean society. In Van Reisen, M. & Mawere, M. (eds), *The Ongoing Tragedy of the Trade in Refugees from Eritrea* (pp. 318–347). Bamenda, Cameroon: Langaa Research & Publishing CIG.

Kim, W., Pae, C. U., Chae, J. H., Jun, T. Y., & Bahk, W. M. (2005). The effectiveness of mirtazapine in the treatment of post-traumatic stress disorder: A 24-week continuation therapy. *Psychiatry and Clinical Neurosciences* 59 (6), 743–747.

Kimhi, S., & Shamai, M. (2004). Community resilience and the impact of stress: Adult response to Israel's withdrawal from Lebanon. *Journal of Community Psychology* 32, 439–602.

King, D. W., King, L. A., Foy, D. W., Keane, T. M., & Fairbank, J. A. (1999). Posttraumatic stress disorder in a national sample of female and male Vietnam veterans: Risk factors, war-zone stressors, and resilience- recovery variables. *Journal of Abnormal Psychology* 108 (1), 164–170.

Kingsley, P. (2015). It's not at war, but up to 3% of its people have fled. What is going on in Eritrea? *The Guardian,* Inside Eritrea, 22 July 2015. Available at: https://www.theguardian.com/world/2015/jul/22/eritrea-migrants-child-soldier-fled-what-is-going (accessed 3 February 2021).

Kordon, D. R., Edelman, L. I., Lagos, D. M., Nicoletti, E., & Bozzolo, R. C. (1988). *Psychological effects of political repression.* Buenos Aires: Sudamericana/Planeta.

Kushner, M. G., Riggs, D. S., Foa, E. B., & Miller, S. M. (1993). Perceived controllability and the development of posttraumatic stress disorder (PTSD) in crime victims. *Behaviour Research and Therapy* 31 (1), 105–110.

Laban, C. J., Gernaat, H. B., Komproe, I. H., Van der Tweel, I., & De Jong, J. T. (2005). Postmigration living problems and common psychiatric disorders in Iraqi asylum seekers in the Netherlands. *Journal of Nervous and Mental Disease* 193 (12), 825–832.

Laban, C. J., Hurulean, E., & Attia, A. (2009). Treatment of asylum seekers: Resilience-oriented therapy and strategies (ROTS): Implications of study results into clinical practice. In De Jong, J. & Colijn, S. (eds), *Handboek Culturele Psychiatrie en Psychotherapie* (pp., 127–146). Utrecht: De Tijdstroom.

Lahad, S., & Ben Nesher, U. (2005). From improvisation during the traumatic situation to the development of guidelines for interventions: Communities coping with terror events preparation, intervention and rehabilitation. In Somer, E. & Bleich, A. (eds),

Mental Health in Terror's Shadow: The Israeli Experience (pp. 259–270). Tel Aviv, Israel: Ramot Publication-Tel Aviv University (in Hebrew).

Lal, S., & Adair, C. E. (2014). E-mental health: A rapid review of the literature. *Psychiatric Services* 65 (1), 24–32.

Landau, J., & Saul, J. (2004). Facilitating family and community resilience in response to major disaster. In Walsh, F. & McGoldrick, M. (eds), *Living Beyond Loss* (pp. 285–309). New York, NY: Norton.

Landau, J., Mittal, M., & Wieling, E. (2008). Linking human systems: Strengthening individuals, families, and communities in the wake of mass trauma. *Journal of Marital and Family Therapy* 34 (2), 193–209.

Landau-Stanton, J. (1990). Issues and methods of treatment for families in cultural transition. In M. P. Mirkin (ed.), *The Social and Political Contexts of Family Therapy* (pp. 251–275). Needham Heights, MA: Allyn & Bacon.

Lanni, A. (2016). 5 things everyone should know about Eritrean refugees. Open Migration [website]. Available at: https://openmigration.org/en/analyses/5-things-everyone-should-know-about-eritrean-refugees/ (accessed 3 February 2021).

Latonero, M., Poole, D., & Berens, J. (2018). *Refugee connectivity. A survey of mobile phones, mental health, and privacy at a Syrian refugee camp in Greece.* Harvard Humanitarian Initiative and Data & Society Research Institute.

Lattanzi-Licht, M., & Doka K.J. (eds). (2003). *Living with grief: Coping with public tragedy.* New York, NY: Brunner-Routledge.

Lazarus, R. S., & Folkman, S. (1984). *Stress, appraisal, and coping.* New York, NY: Springer.

Ledgerwood, J., Ebihara, M. M., & Mortland, C. A. (1994). Introduction. In Ebihara, M. M., Mortland, C. A., & Ledgerwood, J. (eds), *Cambodian Culture Since 1975: Homeland and Exile* (pp. 1–26). Ithaca, NY: Cornell University Press.

LeDoux, J. (1996). *The emotional brain: The mysterious underpinning of emotional life*. New York, NY: Simon & Schuster.

Lee, E. S. (1966). A theory of migration. *Demography* 3 (1), 47–57.

Leganger, A., Kraft, P., & Røysamb, E. (2000). Perceived self-efficacy in health behaviour research: Conceptualisation, measurement and correlates. *Psychology and Health* 15 (1), 51–69.

Lerner, C. F., & Kennedy, L.T. (2000). Stay-leave decision making in battered women: Trauma, coping and self-efficacy. *Cognitive Therapy and Research* 24 (2), 215–232.

Levi, P. (1986). *Survival in Auschwitz; and the reawakening: Two memoirs*. New York, NY: Summit Books.

Levine, P., & Frederick, A. (1997). *Waking the tiger: Healing trauma*. Berkley, CA:
North Atlantic Books.

Litt, M. D., Nye, C., & Shafer, D. (1993). Coping with oral surgery by self-efficacy enhancement and perceptions of control. *Journal of Dental Research* 72 (8), 1237–1243.

Litz, B. T, & Gray, M. J. (2004). Early intervention for trauma in adults: A framework for first aid and secondary prevention. In Litz, B. T. (ed.), *Early Intervention for Trauma and Traumatic Loss* (pp. 87–11). New York, NY: Guilford Press.

Lo, A. Y., Xu, B., Chan, F., & Su, R. (2016). Household economic resilience to catastrophic rainstorms and flooding in a Chinese megacity. *Geographical Research*. doi: 10.1111/1745-5871.12179.

Lupien, S. J., Maheu, F., Tu, M., Fiocco, A., & Schramek, T.E. (2007). The effects of stress and stress hormones on human cognition: implications for the field of brain and cognition. *Brain and Cognition* 65 (3), 209–237.

Lykes, B. (2001). Human rights violations as structural violence. In Christie, D., Wagner, R. V. & Winter, D. (eds), *Peace, Conflict, and Violence* (pp. 158–167). Upper Saddle River, NJ: Prentice-Hall.

MacLean, P. D. (1990). *The triune brain in evolution: Role in paleocerebral functions.* New York, NY: Plenum Press.

Maercker, A., & Schützwohl, M. (1998). Erfassung von psychischen Belastungsfolgen: Die Impact of Event Skala-revidierte Version (IES-R) [Assessment of post-traumatic stress reactions: The Impact of Event Scale-Revised (IES-R)]. *Diagnostica* 44 (3), 130–141.

Manz, B. (2002). Terror, grief and recovery: Genocidal trauma in a Mayan village in Guatemala. In Hinton, A. L. (ed.), *Annihilating Difference. The Anthropology of Genocide* (pp. 292–309). Berkeley, CA: University of California Press.

Marsella, A., Friedman, M., Gerrity, E., & Surfield, R. (eds). (1996). *Ethno-cultural aspects of posttraumatic stress disorder.* Washington, DC: American Psychological Association.

McEwen, B. S. (2003). Mood disorders and allostatic load. *Biological Psychiatry* 54 (3), 200–207.

Meger, S. (2010). Rape of the Congo: Understanding sexual violence in the conflict in the Democratic Republic of Congo. *Journal of Contemporary African Studies* 28 (2), 119–135.

Melicherova, K. (2018). *Refugees and livelihood: A case study from Hitsats.* Research Report. Tilburg: Tilburg University.

Mikulincer, M., Glaubman, H., Wasserman, O., Porat, A., & Birger, M. (1989). Control-related beliefs and sleep characteristics of posttraumatic stress disorder patients. *Psychological Reports* 65 (2), 567–576.

Miller, K. E., & Rasco, L. M. (eds). (2004). *The mental health of refugees: Ecological approaches to healing and adaptation*. Mahwah, NJ: Lawrence Erlbaum.

Modvig, J., & Jaranson, J. M. (2004). A global perspective of torture, political violence, and health. In Wilson, J. P. & Drozdek, B. (eds), *Broken Spirits: The Treatment of Traumatized Asylum Seekers, Refugees, War and Torture Victims* (pp. 33–52). New York, NY: Brunner-Routledge Press.

Molina, B. S., Donovan, J. E., & Belendiuk, K. A. (2010). Familial loading for alcoholism and offspring behavior: mediating and moderating influences. *Alcoholism: Clinical and Experimental Research* 34 (11), 1972–1984.

Mollica, R. F. (2000). Invisible wounds. *Scientific American* 282 (6), 54–57.

Mollica, R. F., McInnes, K., Sarajlić, N., Lavelle, J., Sarajlić, I., & Massagli, M. P. (1999). Disability associated with psychiatric comorbidity and health status in Bosnian refugees living in Croatia. *Journal of the American Medical Association* 282 (5), 433–439.

Mooren, T., De Jong, K., Kleber, R. J., & Ruvic, J. (2003). The efficacy of a mental health program in Bosnia Herzegovina: Impact on coping and general health. *Journal of Clinical Psychology* 59 (1), 57–69.

Morahan-Martin, J. M. (2004). How Internet users find, evaluate, and use online health information: A cross-cultural review. *CyberPsychology & Behavior* 7 (5), 497–510.

Murphy, S. A., Norbeck, J. S., Weinert, C., Cardea, J. M., & Lenz, E. R. (1987). Self-efficacy and social support: Mediators of stress on mental health following a natural disaster. *Western Journal of Nursing Research* 9 (1), 58–86.

Murray, E., Lo, B., Pollack, L., Donelan, K., Catania, J., White, M., Zapert, K., & Turner, R. (2003). The impact of health information on the Internet on the physician-patient relationship: patient perceptions. *Archives of Internal Medicine* 163 (14), 1727–1734.

Murthy, R. S., & Lakshminaryana, R. (2006). Mental health consequences of war: A brief review of research findings. *World Psychiatry* 5 (1), 25–30.

Muscat, R. J. (2004). Mental disabilities post-conflict economic and social recovery. In Mollica, R. F, Guerra, R., Bhasin R. & Lavelle, J. (eds), *Book of Best Practices Trauma and the Role of Mental Health in Post-Conflict Recovery* (pp. 309–325). Rome: World Bank Group.

National Institute for Clinical Excellence (NICE). (2005). *Post-traumatic stress disorder: management*. Clinical guideline [CG26]. Available from: https://www.nice.org.uk/guidance/cg26 (accessed 4 February 2021).

Neema, C. M., Kroon, S., Van Der Aa, J., & Draulans, V. (2018). Ethnographic monitoring through phone-in radio programs: An example from Ankore, Uganda. In Mawere, M. (ed.). *The Political Economy of Poverty, Vulnerability and Disaster Risk Management: Building Bridges of Resilience, Entrepreneurship and Development in Africa's 21st Century* (pp. 205–226). Bamenda, Cameroon: Langaa RPCI.

Neimeyer, R. (2005). Grief, loss, and the quest for meaning. *Bereavement Care* 24 (2), 27–30.

Neumayer, E. (2005). Bogus refugees? The determinants of asylum migration to Western Europe. *International Studies Quarterly* 49 (3), 389–410.

Norris, F., & Stevens, S. (2008). Community resilience and the principles of mass trauma intervention. *Psychiatry: Interpersonal and Biological Processes* 70 (4), 320–328.

Norris, F. H., Friedman, M. J., Watson, P. J., Byrne, C. M., Diaz, E., & Kaniasty, K. (2002a). 60,000 disaster victims speak: Part I. An empirical review of the empirical literature, 1981–2001. *Psychiatry: Interpersonal & Biological Processes* 65 (3), 207–239.

Norris, F. H., Friedman, M. J., & Watson, P. I. (2002b). 60,000 disaster victims speak: Part II. Summary and implications of disaster mental health research. *Psychiatry: Interpersonal & Biological Processes* 65 (3), 240–260.

Norris, F. H., Stevens, P. S., Pfefferbaum, B., Wyche, K. F., & Pfefferbaum, R. L. (2008). Community resilience as a metaphor, theory, set of capacities, and strategy for disaster readiness. *American Journal of Community Psychology* 41 (1–2), 127–150.

Oakes, J. M., & Rossi, P. H. (2003). The measurement of SES in health research: current practice and steps toward a new approach. *Social Science & Medicine* 56 (4), 769–784.

O'Brien, P. (2015). Migrant crisis: from Eritrea across Europe by rail. *Channel 4 News*, 20 June 2015. Available at: https://www.channel4.com/news/migrant-crisis-from-eritrea-across-europe-by-rail (accessed 3 February 2021).

Ogden, P., Pain, C., & Fisher, J. (2006). A sensorimotor approach to the treatment of trauma and dissociation. *Psychiatric Clinics of North America* 29 (1), 263–279.

Orcutt, H. K., Erickson, D. J., & Wolfe, J. (2004). The course of PTSD symptoms among Gulf War veterans: A growth mixture modelling approach. *Journal of Traumatic Stress* 17 (3), 195–202.

Park, J., Wood, J., Bondi, C., Del Arco, A., & Moghaddam, B. (2016). Anxiety evokes hypofrontality and disrupts rule-relevant encoding by dorsomedial prefrontal cortex neurons. *Journal of Neuroscience* 36 (11), 3322–3335.

Passaris, C. (1989). Immigration and the evolution of economic theory. *International Migration* 27 (4), 525–542.

Pastor, L. H. (2004). Culture as casualty: Examining the cause and consequences of collective trauma. *Psychiatric Annals* 34 (8), 616–622.

Patton, D., & Johnston, D. (2001). Disasters and communities: vulnerability, resilience and preparedness. *Disaster Prevention and Management: An International Journal* 10 (4), 270–277.

Patton, M. Q. (2002). Two decades of developments in qualitative inquiry: A personal, experiential perspective. *Qualitative Social Work* 1 (3), 261–283.

Pederson, D. (2002). Political violence, ethnic conflict: and contemporary wars: Broad implications for health and social well-being. *Social Science and Medicine* 55 (2), 175–190.

Perkins, D. D., & Long, D. A. (2002). Neighborhood sense of community and social capital: A multi-level analysis. In Fisher, A., Sonn, C. & Bishop, B. (eds), *Psychological Sense of Community: Research, Applications, and Implications* (pp. 291–318). New York, NY: Plenum.

Perry, B. D. (2002). Childhood experience and the expression of genetic potential: What childhood neglect tells us about nature and nurture. *Brain and Mind* 3 (1), 79–100.

Pesutic, S. (1989). *Persona, estadi, poder (individual, state, power)*. Santiago de Chile: CODEPU.

Pham, M. T. (2004). The logic of feeling. *Journal of Consumer Psychology* 14 (4), 360–369.

Pham, P., Vinck, P., & Stover, E. (2007). *Abducted: The Lord's Resistance Army and forced conscription in Northern Uganda.* Berkeley, CA: University of California, Berkeley, Human Rights Center.

Pierce, C. A., Block, R. A., & Aguinis, H. (2004). Cautionary note on reporting eta-squared values from multifactor ANOVA designs. *Educational and Psychological Measurement* 64 (6), 916–924.

Pietrantonio, F., De Gennaro, L., Paolo, M., & Solano, L. (2003). The Impact of Event Scale: Validation of an Italian version. *Journal of Psychosomatic Research* 55 (4), 389–393.

Possick, C., Sadeh, R. A., & Shamai, M. (2008). Parents' experience and meaning construction of the loss of a child in a national terror attack. *American Journal of Orthopsychiatry* 78 (1), 93–102.

Prandi, S. (2016). Eritrean refugees in Ethiopia. *Aljazeera*, 10 March 2016. Available at: http://www.aljazeera.com/indepth/inpictures/2016/03/eritrean-refugees-ethiopia-160306065928790.html (accessed 8 February 2021).

Putnam, R. D. (2000). Bowling alone: America's declining social capital. In *Culture and Politics* (pp. 223–234). New York: Palgrave Macmillan.

Rahman, A., Iqbal, Z., Bunn, J., Lovel, H., & Harrington, R. (2004). Impact of maternal depression on infant nutritional status and illness: A cohort study. *Archives of General Psychiatry* 61 (9), 946–952.

Ravenstein, E. G. (1885). The laws of migration. *Journal of the Statistical Society of London* 48 (2), 167–235.

Ravenstein, E. G. (1889). The laws of migration. *Journal of the Royal Statistical Society* 52 (2), 241–305.

Reed, S. B. (2007). *Measuring the emotional impact of an event – How to use an effective PTSD test.* Available at: https://psychotherapy-center.com/counseling-issues/trauma-and-stressors/ptsd-post-traumatic-stress-disorder-therapy/measuring-the-emotional-impact-of-an-event/ (accessed 8 February 2021).

Regehr. C. R, Cadell, S., & Jansen, K. (1999). Perceptions of control and long-term recovery from rape. *American Journal of Orthopsychiatry* 69 (1), 110–115.

Reger, M. A, & Gahm, G. A. (2009). A meta-analysis of the effects of Internet- and computer-based cognitive-behavioural treatments for anxiety. *Journal of Clinical Psychology* 65 (1), 53–75.

Rheingold, A. A., Acierno, R., & Resnick, H. S. (2004). Trauma, post-traumatic stress disorder, and health risk behaviours. In Schnurr, P.P. & Green, B.L. (eds), *Trauma and Health: Physical Health Consequences of Exposure to Extreme Stress* (pp. 217–243). Washington, DC: American Psychological Association.

Ritchie, L. A. (2012). Individual stress, collective trauma, and social capital in the wake of the Exxon Valdez oil spill. *Sociological Inquiry* 82 (2), 187–211.

Roback, J. (1982). Wages, rents, and the quality of life. *Journal of Political Economy* 90 (6), 1257–1278.

Roback, J. (1988). Wages, rents, and amenities: Differences among workers and regions. *Economic Inquiry* 26 (1), 23–41.

Rohrmann, B. (2008). Risk perception, risk attitude, risk communication, risk management: a conceptual appraisal (Keynote). In The International Emergency Management Society (ed.), *Global co-operation in emergency and disaster management – 15th*

TIEMS Conference booklet. Prague, Czech Republic: International Emergency Management Society.

Rosenthal, M. (2012). PTSD and decision making: How to put power in your process. *HealthyPlace,* 19 September 2012.

Rothbaum, B. O., Foa, E. B., Riggs, D. S., Murdock, T., & Walsh, W. (1992). A prospective examination of posttraumatic stress disorder in rape victims. *Journal of Traumatic Stress* 5 (3), 455–475.

Rothman, L., & Ronk, L. (2015). This is what Europe's last major refugee crisis looked like. *Time,* 11 September 2015.

Saigh, P. A., Mroueh, M., Zimmerman, B. J., & Fairbank, J. A. (1995). Self-efficacy expectations among traumatized adolescents. *Behaviour Research and Therapy* 33 (6), 701–704.

Salehyan, I. (2008). The externalities of civil strife: Refugees as a source of international conflict. *American Journal of Political Science* 52 (4), 787–801.

Salkovskis, P. M. (1996). The cognitive approach to anxiety: Threat beliefs, safety-seeking behaviour and the special case of health anxiety and obsessions. In Salkovskis, P. M. (ed.), *Frontiers of Cognitive Therapy* (pp. 48–74). New York, NY: Guilford Press.

Salter, A. (1995). *Transforming trauma: A guide to understanding and treating adult survivors of child sexual abuse.* Thousand Oaks, CA: Sage Publications.

Samuel Hall Consulting. (2014). *Living out of camp: Alternatives to camp-based assistance for Eritrean refugees in Ethiopia.* Report commissioned by Norwegian Refugee Council.

Sanderson, W. C., Rapee, R. M., & Barlow, D. H. (1989). The influence of an illusion of control on panic attacks induced via inhalation of 5.5% carbon dioxide-enriched air. *Archives of General Psychiatry* 46 (2), 157–162.

Saraceno, B., & Saxena, S. (2004). Mental health resources in the world: Results from Project Atlas of the WHO. *World Psychiatry* 1 (1), 40–44.

Saul, J. (2014). *Collective trauma, collective healing: Promoting community resilience in the aftermath of disaster* (Vol. 48). New York, NY: Routledge.

Saxena, S., Levav, I., Maulik, P., & Saraceno, B. (2003). How international are the editorial boards of leading psychiatry journals? *The Lancet* 361 (9357), 609.

Schoenmaeckers, R. (2018). *Living rights to education in emergencies A case study to the perceptions of educational rights of unaccompanied Eritrean refugee children and youth*. MA Thesis, University of Amsterdam.

Schuller, T., Baron, S. & Field, J., (eds). (2000). *Social capital: Critical perspectives*. Oxford: Oxford University Press.

Schuster, M. A., Stein, B. D., Jaycox, L. H., Collins, R. L., Marshall, G. N., Elliott, M. N., Zhou, A. J. … & Berry, S. H. (2001). A national survey of stress reactions after the September 11, 2001 terrorist attacks. *The New England Journal of Medicine* 345, 1507–1512.

Schwarz, N. (2012). Feelings-as-information theory. In Van Lange, P. A. M., Kruglanski, A. W., & Higgins, E. T. (eds), *Handbook of Theories of Social Psychology* (pp. 289-308). Thousand Oaks, CA: Sage Publications Ltd.

Schwarz, N., & Clore, G. L. (2007). Feelings and phenomenal experiences. In Kruglanski, A. W. & Higgins, E. T. (eds), *Social Psychology: Handbook of Basic Principles* (2nd Edition) (pp. 385–407). New York, NY: Guilford Press.

Selassie, B., & Van Reisen, M. (2019). Peace, but no progress: Eritrea, an unconstitutional state. In Van Reisen, M., Mawere, M., Stokmans, M. & Gebre-Egziabher, K. A. (eds), *Roaming Africa: Migration, Resilience and Social Protection.* Bamenda, Cameroon: LRPCIG.

Selmi, P. M., Klein, M. H., Greist, J. H., Sorrell, S. P., & Erdman, H. P. (1990). Computer-administered cognitive-behavioural therapy for depression. *American Journal of Psychiatry* 1 (147), 52–56.

Semple, W. E., Goyer, P. F., McCormick, R., Donovan, B., Muzic, R. F., Rugle, L., McCutcheon, K., Lewis, C., Liebling, D., Kowaliw, S., Vapenik, K., Semple, M. A., Flener, C. R., & Schulz, S. C. (2000). Higher brain blood flow at amygdala and lower frontal cortex blood flow in PTSD patients with comorbid cocaine and alcohol abuse compared with normal. *Psychiatry* 63 (1), 65–74.

Sen, A. M. (1993). *Positive affect and decision making.* In Lewis, M. & Haviland, J. (eds), *Handbook of Emotion* (pp. 261–277). New York, NY: Guilford Press.

Shadish, W. R., Cook, T. D., & Campbell, D. T. (2002). *Experimental and quasi-experimental designs for generalized causal inference.* Boston: Houghton Mifflin.

Shamai, M. (2015). *Systemic interventions for collective and national trauma: Theory, practice, and evaluation.* New York, NY and London: Routledge.

Shapiro, F. (1989). Efficacy of the eye movement desensitization procedure in the treatment of traumatic memories. *Journal of Traumatic Stress* 2 (2), 199–223.

Shapiro, F. (2012). *Getting past your past: Take control of your life with self-help techniques from EMDR therapy.* New York, NY: Rodale.

Shiv, B., & Fedorikhin, A. (1999). Heart and mind in conflict: The interplay of affect and cognition in consumer decision-making. *Journal of Consumer Research* 26 (3), 278–292.

Siegel, D. J. (1999). *The developing mind: How relationships and the brain interact to shape who we are.* New York, NY: Guilford Press.

Siegel, D. J. (2001). Toward an interpersonal neurobiology of the developing mind: Attachment relationships, 'mindsight', and neural integration. *Infant Mental Health Journal* 22 (1–2), 67–94.

Siegel, D. J. (2003). An interpersonal neurobiology of psychotherapy: The developing mind and the resolution of trauma. In Solomon, M. & Siegel, D. J. (eds), *Healing Trauma: Attachment, Mind, Body, and Brain* (pp. 1–56). New York, NY: W.W. Norton & Company.

Silk, J. (1999). The dynamics of community, place, and identity. Guest editorial. *Environment and Planning A*, 31 (1), 5–17.

Silove, D., & Steel, Z. (1998). *The mental health and well-being of on-shore asylum seekers in Australia.* Sydney: Psychiatry Research and Teaching Unit, School of Psychiatry, University of New South Wales.

Silove, D., Ekblad, S., & Mollica, R. (2000a). The rights of the severely mentally ill in post-conflict societies. *The Lancet* 355 (9214), 1548–1549. doi: 10.1016/S0140-6736(00)02177-2. PMID: 10801189.

Silove, D., Steel, Z., & Watters, C. (2000b). Policies of deterrence and the mental health of asylum seekers. *Journal of the American Medical Association*, 284 (5), 604–611.

Silove, D., Liddell, B., Rees, S., Chey, T., Nickerson, A., Tam, N., Zwi, A. B., Brooks, R., Sila, L. L., & Steel, Z. (2014). Effects of recurrent violence on post-traumatic stress disorder and severe distress in conflict-affected Timor-Leste: a 6-year longitudinal study. *The Lancet Global Health* 2 (5), e293–e300.

Silove, D., Ventevogel, P., & Rees, S. (2017). The contemporary refugee crisis: an overview of mental health challenges. *World Psychiatry* 16 (2), 130–139.

Sirleaf, E. J., & Rehn, E. (2002). *Women, war and peace: The independent experts' assessment on the impact of armed conflict on women and women's role in peace-building.* New York, NY: United Nations Development Fund for Women.

Skeldon, R. (1990). *Population mobility in developing countries: A reinterpretation.* London: Belhaven Press.

Slovic, P., MacGregor, D., & Kraus, N. N. (1987). Perception of risk from automobile safety defects. *Accident Analysis & Prevention* 19 (5), 359–373.

Snow, D. A., Morrill, C., & Anderson, L. (2003). Elaborating analytic ethnography: Linking fieldwork and theory. *Ethnography* 4 (2), 181–200.

Solomon, Z. (2013). *Coping with war-induced stress: The Gulf War and the Israeli response.* New York, NY: Springer Science & Business Media.

Somasundaram, D. (2014). Addressing collective trauma: Conceptualisations and interventions. *Intervention* 12 (1), 43–60.

Spradley, J. P. (1979). *The ethnographic interview.* New York, NY: Holt, Rinehart & Winston.

Starcke, K., & Brand, M. (2012). Decision making under stress: A selective review. *Neuroscience & Biobehavioral Reviews* 36 (4), 1228–1248.

Steed, L., & Bicknell, J. (2001). Trauma and the therapist: The experience of therapists working with the perpetrators of sexual abuse. *The Australasian Journal of Disaster and Trauma Studies* 1 (5), 527–540.

Steimel, S. J. (2010). Refugees as people: The portrayal of refugees in American human interest stories. *Journal of Refugee Studies* 23 (2), 219–237.

Suhrke, A. (1995). *Analysing the Causes of Contemporary Refugee Flows. Causes of International Migration.* Luxembourg: Office for Official Publications of the European Communities

Summerfield, D. (1995). Addressing human response to war and atrocity. In Kleber, R.J., Figley, C.R. & Gersons, B. P. R. (eds), *Beyond Trauma: Cultural and Societal Dynamics* (pp. 17–29). New York, NY: Plenum Press.

Summerfield, D. (1996). The psychological legacy of war and atrocity: The question of long term and trans generational effects and the need for a broad view. *Journal of Nervous and Mental Disease* 184 (1), 375–377.

Sundin, E. C., & Horowitz, M. J. (2002). Impact of Event Scale: Psychometric properties. *The British Journal of Psychiatry* 180 (3), 205–209.

Tedeschi, R. G., & Calhoun, L. G. (2004). Target article: Posttraumatic growth: Conceptual foundations and empirical evidence. *Psychological Inquiry* 15 (1), 1–18.

Teitelbaum, M. S. (1984). Immigration, refugees, and foreign policy. *International Organization*, 38 (3), 429–450.

Thoresen, S., Tambs, K., Hussain, A., Heir, T., Johansen, V. A., & Bisson, J. I. (2010). Brief measure of posttraumatic stress reactions:

Impact of Event Scale-6. *Social Psychiatry and Psychiatric Epidemiology* 45 (3), 405–412.

Tsigos, C., & Chrousos, G. P. (2002). Hypothalamic-pituitary-adrenal axis, neuroendocrine factors and stress. *Journal of Psychosomatic Research* 53 (5), 865–871.

Tull, M. T., Weiss, N. H., & McDermott, M. J. (2016). Post-traumatic stress disorder and impulsive and risky behavior: Overview and discussion of potential mechanisms. In Martin, C., Preedy, V., & Patel V. (eds), *Comprehensive Guide to Post-Traumatic Stress Disorders* (pp. 803–816). Cham: Springer.

Turner, S. W., Bowie, C., Dunn, G., Shapo, L., & Yule, W. (2003). Mental health of Kosovar Albanian refugees in the UK. *British Journal of Psychiatry* 182 (5), 444–448.

Ugalde, A., Richards, P., & Zwi, A. (1999). Health consequences of war and political violence. *Encyclopedia of Violence, Peace and Conflict* 2, 103–121.

UK Home Office. (2015a). *Country information and guidance Eritrea: Illegal exit.* Country Report, 7 September 2015, Version 2.0e. London: UK Home Office.

UK Home Office. (2015b). *Country information and guidance Eritrea: National (incl. military) service.* Country Report, September 2015, Version 2.0. London: UK Home Office.

UN General Assembly. (1951). *Convention relating to the status of refugees.* United Nations, Treaty Series, Vol. 189. New York, NY: United Nations, p. 137.

UNHCR. (2014). Sharp increase in number of Eritrean refugees and asylum-seekers in Europe, Ethiopia and Sudan. News Briefing Notes, 14 November 2014, UNHCR Asia Pacific. Available at: https://www.unhcr.org/news/briefing/2014/11/5465fea1381/sha

rp-increase-number-eritrean-refugees-asylum-seekers-europe-ethiopia.html (accessed 3 February 2021).

UNHCR. (2016). *Connecting refugees: How Internet and mobile connectivity can improve refugee well-being and transform humanitarian action.* Geneva: UNHCR.

UNHCR. (2017). *Refugee/migrants response – Mediterranean.* Geneva: UNHCR.

UNHCR. (2018). Figures at a glance. Available at: http://www.unhcr.org/en-us/figures-at-a-glance.html (accessed 9 February 2021).

UN Human Rights Council. (2015). *Report of the detailed findings of the commission of inquiry on human rights in Eritrea.* A/HRC/29/CRP. New York: United Nations Human Rights Council.

UN Secretary General. (2013). *Sexual violence in conflict.* Report of the Secretary-General, A/67/792; S/2013/149. New York, NY: United Nations.

UN Secretary General. (2014). *Children and armed conflict.* Report of the Secretary-General, A/68/878; S/2014/339. New York, NY: United Nations.

Van den Berg, S., Shapiro, D. A., Bickerstaffe, D., & Cavanagh, K. (2004). Computerized cognitive–behaviour therapy for anxiety and depression: A practical solution to the shortage of trained therapists. *Journal of Psychiatric and Mental Health Nursing* 11 (5), 508–513.

Van der Hart, O., Nijenhuis, E. R. S., & Steele, K. (2006). *The haunted self: Structural dissociation and the treatment of chronic traumatization.* New York, NY: Norton.

Van der Kolk, B. (2014). *The body keeps the score: Brain, mind and body in the healing of trauma.* New York, NY: Viking.

Van der Kolk, B. A., & Fisler, R. (1995). Dissociation and the fragmentary nature of traumatic memories: Overview and exploratory study. *Journal of Traumatic Stress* 8 (4), 505–525.

Van der Kolk, B., & McFarlane, A. (1996). *The black hole of trauma.* In Van der Kolk, B., McFarlane, A. & Weisaeth, L. (eds), *Traumatic Stress: The Effects of Overwhelming Experience on Mind, Body and Society* (pp. 3–23). New York, NY: The Guilford Press.

Van der Kolk, B., Spinazzola, J., Blaustein, M., Hopper, J., Hopper, E., Korn, D., & Simpson, W. (2007). A randomized clinical trial of eye movement desensitization and reprocessing (EMDR), fluoxetine, and pill placebo treatment of posttraumatic stress disorder: treatment effects and long-term maintenance. *Journal of Clinical Psychiatry* 68 (1), 37–46.

Van Oortmerssen, G. (2015). Technology and the power to connect: Participation of women in supporting activities through Internet communities. In Van Reisen, M. (ed.), *Women's Leadership in Peace Building Conflict, Community and Care* (pp. 213–227). place: Trenton, NJ: Africa World Press.

Van Reisen, M., Estefanos, M., & Rijken, C. (2012). *Human trafficking in the Sinai: Refugees between life and death.* Oisterwijk: Wolf Legal Publishers.

Van Reisen, M. E. H., Estefanos, M., & Rijken, C. R. J. J. (2014). *The human trafficking cycle: Sinai and beyond.* Oisterwijk: Wolf Legal Publishers.

Van Reisen, M., & Gerrima, Z. (2016). The order of things: Changing identities in Eritrea through ICTs. In Mawere, M. & Marongwe, N. (eds), *Violence, Politics and Conflict Management in Africa:*

Envisioning Transformation, Peace and Unity in the Twenty-first Century (pp. 367–400). Bamenda, Cameroon: Langaa RPCIG.

Van Reisen, M., Gerrima, Z., Ghilazghy, E., Kidane, S., Rijken, C., & Stam, G. J. (2017). Tracing the emergence of ICT-enabled human trafficking for ransom. In Rijken, C. (ed.), *Handbook for Human Trafficking* (pp. 146–156). Routledge: London.

Van Reisen, M., & Kidane, S. (2017). Collective trauma from Sinai trafficking: A blow to the fabric of Eritrean society. In Van Reisen, M. & Mawere, M. (eds), *Human Trafficking and Trauma in the Digital Era: The Ongoing Tragedy of the Trade in Refugees from Eritrea* (pp. 317–345). Bamenda, Cameroon: Langaa RPCIG.

Van Reisen, M., & Mawere, M. (2017). *Human trafficking and trauma in the digital era.* Bamenda, Cameroon: Langaa RPCIG.

Van Reisen, M., & Rijken, C. (2015). Sinai trafficking: Origin and definition of a new form of human trafficking. *Social Inclusion* 3 (1), 113–124.

Van Reisen, M., Stokmans, M., Kidane, S., Melicherova, K., & Schoenmaeckers, R. (2018a). *Causes and dynamics of mixed unskilled migrants trafficked within the Horn region. A study including Eritrea, Ethiopia and Sudan.* Synthesis Report. Tilburg: Tilburg University.

Van Reisen, M., Stokmans, M., Nakazibwe, P., Vallejo, B., & Kidane, S. (2018b). *Livelihood-support and trauma relief in relation to social-economic resilience in Northern Uganda and northern Ethiopia.* Research Summary, NWO Report. Tilburg: Tilburg University.

Van Reisen, M., Saba, M., & Smits, K. (2019). 'Sons of Isaias': Slavery and indefinite national service in Eritrea. In Van Reisen, M., Mawere, M., Stokmans, M., & Gebre-Egziabher, K. A. (eds), *Mobile Africa: Human Trafficking and the Digital Divide* (pp. 115–157). Bamenda, Cameroon: Langaa RPCIG.

Van Reisen, M., Smits, K., & Wirtz, M. (2019). Lawless Libya: Unprotected refugees kept powerless and silenced. In Van Reisen, M., Mawere, M., Stokmans, M., & Gebre-Egziabher, K. A. (eds), *Mobile Africa: Human Trafficking and the Digital Divide* (pp. 261–293). Bamenda, Cameroon: Langaa RPCIG.

Van Reisen, M., Stokmans, M., Mawere, M., & Gebre-Egziabher, K. A. (2019a). Roaming Africa: A social analysis of migration and resilience. In Van Reisen, M., Mawere, M., Stokmans, M., & Gebre-Egziabher, K. A. (eds), *Roaming Africa: Migration, Resilience and Social Protection* (pp. 3–36). Bamenda, Cameroon: Langaa RPCIG.

Van Reisen, M., Stokmans, M., Nakazibwe, P., Malole, Z., & Vallejo, B. (2019b). Is trauma counselling the missing link? Enhancing socio-economic resilience among post-war IDPs in Northern Uganda. In Van Reisen, M., Mawere, M., Stokmans, M. & Gebre-Egziabher, K. A. (eds), *Roaming Africa: Migration, Resilience and Social Protection* (pp. 435–458). Bamenda, Cameroon: LRPCIG.

Van Reisen, M., Stokmans, M., Malole, Z. & Kidane, S. (2021, forthcoming). Hidden costs of psychosocial support in social protection programs in Uganda

Veronese, G., & Pepe A. (2013). Psychometric proprieties of the Impact of Event Scale (short version) in contexts of military violence. *Research on Social Work Practice* 23 (6), 710–718.

Walsh, F. (2006). *Strengthening family resilience* (2nd Edition). New York, NY: Guilford Press.

Walsh, F. (2007). Traumatic loss and major disasters: Strengthening family and community resilience. *Family Process* 46 (2), 207–228.

Warda, G., & Bryant, R. A. (1998). Cognitive bias in acute stress disorder. *Behaviour Research and Therapy* 36 (12), 1177–1183.

Watts, S., Kavanagh, J., Frederick, B., Norlen, T. C., O'Mahony, A., Voorhies, P., & Szayna, T. S. (2017). *Understanding conflict trends: A review of the social science literature on the causes of conflict*. Santa Monica, CA: Rand Corporation.

Wegner, E. (2000). *Communities of practice: Learning, meaning, and identity*. Cambridge: Cambridge University Press.

Weisaeth, L. (1991). The information and support center: Preventing the after-effects of disaster trauma. In Sorensen, T., Abrahamsen, P. & Torgersen, S. (eds), *Psychiatric Disorders in the Social Domain* (pp. 50–58). Oslo: Norwegian University Press.

Weisaeth, L. (1992). Prepare and repair: Some principles in prevention of psychiatric consequences of traumatic stress. *Psychiatria Fennica* 23, 11–18.

Weiss, D. S. (2004). The Impact of Event Scale (Revised). In Wilson, J. P. & Keane, T. M. (eds), *Assessing Psychological Trauma and PTSD* (2nd Edition) (pp. 168–189). New York, NY: Guilford Press.

Weiss, D. S., Marmar, C. R., Metzler, T. J., & Ronfeldt, H. M. (1995). Predicting symptomatic distress in emergency services personnel. *Journal of Consulting and Clinical Psychology* 63 (3), 361–368.

Weiss, D. S., Marmar, C. R., Zatzick, D. F., Browner, W. S., Metzler, T. J., Golding, J. M., ... & Wells, K. B. (1997). Posttraumatic stress disorder and functioning and quality of life outcomes in a nationally representative sample of male Vietnam veterans. *American Journal of Psychiatry* 154 (12), 1690–1695.

Wessells, M. G., & Monteiro, C. (2001). Psychosocial interventions and post-war reconstruction in Angola. In Christie, D., Wagner, R.V. & Winter, D. (eds), *Peace, Conflict, and Violence* (pp. 262–275). Upper Saddle River, NJ: Prentice Hall.

Williams, D. (2006). On and off the Net: Scales for social capital in an online era. *Journal of Computer-Mediated Communication* 11 (2), 593–628.

Williams, A.M., & Baláž, V. (2012). Migration, risk, and uncertainty: Theoretical perspectives. *Population, Space and Place* 18 (2), 167–180.

Wind, T. R., & Komproe, I. H. (2012). The mechanisms that associate community social capital with post-disaster mental health: A multilevel model. *Social Science & Medicine Journal* 75 (17), 1715–1720.

Wisdom, J., & Creswell, J. W. (2013). *Mixed Methods: Integrating Quantitative and Qualitative Data Collection and Analysis While Studying Patient-Centered Medical Home Models*. Rockville, MD: Agency for Healthcare Research and Quality.

World Health Organization. (2013). *Guidelines for the management of conditions specifically related to stress*. Geneva: WHO.

Wu, K. K., & Chan, K. S. (2003). The development of the Chinese version of Impact of Event Scale-Revised (CIES-R). *Social Psychiatry Psychiatric Epidemiology* 38 (2), 94–98.

Yehuda, R. (2002). Post-traumatic stress disorder. *New England Journal of Medicine* 346 (2), 108–114.

Yehuda, R., Schmeidler, J., Wainberg, M., Binder-Brynes, K., & Duvdevani, T. (1998). Vulnerability to posttraumatic stress disorder in adult offspring of Holocaust survivors. *American Journal of Psychiatry* 155 (9), 1163–1171.

Zaghrout-Hodali, M., Alissa, F., & Dodgson, P. W. (2008). Building resilience and dismantling fear: EMDR group protocol with children in an area of ongoing trauma. *Journal of EMDR Practice and Research* 2 (2), 106–113.

Zang, Y., Hunt, N., & Cox, T. (2013). A randomised controlled pilot study: The effectiveness of narrative exposure therapy with adult survivors of the Sichuan earthquake. *BMC Psychiatry* 13 (1), 41.

Zilberg, N. J., Weiss, D. S., & Horowitz, M. J. (1982). Impact of Event Scale: A cross-validation study and some empirical evidence supporting a conceptual model of stress response syndromes. *Journal of Consulting and Clinical Psychology* 50 (3), 407.

Zimmermann, S. E. (2011). Reconsidering the problem of 'Bogus' refugees with 'socioeconomic motivations' for seeking asylum. *Mobilities* 6 (3), 335–352.

Appendix 1. Baseline questionnaire

መጸናዕቲ ስማዕቲ ሬድዮ
(ጎኤርትሪፎውያን)

ሽም: _____

መግለስከር (ትኅብርሊ ከተጣ: _____

ኢ መዋይል ወይ ቁ ጸረ ተለፎን: _____

ጾታ: ተባዕታይ   ኣንስታይ

ዕድmi: ☐   ☐

1. ገከጋደይ ዝላኣል ተቆሟጥሳ (ኪ) ኣብ ሱ-ዳግ: _____

287

2. ናይ ፊደዮ ናይ ሞባይል ልምድታት

ሂያዋይ መደበር ፊደዮ ኢ ኸ (ሺ) ትስምዕ (ግ)	ኣብ ከኸንደይ ትስምዕ (ግ)		
	መዓልታዊ	ሰሙናዊ	ሰሙኑ

ትቅበሎሎም/ትቅምሎም ቍንቋታት ኣዮኖት እዮም?				
ትግራኛ	ዓረብኛ	ትግረይት	ካልእ ናይ ዉሽጢ ሃገር ቍንቋ	ካልእ ኣህጉራዊ ቍንቋ

3. ፊደዮ ትስምዓሉ/ትስምዕሉ ኣገባባት?

ሕብረትስብኣዊ ፈጋዌ ሬዲዮ
ናይ ሓበር ሬዲዮ ኣብ ገዛ
ኣብ ተንቀሳቐሲት ተሌፎን
ኣብ ኢንተርነት
ካልእ

288

4. አየኖት ማሕበራዊ መሪኸብታት ሊኸ (ኺ) ትጥቀም (ሟ)?

ፌስቡክ (Facebook)	
ፓልቶክ (Pal Talk)	
ቫይበር (Viber)	
ስካይፕ (Skype)	
ትዊተር (Twitter)	
ዋትስኣፕ (WhatsApp)	
ወላ ሓደ ኢይጥቀምን (None)	
ካልእ	

5. ኣብ ከመብኸ (ኺ) ምስ ሱዳናውያን ትዃዓሪኸ (ኺ) ትቃረርብ (ቢ) ዲኸ (ኺ)?

ኩሎ ጊዜ	ሳሕቲ	ብጥራሽ

289

6. ምስ ሱዳናውያን አዕራኽትኻ/መሳዝብትኺ ተዕልልዎም ጕዳያት እንታይ እዮም?

መንዚቃ: ስፖርት: ፊልም			
ፖለቲካ			
ስደት/ፍልሰት			
ገንዘብባን ስራሕን			
ወልቃዊ ጕዳያት: ጥዕና: ስድራቤታዊ ጕዳያት			
ድስነገትን ጸወታን			
ካልእ			

7. ንሱዳንን ሱዳናውያንን ዝምልከት ሓበሬታኻ (ኺ) ካበይ ትረክስ (ብዩ)?

ካብ ኤርትራውያን	
ካብ ሱዳናውያን	
ካብ ጋዜጣታን መደበት ፈደዮን ተለቪዥንን	
ካብ ኢንተርኔት ማሕበራዊ መገናኛ መካታትን	
ካብ ካልእ	

290

8. ኣብ ከባቢኻ (ኺ) ዘለዉ ሱዳናውያን ጉኣርትራውያን ይርድኡኹም እዮም፡ ከምኡ ‘ውን ለገዝ ኣብ ዝደልዩሉ፡ ከሕግዝዎም ይኽእሉ እዮም ኢልካ (ኺ) ዶ ትሓስብ (ቢ)?

ኩሉ ጊዜ	ሓደ-ሓደ ጊዜ	ብጥራሽ

Baseline Study for Radio Programme

(ERITREANS)

Name: _____

Camp (city of residence): _____

Email or phone number: _____

Gender: Male   Female

Age: [ ] [ ]   _____

1. How long have you lived in Ethiopia/Sudan? _____

2. Radio listening habits

What radio station do you listen to	How often			What language is used				
	Daily	Weekly	Rarely	Amharic	Arabic	Tigrigna	Other local	Other international

1. How do you listen to the radio?

Communal broadcast in the camp	
Shared radio at home	
On my mobile phone	
On the Internet	
Other	

2. What social media outlet do you use?

Facebook	
Pal Talk	
Viber	
Skype	
Twitter	
None	
Other	

3. Do you socialise with Ethiopians in your locality?

Always	Rarely	Never

4. What sort of things do you discuss with your Ethiopian friends?

Music, sport and films	
Migration	
Money and work	
Personal issues, health and family matters	
Safety and security	
Other	

5. Where do you get your information about Ethiopia and Ethiopians?

From other Eritreans	
From Ethiopians	
Newspapers, radio and TV programmes	
On the Internet and social media	
Other	

6. Do you think Ethiopians in your locality understand Eritreans and would help them if needed?

Always	Occasionally	Never

Appendix 2. Social and Economic Resilience Scale (SER)

Name				
Age	18–21	22–24	25–30	Over 30
Who do you live with?	On my own	With family	With friends	Other
Level of education	Never been to school	Number of years of primary education	Number of years in secondary education	Number of years in higher education
Gender	Male	Female		
How long ago did you leave Eritrea?				
Have you ever experienced a very difficult event that you thought was life threatening?	Yes	No		
Do you own a smartphone?	Yes	No		
How important is your mobile phone?	Very important	Relatively important	Not at all important	

What do you use your phone for?	To stay in touch with friends and family on social media	To access news and information	For entertainment	To learn new skills	To stay in touch with friends and family via voice calls	To stay in touch with friends and family via short text messages
Do you expect to be at this location six months from now?	Yes	No	Alternative contact details		(Facebook, Viber, WhatsApp etc.)	

Social and Economic Resilience						

Part 1: Income

		Strongly disagree	Disagree	Neutral	Agree	Strongly agree
1.	I am able to meet my financial needs.	1	2	3	4	5
2.	I am able to save money.	1	2	3	4	5
3.	I will have good means of earning money in the next six months.	1	2	3	4	5

#	Statement	1	2	3	4	5
4.	I am able to survive in times of hardship.	1	2	3	4	5
Part 2: Empowerment						
5.	I am able to get more time for productive activities.	1	2	3	4	5
6.	I am able make my own decisions.	1	2	3	4	5
7.	I feel improvement in my self-worth.	1	2	3	4	5
Part 3: Trust in the system						
8.	I feel I am able to exercise my rights.	1	2	3	4	5
9.	I am able to access the support services that I need easily.	1	2	3	4	5
10.	I understand organisations offering support services in the refugee camp work.	1	2	3	4	5
Part 4: Worriedness						
11.	I am worried that conflict/war may erupt again.	1	2	3	4	5
12.	I am worried that I will fail to provide for myself and/or my family.	1	2	3	4	5
13.	I am worried that support organisations will not treat me fairly.	1	2	3	4	5

		1	2	3	4	5
14.	I am worried that my physical or emotional health will deteriorate.	1	2	3	4	5
15.	I am worried that I may not have enough money to meet my needs.	1	2	3	4	5
16.	I am worried about my safety in the camp.	1	2	3	4	5

Part 5: Capacity

		1	2	3	4	5
17.	I feel I can get information about anything I want.	1	2	3	4	5
18.	I have acquired new skills to improve my life.	1	2	3	4	5
19.	I feel change in the amount of knowledge I hold.	1	2	3	4	5

Part 6: Social embeddedness

		1	2	3	4	5
20.	I feel my relationship with the rest of the community has improved.	1	2	3	4	5
21.	I feel my contact with the leadership in the camp has improved.	1	2	3	4	5
22.	I feel that I trust my community.	1	2	3	4	5

Appendix 3. Impact of Events Scale-Short (IES-S)

INSTRUCTIONS: Below is a list of difficulties people sometimes have after stressful life events. Please read each item, and then indicate how stressful each difficulty has been for you DURING THE PAST SEVEN DAYS with respect to.............. (event) that occurred on.................(date). How much have you been distressed or bothered by these difficulties?

	Strongly disagree	Disagree	Neutral	Agree	Strongly agree
1. Other things kept making me think about it.	1	2	3	4	5
2. I stayed away from reminders of it.	1	2	3	4	5
3. I had trouble falling asleep.	1	2	3	4	5
4. I had waves of strong feelings about it.	1	2	3	4	5
5. I had trouble concentrating.	1	2	3	4	5
6. Reminders of it caused me to have physical reactions, such as sweating, trouble breathing, nausea, or a pounding heart.	1	2	3	4	5
7. I tried not to talk about it.	1	2	3	4	5

Appendix 4. Internet Social Capital Scale (ISCS)

Please tick to indicate whether or not you agree with these statements, in relation to your online and offline interactions.	Online					Offline				
	Strongly disagree	Disagree	Neutral	Agree	Strongly agree	Strongly disagree	Disagree	Neutral	Agree	Strongly agree
Bonding subscale										
1. There are several people online/offline I trust to help solve my personal problems.	1	2	3	4	5	1	2	3	4	5
2. There is someone online/offline I can turn to for advice about making very important decisions.	1	2	3	4	5	1	2	3	4	5
3. There is no one online/offline that I feel comfortable talking to about	1	2	3	4	5	1	2	3	4	5

	1	2	3	4	5		1	2	3	4	5
intimate personal problems. (reversed)											
4. When I feel lonely, there are several people online/offline I can talk to.	1	2	3	4	5		1	2	3	4	5
5. If I needed an emergency loan, I know someone online/offline I can turn to.	1	2	3	4	5		1	2	3	4	5
6. The people I interact with online/offline would recommend me to people in their network.	1	2	3	4	5		1	2	3	4	5
7. The people I interact with online/offline would be good job references for me.	1	2	3	4	5		1	2	3	4	5
8. The people I interact with online/offline would share their last dollar/food/clothing with me.	1	2	3	4	5		1	2	3	4	5

	1	2	3	4	5		1	2	3	4	5
9. I do not know people online/offline well enough to help me get ahead. (reversed)	1	2	3	4	5		1	2	3	4	5
10. The people I interact with online/offline would help me fight an injustice.	1	2	3	4	5		1	2	3	4	5
11. I have a good network of friends and family	1	2	3	4	5		1	2	3	4	5

Appendix 5. Interview topic list

Interview list

1. Experiences of the original trauma
    1.1 Traumatic experience
    1.2 Symptoms (how does trauma affect you on a day-to-day basis?)

2. Experiences of the trauma intervention
    2.1 Impressions
    2.2 Changes experienced
    2.3 What other people saw (changes seen by friends, family members and others)

3. Post-intervention experiences
    3.1 Has anything changed for you?
    3.2 Do others notice this change?
    3.3 Have you got new plans and new things you do now?
    3.4 Would you teach the techniques to others?

Observation format

Site	Examples of change in traumatic stress level	Examples of change in social capital	Examples of change in SER	Examples of familiarity with the techniques	Examples of disseminating the learning

Appendix 6. Research funding

Gratefully acknowledgement to the following research funding received for this research.

- June 2018 to August 2018 (0.2fte). 'Causes and dynamics of mixed unskilled migrants trafficked within the Horn region. A study including Eritrea, Ethiopia, and Sudan'. Funder: NWO-WOTRO (Security and Rule of Law (SRoL). Project number: W08.40016.10034
  Participants: Tilburg University, ZOA, Mekelle University Africa Monitors

- June 2015 to December 2017 (0.2fte). 'Cost-benefit analysis of cash transfer programmes and post-trauma services for economic empowerment of women in Uganda'. Funder: NWO-WOTRO (Research for Inclusive Development in sub-Saharan Africa (RIDSSA)). Project number: W 08.390.001
  Participants: Tilburg University, Mbarara University of Science and Technology, Makerere University, Isis-WICCE.

- January 2016 to December 2017. 'Youth in the Horn of Africa (involving Eritrea, Ethiopia, Sudan)'. European Union proposal number PP-AP/2014/037-724. Pilot project – Strategic investment in sustainable peace and democratization in the Horn of Africa.
  Participants: Tilburg University, EEPA, SORD, Africa Monitors

- 2016-2018 and 2019-2021. Europe-Africa Response to Human Trafficking and Mixed Migration Flows.
  Participants: Europe External Programme in Africa (EEPA)

CPSIA information can be obtained
at www.ICGtesting.com
Printed in the USA
BVHW090831111021
618671BV00010B/383

9 789956 552504